Footprint Handbook
Rio de Janeiro
& Min

ALEX & GARD

This is
Rio de Janeiro
& Minas Gerais

Even those who know nothing else of Brazil will have heard of Rio, its Mardi Gras carnival and its spectacular beach and mountain scenery. What many do not realize is that Rio is redolent with contemporary culture too – from the jazzy jilt of *chorinho* and the breezy sway of bossa nova in the bars of Copacabana and the sultry samba and *forró* rhythms which reverberate around Lapa in the centre to the state-of-the-art museums and galleries renovated or rebuilt in anticipation of the Olympics.

And Rio de Janeiro is a state as well as a city – with some of Brazil's emptiest beaches, wildlife-filled forests and mist-covered mountain ranges big enough to generate their own rain which drips down the slopes in waterfalls. The hills are patchworked with protected areas overflowing with wildlife, like Itatiaia National Park, the REGUA reserve and the Serra dos Órgãos. Little mountain towns like Petrópolis sit between them: pink with wedding-cake palaces and faux Bavarian mansions built by a Portuguese royal family in exile from Europe.

The southern coast, or Costa Verde, is a rugged fold of ridges broken by emerald-green coves and bays dotted with islands, and pocked with national parks. To the northeast Rio state dries into maquis and coastal flats covered in restinga scrub. Near Cabo Frio these run around saltwater lagoons to white-sand beaches. Further north around the cruise-ship crowded resort town of Búzios they fringe a rocky cape cut with half-moon bays and swathes of sand backed by gated villa communities.

The land-locked state of Minas Gerais lies to the north of Rio. Its rolling hills and rocky crags are dotted with colonial mining towns such as Ouro Preto, whose cobbled streets are lined with some of the finest baroque buildings in Latin America.

Alex Robinson

Gardênia Robinson

Best of
Rio de Janeiro
& Minas Gerais

❶ Church of São Francisco da Penitência

The modest façade of this Portuguese church hides one of Latin America's most exquisite interiors – a lavish, swirling array of intricately carved gilt wood by Francisco Xavier de Brito who introduced baroque to Brazil. And it only receives a handful of visitors. Page 45.

❷ Views of Christ on Corcovado

Rio's famous Christ statue can be seen from all over the city perched high on Corcovado mountain. Climb to the top of the Morro dos Cabritos or take a cable car up Sugar Loaf mountain for the best views. And be sure to see Rio from the statue's feet. Page 62.

❸ Copacabana and Ipanema beaches

These two sweeps of crescent sand washed by a bottle-green ocean have become synonymous with Rio's glamorous beach life. Take time for a wander along one of them, stopping for an ice-cold, freshly cracked coconut at one of the beachside kiosks. Pages 64 and 67.

❹ Pontal and Prainha beaches

Pounded by powerful surf and watched over by lookouts reached by winding forest trails, Rio's far southern beaches are long, broad and washed by the cleanest sea in the city. They are perfectly positioned for the Olympic Park and they're almost empty during the week. Page 72.

To Diamantina

Parque Nacional
da Serra do Cipó

Sete Lagoas

Gruta de
Lapinha

Ipatinga

Belo
Horizonte

Sabará

Caeté

Parque
Nacional
Caparaó

Nova Lima

Caraça

8 Ouro Preto

Congonhas
do Campo

Mariana

Viçosa

Prados

Tiradentes

Itaperuna

São João
del Rei

Barbacena

MINAS GERAIS

Lavras

Church of São
Francisco da
Penitência **1**

São Tomé
das Letras

Santos Dumont

2

Corcovado
Mountain

Santo
Antônio
de Pádua

Ibitipoca

Caxambu

Lima
Duarte

3

Copacabana
Beach

Juiz de Fora

Itaocara

Matias Barbosa

5

Vidigal
Favela

Ipanema
Beach

Parque Nacional
do Itatiaia

Rio Preto

Três Rios

Penedo

Visande
de Mauá

Conservatória

Valença

RIO DE JANEIRO

Resende

Vassouras

Miguel
Pereira

Reserva Ecológica
de Guapi Assu

Novo Friburgo

Rio Paraíba Do Sul

Getulândia

Japeri

Teresópolis

Petrópolis

Macaé

Itauruçá

Itaguaí

Neves

Rio das Ostras

PN da Serra
da Bocaina

Mangaratiba

Muriqui

**Rio de
Janeiro**

Barra de São João

Angra
dos Reis

Niterói

Araruama

Búzios

7

Paraty

Ilha Grande
Aventureiro

Abraão

4

Prainha
Beach

Pontal
Beach

Costa do Sol

L de Araruama

Cabo Frio

Trinidade

Lopes
Mendes
Beach

Dois
Rios

6

Saquarema

Arraial
do Cabo

N

Atlantic Ocean

30 km

30 miles

❺ A favela hike

Rio is a city of wonderful views. Some of the best are from the summits of hills that sit above the favelas in the south of the city. Hike with local guides from Tabajaras-Cabritos or Vidigal for views from the Pedra do Marroca and the Dois Irmãos. Page 72.

❻ Lopes Mendes beach, Ilha Grande

Along Rio state's Costa Verde (Green Coast), rainforest-covered mountain ridges drop into an emerald sea, emerging offshore as rugged islands. The prettiest is Ilha Grande, where trails lead to stunning beaches like Lopes Mendes. Page 131.

❼ Paraty

With brightly painted fishing boats bobbing in the water, whitewashed bell towers set against rainforest-green mountains and donkeys clip-clopping along cobbled streets, Paraty is one of Brazil's most enchanting coastal towns and the perfect place to spend a tranquil day or two. Page 135.

❽ Ouro Preto

Wander winding cobbled-streets lined with ornate baroque churches glistening with gold in this historic mining town set in the rolling hills of Minas Gerais state. One of the most important colonial towns in Brazil, Ouro Preto is a UNESCO World Heritage Site. Page 160.

Capuchin monkey

Route
planner

With the Christ statue embracing the city, the famous carnival and those long talcum powder-fine beaches, Rio de Janeiro is a must-see for most first-time visitors to Brazil. But there's far more to the region than its capital city. A southeastern itinerary beginning and ending here can take in the rainforests and islands of the Costa Verde, a series of national parks and the colonial mining towns of Minas Gerais with their lavish baroque churches.

One to two weeks
beaches, baroque churches and Rio nightlife

A trip of one to two weeks is enough to see a little of Rio and visit a destination on the Costa Verde. Allow at least two days for Rio, taking a full day to visit the Christ Corcovado mountain and the Sugar Loaf. Take the Trem do Corcovado funicular railway from Cosme Velho through the rainforest to Corcovado and spend a few hours admiring the superb views over Rio's myriad beaches, bays and islands. Be sure to enjoy an ice-cold coconut on the beach in the early morning, take a stroll through the Botanical Gardens (nestled under Corcovado) and dance the night away in one of the many samba clubs in Rio's bustling and bohemian Lapa neighbourhood.

Save some valuable time by booking a direct transfer to one of the sights on the Costa Verde. If you have just a week, make it Paraty and stay for two days. Close to Paraty are some beautiful beaches, especially near Trindade.

With two weeks you can visit Ilha Grande too for two or three days. It's a car-free, mountainous island cut with hiking trails through the rainforest, and fringed with gorgeous tropical beaches. You'll need to double back to Rio. If you have a couple of weeks try and fit in a side trip to Ouro Preto in Minas Gerais – one of colonial Brazil's prettiest towns reachable on a long bus journey or a short flight via Belo Horizonte.

Three to four weeks will allow you to get to know Rio with plenty of time for long side trips. Spend a week in the city itself. After taking in the Sugar Loaf and Corcovado see more of the world's best urban views on a head-spinning hike through the favelas and forest to the Morro dos Dois Irmãos or Cabritos peaks. Surf in Prainha, hang-glide over São Conrado, samba in Lapa, sip a caipirinha on the sand in Niterói (as the sun sinks behind the skyline), or stroll through the new museum areas around Porto Maravilha in Rio's renovated city centre. Then using Rio as a hub and doubling back in between, take two weeks to see the gold-rich mining towns of Minas Gerais: Ouro Preto, Congonhas, Mariana and Tiradentes, the wildlife-filled forests of Itatiaia national park and the Portuguese port villages, coconut shaded coves and rugged islands of the Costa Verde.

When to go

The best time to visit Rio is from April to June, and August to October. Business visitors should avoid mid-December to the end of February, when it is hot and people are on holiday. In these months, hotels, beaches and transport tend to be very crowded. July is a school holiday month. Be aware that some tourist sights may be closed for renovation in low season.

Rio has one of the healthiest climates in the tropics, with trade winds keeping the air fresh. July and August are the coolest months. December to March is hot and humid, while October to March is the rainy season.

Festivals

Carnaval dates depend on the ecclesiastical calendar and so vary from year to year. The party begins on the Friday afternoon before Shrove Tuesday, officially ending on Ash Wednesday and unofficially on the following Sunday. The festival takes place all over Brazil and not just in Rio. Ouro Preto and Paraty are smaller-scale events but equally lively alternatives to Rio.

Carnival dates
2017 23 February-1 March
2018 8-14 February
2019 28 February-6 March

But carnival is not Rio de Janeiro's biggest party as even more crowds come for New Year, cramming Copacabana to watch live music and fireworks erupting from the bay and cascading down the skyscrapers.

Weather Rio de Janeiro city					
January	**February**	**March**	**April**	**May**	**June**
23°C 33°C 120mm	23°C 33°C 130mm	23°C 32°C 120mm	21°C 30°C 100mm	19°C 28°C 70mm	18°C 27°C 50mm
July	**August**	**September**	**October**	**November**	**December**
17°C 26°C 40mm	18°C 27°C 40mm	19°C 28°C 60mm	20°C 28°C 80mm	21°C 29°C 90mm	22°C 31°C 130mm

ON THE ROAD

Carnaval

Carnaval in Rio is as spectacular as its reputation suggests – a riot of colour, flamboyance and artistry unrivalled outside Brazil. On the Friday before Shrove Tuesday, the mayor of Rio hands the keys of the city to *Rei Momo*, the Lord of Misrule, signifying the start of a five-day party. Imagination runs riot, social barriers are broken and the main avenues, full of people and children wearing fancy dress, are colourfully lit. Areas throughout the city such as the Terreirão de Samba in Praça Onze are used for shows, music and dancing. Spectacularly dressed carnival groups throng around the Sambódromo (Oscar Niemeyer's purpose-built stadium, see page 48) strutting, drumming and singing in preparation for their parade. And there are *blocos* (parades) throughout the city, in neighbourhoods such as Santa Teresa and Ipanema. It can be ghostly quiet in the southern beach zones during this time.

Unlike Salvador, which remains a wild street party, Rio's Carnaval is a designated parade, taking place over a number of days and contained within the Sambódromo stadium. Alongside the parade are a number of *bailes* (parties) held within designated clubs, street shows like those held around Praça Onze.

There are numerous samba schools in Rio, which are divided into two leagues before they parade through the Sambódromo. The 14 schools of the *Grupo Especial* parade on Sunday and Monday while the *Grupos de Acesso* A and B parade on Saturday and Friday respectively. There is also a *mirins* parade (younger members of the established schools) on Tuesday. Judging takes place on Wednesday afternoon and the winners of the groups parade again on the following Saturday. Tickets to these winners' parades are always easy to get hold of even when all others are sold out.

Every school comprises 2500-6000 participants divided into *alas* (wings) each with a different costume and parading on or around five to nine *carros alegóricos* (beautifully designed floats). Each school chooses an *enredo* (theme) and composes a samba that is a poetic, rhythmic and catchy expression of the theme. The *enredo* is further developed through the design of the floats and costumes. A *bateria* (percussion wing) maintains a reverberating beat that must keep the entire school, and the audience, dancing throughout the parade. Each procession follows a set order with the first to appear being the *comissão de frente* (a choreographed group that presents the school and the theme to the public). Next comes the *abre alas* (a magnificent float usually bearing the name or symbol of the school). The *alas* and other floats follow as well as *porta bandeiras* (flag bearers) and *mestre salas* (couples dressed in 18th-century costumes bearing the school's flag), and *passistas* (groups traditionally of mulata dancers). An *ala of baianas* (elderly women with circular skirts that swirl as they dance) is always included as is the *velha guarda* (distinguished members of the school) who close the parade. Schools are given between 65 and 80 minutes and lose points for failing to keep within this time. Judges award points to each school for components of their procession, such as costume, music and design, and make deductions for lack of energy, enthusiasm or discipline. The winners of the *Grupos de Acesso* are promoted to the next higher group while the losers, including those of the *Grupo Especial*, are relegated to the next lowest group. Competition is intense and the winners gain a monetary prize funded by the entrance fees.

The Carnaval parades are the culmination of months of intense activity by community groups, mostly in the city's poorest districts. Rio's *bailes* (fancy-dress balls) range from the sophisticated to the wild. The majority of clubs and hotels host at least one. The **Copacabana Palace**'s is elegant and expensive whilst the **Scala** club has licentious parties. It is not necessary to wear fancy dress; just join in, although you will feel more comfortable if you wear a minimum of clothing to the clubs, which are crowded, hot and rowdy. The most famous are the **Red and Black Ball** (Friday) and the **Gay Ball** (Tuesday) which are both televized. Venues for these vary.

Bandas and *blocos* can be found in all neighbourhoods and some of the most popular and entertaining are: **Cordão do Bola Preta** (meets at 0900 on Saturday, Rua 13 de Maio 13, Centro); **Simpatia é Quase Amor** (meets at 1600 on Sunday, Praça General Osório, Ipanema) and the transvestite **Banda da Ipanema** (meets at 1600 on Saturday and Tuesday, Praça General Osorio, Ipanema). It is necessary to join a bloco in advance to receive their distinctive T-shirts, but anyone can join in with the *bandas*. The expensive hotels offer special Carnaval breakfasts from 0530.

Even if you're coming independently it's wise to book your carnival tickets in advance with a tour operator like **Brazil Revealed** (www.brazilrevealed.co.uk) or **Journey Latin America** (www.journeylatinamerica.co.uk). See also Festivals, page 92.

What to do

Birdwatching

Almost a fifth of the world's bird species are Brazilian. The country is home to some 1750 species, of which 218 are endemic, the highest number of any country in the world. Brazil also has the largest number of globally threatened birds: 120 of 1212 worldwide. This is accounted for partly by the numbers of critically threatened habitats that include the Atlantic coastal rainforest, which recently lost the Alagoas currassow, the *caatinga*, which has lost Spix's macaw, and the Cerrado which is being cut at an alarming rate to feed the demand for soya.

Compared to Costa Rica or Ecuador, birding in Brazil is in its infancy, but awareness is increasing and there are some excellent birding guides in Brazil. It is no longer necessary to organize a birding trip through an international company (though many choose to do so; see operators below). The best time for birding is September-October as it is quiet, relatively dry and flights are cheapest.

The Rio region offers some of Brazil's best birding, especially in the **Serra dos Tucanos** (www.serradostucanos.com.br), and at **Reserva Ecológica de Guapi Assu (REGUA)**, both of which have expert guides, excellent facilities and extensive species lists. **Edson Endrigo** (www.avesfoto.com.br) offers guided trips into Itatiaia national park and in the rainforests of Rio's coastal mountains. See page 202 for a list of international companies offering Brazilian birdwatching and wildlife tours. Two comprehensive websites are www.worldtwitch.com and www.camacdonald.com.

Climbing and hill walking

Rio is one of the best cities anywhere for rock-climbing and hill walking. **CEESC, Rio Hiking, Morro dos Dois Irmãos** and a string of other companies can organize day hikes of varying degrees of difficulty as well as rock climbs up the Sugar Loaf or the Pedra da Gávea, the world's largest coastal monolith; see page 97.

The Serra dos Órgãos just outside the city is equally as spectacular and more challenging, not least the Dedo de Deus (God's Finger), a pinnacle of sheer granite set in forest-swathed mountains. Contact www.ancoraue.com, www.climbinrio.com and www. rioadventures.com for more details.

Pedra Branca and the Serra do Cipó are recommended climbing locations in Minas Gerais.

10 of the best beaches

Praia Urca, Rio, for sunset beers; see page 59.
Copacabana, Rio, for people-watching; see page 64.
Ipanema-Leblon, Rio, for urban sunbathing; see page 67.
Praia Joatinga, Rio, for privacy; see page 71.
Praia do Pontal, Rio, for surf and empty sand; see page 72.
Prainha, Rio, for surf and trail walking; see page 72.
Itacoatiara, Niterói, for surfing and scenery; see page 107.
Arraial do Cabo, Região dos Lagos, for bone-white sand and blue sea; see page 109.
Lopes Mendes, Ilha Grande, for scenery and walking; see page 131.
Trindade, Costa Verde, for rainforest running to the ocean; see page 142.

Cycling

With a public bike rental scheme, cycle tracks linking Barra to Copacabana via the beaches inaugurated in 2016 and a proliferation of pelotons practicing climbs on the hilly roads of Tijuca national park, Rio is now a decent place for cyclists. Bikes can be rented through **Velobike** (see page 100), through most hostels and through tour operators like **Rio Connexions** (see page 99) and **Rio Hiking** (see page 98).

Serra da Canastra in Minas Gerais is a popular area for mountain biking.

Diving and snorkelling

The water around Rio is cool, and while there are no coral reefs, the rocks around the islands near Angra and the pinnacles around Cabo Frio offer decent diving, though species diversity is low compared to Belize or the Caribbean. **CEESC** (see page 96) can organize snorkelling trips. **Rio Adventures** (www.rioadventures.com) and **Océan** (www.ocean.com.br) offer dive trips.

Hang-gliding and paragliding

There are state associations affiliated with the **Associação Brasileira de Vôo Livre**, or **ABVL**, the **Brazilian Hang-gliding Association** (T021-3322 0266, www.abvl. com.br), the national umbrella organization for hang-gliding and paragliding associations, and there are a number of operators offering tandem flights for those without experience. *Rampas* (launch sites) are growing in number. The best known and most spectacular is Pedra Bonita in Gávea in Rio de Janeiro city, and there are others in the state. See page 97 for a full list of operators.

Guia 4 Ventos Brasil (www.guia4ventos. com.br) has a full list of launch sites (and much else besides).

Horse riding

There are good horse trails in Minas Gerais along the routes that used to be taken by the mule trains which transported goods between the coast and the interior.

ON THE ROAD

Brazil's World Cup tragedies

Brazilians love football like Indians love cricket and seeing a match live is an unforgettable experience. The crowd is a sea of waving banners and the noise from the jeers and cheers, drums and whistles is deafening. Football in Brazil is treated with religious reverence. Work is put on hold during an important game. And the country quite literally closes for business during a FIFA World Cup™.

Once Brazilians were certain that they were and would always be the best in the world at the sport. That has changed in the last few years, after the national team failed dismally in the 2014 FIFA World Cup™, which returned to Brazil after a 64-year absence. Brazil played poorly in the opening rounds but nonetheless made it through to the semi-final undefeated where they faced Germany. The crowd began jauntily, waving flags, blowing whistles and full of enthusiasm born of the inevitability of Brazilian victory. They were soon stunned into silence as Germany slipped four goals past the team in just six minutes, going on to thrash Brazil 7-1 – the largest ever margin of victory in a World Cup semi-final.

The night of horror has since been christened the *Mineirazo* after the Mineirao stadium where the game was played, and echoing the *Maracanazo*, a national football tragedy which had occurred the previous time Brazil staged the tournament in 1950. On that occasion the team had stormed through the competition. Before they had even played in the final they were already being hailed as the world champions. The fans were smug, treating the Uruguayan opponents with a mixture of derision and pity and the front pages of the daily paper *O Mundo* printed an early edition of their final evening run showing a photograph of the Brazilian team with the caption "These are the world champions". The Uruguayans were furious. Their captain, Obdulio Varela, bought as many copies of the paper as he could, laid them on his bathroom floor and encouraged his teammates to urinate on them. They players went into the game bent on revenge, played their football socks off and defeated Brazil 2-1. Stripped of a title they had already considered theirs, the fans' silence was, in the words of FIFA chairman, Jules Rimet, "morbid and sometimes too difficult to bear".

The loss became known as the *Maracanazo* (after the Maracanã stadium in Rio where the match was held), a word which has become shorthand for any tragedy in Brazil ever since. To see a game in Rio, see Maracanã stadium, page 49.

Motorbike tours

Rio has a traffic problem and car-based tours operating over the rush hours (usually 0700-0930 and 1730-2000) can involve delays in jams. Motorbike tours, where passengers ride pillion, avoid these and can be organized through **CEESC** (see page 96).

Rafting

Whitewater rafting is popular around Rio in Casmimiro de Abreu, some two hours from the city, meaning a rafting trip will take a full day. The river is 80 km long with a rafting course of 8 km and a rafting experience of about two hours. Rapids range from Grade I-V in summer, I-IV in spring, I-III in autumn and I-II in winter. See Tour operators and guides, page 98.

Surfing

Brazilians love to surf and are well-represented in international competitions. Many of the local tour companies offer surf trips or lessons and you can find a selection listed on page 98.

Rio's best surf breaks are as follows:

Arpoador Breaks next to the rocks, gets good, the beach is illuminated making night surfing possible.

Barra da Guaratiba Rivermouth, perfect and powerful waves in the right conditions.

Barra da Tijuca 18-km beach with sand banks, closes out when big.

Copacabana Posto 5, needs a big swell and the water can be dirty.

Grumari 1-7 feet.

Ipanema Hollow, not much shape, 1-5 feet.

Leblon Hollow next to the breakwater, 1-5 feet.

Quebra Mar Next to the breakwater, hollow in the right conditions, 1-7 feet.

Pepino (São Conrado) Sometimes a good hollow left can break next to the rocks on the left side of the beach. Hang gliders land here, 1-6 feet.

Prainha Wild and good, 1-8 feet.

Recreio dos Bandeirantes Breaks by a rock a few metres from shore, on both sides and in different directions; can handle some size when other spots close out, 2-8 feet.

There is also good surfing on Itacoatiara beach in Niterói, Ilha Grande and around Trindade near Paraty – though you will need your own board to surf here.

Fluir (www.fluir.com.br), the country's biggest surf magazine, has information in Portuguese. Or see www.brazilsurftravel. com (in English).

Wind- and kitesurfing

While it cannot begin to compare to Atins or Jericoacoara in the country's northeast, there is good wind- and kitesurfing around Rio, especially to the east near Cabo Frio (see page 111) and along the beaches south of Barra da Tijuca in the city itself.

Shopping tips

Arts and crafts

Good buys include: beautiful bead jewellery and bags made from Amazon seeds; clay figurines from the northeast, especially from Pernambuco; lace from Ceará; leatherwork, Marajó pottery and fabric hammocks from Amazônia (be sure to buy hooks – *ganchos para rede* – for hanging your hammock at home); carvings in soapstone and in bone; *capim-dourado* gold-grass bags and jewellery from Tocantins; and African-type pottery, basketwork and *candomblé* artefacts from Bahia. Brazilian cigars are excellent for those who like mild flavours. These items can be found in shops around Rio, including in the **Feira do São Cristóvão**, the **Hippie Market** and in **Saara** (see pages 94 and 95).

The best shopping Rio itself is higher end fashion, home decor and arty souvenirs. Shop in the **MAM** store and **Novo Desenho (ND)** (see pages 55 and 94) for home decor and knick-knacks, in Ipanema for fashion, especially beachwear (see page 94), and the galleries of Santa Teresa and the **Hippie Market** in Ipanema for arty knick-knacks (see pages 94 and 95).

Cosmetics and herbal remedies

For those who know how to use them, medicinal herbs, barks and spices can be bought from street markets and in the **Feira do São Cristóvão**. Coconut oil and local skin and haircare products (including fantastic conditioners and herbal hair dyes) are as good though far cheaper than in Europe. Natura and O Boticário are excellent local brands, similar in quality to the Body Shop. There are branches in Rio's shopping malls.

Fashion

Brazil has long eclipsed Argentina as the fashion capital of Latin America. Brazilian cuts, colours and contours are fresh and daring by US and European standards. Quality and variety is very high, from gorgeous bags and bikinis to designer dresses, shoes and denims. In Rio, Ipanema is the place to go for high-end shopping, as well as the **São Conrado Fashion Mall** and **Shopping Leblon**. See Shopping, page 94.

Jewellery

Gold, diamonds and gemstones are good buys and there are innovative designs in jewellery. For something special and high quality, buy at reputable dealers such as **H Stern** or **Antonio Bernado** in Ipanema. Cheap, fun pieces can be bought from street traders. There are interesting furnishings made with gemstones and marble – some of them rather cheesy – and huge slabs of amethyst, quartz and crystal at a fraction of a New Age shop price. More interesting and unusual is the seed and bead jewellery, much of it made with uniquely Brazilian natural products, and based on original indigenous designs.

Music and instruments

Music is as ubiquitous as sunlight in Rio and browsing through a CD shop anywhere will be sure to result in at least one purchase.

Musical instruments are a good buy, particularly Brazilian percussion items. For example: the *berimbau*, a bow with a gourd sound-bell used in *candomblé*; the *cuica* friction drum, which produces the characteristic squeaks and chirrups heard in samba; assorted hand drums including the *surdo* (the big samba bass drum); and the *caixa*, *tambor*, *repinique* and *timbale* (drums that produce the characteristic Brazilian ra-ta-ta-ta-ta). The most Brazilian of hand drums is the tambourine, a misnomer for the *pandeiro* (which comes with bells), as opposed to the *tamborim* (which comes without). There are many unusual stringed instruments too: the *rabeca* (desert fiddle), the *cavaquinho* or *cavaco* (the Portuguese ancestor of ukulele), the *bandolim* (Brazilian mandolin), with its characteristic pear shape, and many excellent nylon-strung guitars. You can buy these in the Feira do São Cristóvão.

Then there's Brazilian music itself. Only a fraction of the best CDs reach Europe or the USA. Browse the selection in **Bossa Nova e Companhia** (see page 96) or **Toca do Vinícius** (see page 96) for a wonderful choice of samba, bossa nova and contemporary Rio samba funk and alternative music.

Improve your travel photography

Taking pictures is a highlight for many travellers, yet too often the results turn out to be disappointing. Steve Davey, author of Footprint's *Travel Photography*, sets out his top rules for coming home with pictures you can be proud of.

Before you go

Don't waste precious travelling time and do your research before you leave. Find out what festivals or events might be happening or which day the weekly market takes place, and search online image sites such as Flickr to see whether places are best shot at the beginning or end of the day, and what vantage points you should consider.

Get up early

The quality of the light will be better in the few hours after sunrise and again before sunset – especially in the tropics when the sun will be harsh and unforgiving in the middle of the day. Sometimes seeing the sunrise is a part of the whole travel experience: sleep in and you will miss more than just photographs.

Stop and think

Don't just click away without any thought. Pause for a few seconds before raising the camera and ask yourself what you are trying to show with your photograph. Think about what things you need to include in the frame to convey this meaning. Be prepared to move around your subject to get the best angle. Knowing the point of your picture is the first step to making sure that the person looking at the picture will know it too.

Compose your picture

Avoid simply dumping your subject in the centre of the frame every time you take a picture. If you compose with it to one side, then your picture can look more balanced. This will also allow you to show a significant background and make the picture more meaningful. A good rule of thumb is to place your subject or any significant detail a third of the way into the frame; facing into the frame not out of it.

This rule also works for landscapes. Compose with the horizon two-thirds of the way up the frame if the fore-ground is the most interesting part of the picture; one-third of the way up if the sky is more striking.

Don't get hung up with this so-called Rule of Thirds, though. Exaggerate it by pushing your subject out to the edge of the frame if it makes a more interesting picture; or if the sky is dull in a landscape, try cropping with the horizon near the very top of the frame.

Fill the frame

If you are going to focus on a detail or even a person's face in a close-up portrait, then be bold and make sure that you fill the frame. This is often a case of physically getting in close. You can use a telephoto setting on a zoom lens but this can lead to pictures looking quite flat; moving in close is a lot more fun!

Interact with people

If you want to shoot evocative portraits then it is vital to approach people and seek permission in some way, even if it is just by smiling at someone. Spend a little time with them and they are likely to relax and look less stiff and formal. Action portraits where people are doing something, or environmental portraits, where they are set against a significant background, are a good way to achieve relaxed portraits. Interacting is a good way to find out more about people and their lives, creating memories as well as photographs.

Focus carefully

Your camera can focus quicker than you, but it doesn't know which part of the picture you want to be in focus. If your camera is using the centre focus sensor then move the camera so it is over the subject and half press the button, then, holding it down, recompose the picture. This will lock the focus. Take the now correctly focused picture when you are ready.

Another technique for accurate focusing is to move the active sensor over your subject. Some cameras with touch-sensitive screens allow you to do this by simply clicking on the subject.

Leave light in the sky

Most good night photography is actually taken at dusk when there is some light and colour left in the sky; any lit portions of the picture will balance with the sky and any ambient lighting. There is only a very small window when this will happen, so get into position early, be prepared and keep shooting and reviewing the results. You can take pictures after this time, but avoid shots of tall towers in an inky black sky; crop in close on lit areas to fill the frame.

Bring it home safely

Digital images are inherently ephemeral: they can be deleted or corrupted in a heartbeat. The good news though is they can be copied just as easily. Wherever you travel, you should have a backup strategy. Cloud backups are popular, but make sure that you will have access to fast enough Wi-Fi. If you use RAW format, then you will need some sort of physical back-up. If you don't travel with a laptop or tablet, then you can buy a backup drive that will copy directly from memory cards.

Recently updated and available in both digital and print formats, Footprint's Travel Photography by Steve Davey covers everything you need to know about travelling with a camera, including simple post-processing. More information is available at www.footprinttravelguides.com

Where to stay

from *pensãos* to *pousadas*

There is a good range of accommodation options in Rio. An *albergue* or hostel offers the cheapest option. These have dormitory beds and single and double rooms. Many are part of **Hostelling International (HI)** ⓘ *www.hihostels.com*; **Hostel World** ⓘ *www.hostelworld.com*, **Hostel Bookers** ⓘ *www.hostelbookers.com*, and **Hostel.com** ⓘ *www.hostel.com*, are all useful portals. **Hostel Trail Latin America** ⓘ *T0131-208 0007 (UK), www.hosteltrail.com*, managed from their hostel in Popayan, is an online network of hotels and tour companies in South America. A *pensão* is either a cheap guesthouse or a household that rents out some rooms. **Favela Experience** (see page 79) organize stays in favelas.

Pousadas

A *pousada* is either a bed & breakfast, often small and family-run, or a sophisticated and frequently charming small hotel. A *hotel* is as it is anywhere else in the world, operating according to the international star system, although five-star hotels are not price controlled and hotels in any category are not always of the standard of their star equivalent in the USA, Canada or Europe. Many of the older hotels can be cheaper than hostels. Usually accommodation prices include a breakfast of rolls, ham, cheese, cakes and fruit with coffee and juice; there is no reduction if you don't eat it. Rooms vary too. Normally an *apartamento* is a room with separate living and sleeping areas and sometimes cooking facilities. A *quarto* is a standard room; *com banheiro* is en suite; and

Price codes

Where to stay	Restaurants
$$$$ over US$150	$$$ over US$12
$$$ US$66-150	$$ US$7-12
$$ US$30-65	$ US$6 and under
$ under US$30	
Price of a double room in high season, including taxes.	Prices for a two-course meal for one person, excluding drinks or service charge.

sem banheiro is with shared bathroom. Finally there are the *motels*. These should not be confused with their US counterpart: motels are used by guests not intending to sleep; there is no stigma attached and they usually offer good value (the rate for a full night is called the '*pernoite*'), however the decor can be a little garish.

It's a good idea to book accommodation in advance in small towns that are popular at weekends with city dwellers (eg near Rio de Janeiro), and it's essential to book at peak times. **Hidden Pousadas Brazil** ⓘ *www.hiddenpousadasbrazil.com*, offers a range of the best *pousadas*.

Luxury accommodation

Much of the best private accommodation sector can be booked through operators. **Angatu** ⓘ *www.angatu.com*, offers the best private homes along the Costa Verde, together with bespoke trips. **Matuete** ⓘ *www.matuete.com*, has a range of luxurious properties and tours throughout Brazil.

Camping

Those with an international camping card pay only half the rate of a non-member at **Camping Clube do Brasil** sites ⓘ *www.campingclube.com.br*. Membership of the club itself is expensive: US$70 for six months. The club has 43 sites in 13 states and 80,000 members. It may be difficult to get into some Camping Clube campsites during high season (January to February). Private campsites charge about US$6-8 per person. For those on a very low budget and in isolated areas where there is no campsite available, it's usually possible to stay at service stations. They have shower facilities, watchmen and food; some have dormitories. There are also various municipal sites. Campsites tend to be some distance from public transport routes and are better suited to people with their own car. Wild camping is generally difficult and dangerous. Never camp at the side of a road; this is very risky.

Homestays

Staying with a local family is an excellent way to become integrated quickly into a city and companies try to match guests to their hosts. **Cama e Café** ⓘ *www.camaecafe.com.br*, organizes homestays in Rio de Janeiro. **Couch surfing** ⓘ *www.couchsurfing.com*, offers a free, backpacker alternative.

Quality hotel associations

The better international hotel associations have members in Brazil. These include: **Small Luxury Hotels of the World** ⓘ *www.slh.com*; the **Leading Hotels** of the World ⓘ *www.lhw.com*; the **Leading Small Hotels of the World** ⓘ *www. leadingsmallhotelsoftheworld.com*; **Great Small Hotels** ⓘ *www.greatsmallhotels. com*; and the French group **Relais et Chateaux** ⓘ *www.relaischateaux.com*, which also includes restaurants.

The Brazilian equivalent of these associations are **Hidden Pousadas Brazil** ⓘ *www.hiddenpousadasbrazil.com*, and their associate, the **Roteiros de Charme** ⓘ *www.roteirosdecharme.com.br*. Membership of these groups pretty much guarantees quality, but it is by no means comprehensive.

Online travel agencies (OTAs)

Services like www.tripadvisor.com and OTAs associated with them – such as www.hotels.com, www.expedia.com and www.venere.com – are well worth using for both reviews and for booking ahead. Hotels booked through an OTA can be up to 50% cheaper than the rack rate. Similar sites operate for hostels (though discounts are far less considerable). They include the **Hostelling International** site, www.hihostels.com, www.hostelbookers.com, www.hostels. com and www.hostelworld.com.

Food
& drink

from a *chope* with *churrasco* to a *pinga* with *pesticos*

While Brazil has some of the best fine dining restaurants in Latin America and cooking has greatly improved over the last decade, everyday Brazilian cuisine can be stolid. Mains are generally heavy, meaty and unspiced. Desserts are often very sweet. In Rio, a heady mix of international immigrants has resulted in some unusual fusion cooking and exquisite variations on French, Japanese, Portuguese, Arabic and Italian traditional techniques and dishes and the regional cooking can be a delight. The Brazilian staple meal generally consists of a cut of fried or barbecued meat, chicken or fish accompanied by rice, black or South American broad beans and an unseasoned salad of lettuce, grated carrot, tomato and beetroot. Condiments consist of weak chilli sauce, olive oil, salt and pepper and vinegar.

The national dish – which is associated with Rio – is a heavy campfire stew called *feijoada*, made by throwing jerked beef, smoked sausage, tongue and salt pork into a pot with lots of fat and beans and stewing it for hours. The resulting stew is sprinkled with fried *farofa* (manioc flour) and served with *couve* (kale) and slices of orange. The meal is washed down with *cachaça* (sugarcane rum). Most restaurants serve the *feijoada completa* for Saturday lunch (up until about 1630). Come with a very empty stomach.

Brazil's other national dish is mixed grilled meat or *churrasco*, served in vast portions off the spit by legions of rushing waiters, and accompanied by a buffet of salads, beans and mashed vegetables. *Churrascos* are served in *churrascarias* or *rodízios*. The meat is generally excellent, especially in the best *churascarias*, and the portions are unlimited, offering good value for camel-stomached carnivores able to eat one meal a day.

In remembrance of Portugal, but bizarrely for a tropical country replete with fish, Brazil is also the world's largest consumer of cod, pulled from the cold north Atlantic, salted and served in watery slabs or little balls as *bacalhau* (an appetizer/bar snack) or *petisco*. Other national *petiscos* include *kibe* (a deep-fried or baked mince with onion, mint and flour), *coxinha* (deep-fried chicken or meat in dough), *empadas* (baked puff-pastry patties with prawns, chicken, heart of palm or meat) and *tortas* (little pies with the same ingredients). When served in bakeries, *padarias* or snack bars these are collectively referred to as *salgadinhos* (savouries).

Eating cheaply

The cheapest dish is the *prato feito* or *sortido*, an excellent-value set menu usually comprising meat/chicken/fish, beans, rice, chips and salad. The *prato comercial* is similar but rather better and a bit more expensive. Portions are usually large enough for two and come with two plates. If you are on your own, you could ask for an *embalagem* (doggy bag) or a *marmita* (takeaway) and offer it to a person with no food (many Brazilians do). Many restaurants serve *comida por kilo* buffets where you serve yourself and pay for the weight of food on your plate. This is generally good value and is a good option for vegetarians. *Lanchonetes* and *padarias* (diners and bakeries) are good for cheap eats, usually serving *prato feitos*, *salgadinhos*, excellent juices and other snacks.

The main meal is usually taken in the middle of the day; cheap restaurants tend not to be open in the evening.

Drink

The national liquor is *cachaça* (also known as *pinga*), which is made from sugar-cane, and ranging from cheap supermarket and service-station firewater, to boutique distillery and connoisseur labels from the interior of Minas Gerais. Mixed with fruit juice, sugar and crushed ice, *cachaça* becomes the principal element in a *batida*, a refreshing but deceptively powerful drink. Served with pulped lime or other fruit, mountains of sugar and smashed ice it becomes the world's favourite party cocktail, caipirinha. A less potent caipirinha made with vodka is called a *caipiroska* and with sake a *saikirinha* or *caipisake.*

Some genuine Scotch whisky brands are bottled in Brazil. They are far cheaper even than duty free; Teacher's is the best. Locally made and cheap gin, vermouth and Campari are pretty much as good as their US and European counterparts.

Wine is becoming increasingly popular and Brazil is the third most important wine producer in South America. The wine industry is mainly concentrated in the south of the country where the conditions are most suitable, with over 90% of wine produced in Rio Grande do Sul. Reasonable national table wines include Château d'Argent, Château Duvalier, Almadén, Dreher, Preciosa and more respectable Bernard Taillan, Marjolet from Cabernet grapes, and the Moselle-type white Zahringer. There are some interesting sparkling wines in the Italian spumante style (the best is Casa Valduga Brut Premium Sparkling Wine), and Brazil produces still wines using many international and imported varieties. The best bottle of red is probably the Boscato Reserva Cabernet Sauvignon, but it's expensive (at around US$20 a bottle); you'll get far higher quality and better value buying Portuguese, Argentine or Chilean wines in Brazil.

Brazilian beer is generally lager, served ice-cold. Draught beer is called *chope* or *chopp* (after the German Schoppen, and pronounced 'shoppi'). There are various national brands of bottled beers, which include Brahma, Skol, Cerpa, Antartica and the best Itaipava and Bohemia. There are black beers too, notably Xingu. They tend to be sweet.

Brazil's myriad fruits are used to make fruit juices or *sucos*, which come in a delicious variety, unrivalled anywhere in the world. *Açai acerola*, *caju* (cashew), *pitanga*, *goiaba* (guava), *genipapo*, *graviola* (chirimoya), *maracujá* (passion fruit), *sapoti*, *umbu* and *tamarindo* are a few of the best. *Vitaminas* are thick fruit or vegetable drinks with milk. *Caldo de cana* is sugar-cane juice, sometimes mixed with ice. *Água de côco* or *côco verde* is coconut water served straight from a chilled, fresh, green coconut. The best known of many local soft drinks is *guaraná*, which is a very popular carbonated fruit drink, completely unrelated to the Amazon nut. The best variety is *guaraná Antarctica*. Coffee is ubiquitous and good tea entirely absent.

Menu reader

A

acarajé deep-fried ball of black-eyed peas and onions, slit open and filled with prawns and cashews, common in Salvador and Espírito Santo

água de côco coconut water served from a green coconut

arroz doce rice pudding

B

bacalhau salt cod

batida cachaça mixed with fruit juice and crushed ice

bauru sandwich made with melted cheese, roast beef and tomatoes

brigadeiros chocolate fudge

C

cachaça sugar cane rum

caipirinha cocktail of crushed fruit (usually limes), *cachaça* and lots of sugar and ice

caju cashew

caldo de cana sugar cane juice

caldo de feijão bean soup

chope/chopp draught beer

churrasco mixed grilled meat

churrasqueira restaurant serving all-you-can-eat barbecued meat

côco verde coconut water served from a chilled, fresh, green coconut

comida por kilo
comida por kilo pay-by-weight food

coxinha shredded chicken or other meat covered in dough and breadcrumbs and deep fried

curau custard flan-type dessert made with maize

cuscuz branco tapioca pudding with coconut milk and sugar

E

empadas or **empadinhas** baked puff-pastry patties with prawns, chicken, palm hearts or meat

F

farofa fried cassava flour

feijoada hearty stew of black beans, sausages and pork

frango churrasco grilled chicken

G

goiaba guava (*goiabada* is a guava paste served with cheese)

K

kibe a petisco deep-fried or baked mince with onion, mint and flour

M

mandioca frita fried manioc root, similar to chips
maracujá passion fruit
misto quente toasted ham and cheese sandwich
moqueca seafood stew cooked with coconut and dende palm oil, typical of Bahia and Espírito Santo

P

padaria bakery
palmito palm heart
pamonha paste of milk and corn boiled in a corn husk
pão de queijo a roll made with cheese, served with meals, especially breakfast
pastéis deep-fried pastries filled with cheese, minced beef, or palm heart
peixe fish
petisco a tapas-style snack
picanha rump, a popular cut of beef in Brazil
pinga sugar cane rum
prato feito/prato comercial set meal

Q

queijo cheese
quindim a sweet made with egg yolks, sugar and shredded coconut, common in Bahia

R

requeijão ricotta-like cream cheese
roupa velha literally meaning 'old clothes', a dish of shredded dried meat served with rice mandiocas

S

salgadinhos savoury snacks such as *empadas* and *tortas*
sortido inexpensive set meal
suco fruit juice

T

tacacá prawn and manioc juice soup served with *jambu* leaves, which leave the mouth tingling
tortas small pies filled with prawns, chicken, palm hearts or meat

V

vatapá fish and prawn stew cooked in a creamy peanut sauce
vitaminas fruit or vegetable drinks with milk

Rio de
Janeiro

Rio de Janeiro city

According to Cariocas – the people of Rio de Janeiro – God made the world in six days and then spent the seventh lying on the beach in Ipanema. For in a city as beautiful as this, they say, only the philistine or the ungrateful would do anything else.

There is far more to the city than Corcovado capped with Christ or the Sugar Loaf; these are overtures to the grand symphony of the scene. Rainforest-covered boulder-mountains as high as Snowdon rise sheer from the sea around the vast Guanabara Bay and stretch to the horizon. Their curves and jags are broken by long sweeping beaches of powder-fine sand pounded by the dazzling green ocean, or by perfect half-moon coves lapped by the gentle waters of the bay. The city clusters around them, climbing over hills and crowding behind beaches and lakes.

Against this magical backdrop, the famous Carioca day leisurely unwinds. When the sun is up the middle classes head for the beach, wearing nothing but tiny speedos or bikinis. Here they surf, play beach volleyball or football, or soak up the rays between dips, with the working day just a brief interruption. When the sun is down, still wearing almost nothing, they head for the *botecos* (street bars) for an ice-cold draught beer or *chope*. Then they go home, finally put some clothes on and prepare to go out until the early hours of the morning.

Essential Rio de Janeiro city

Finding your feet

International flights arrive at **Aeroporto Internacional Tom Jobim** (also known as **Galeão**), 15 km north of the city centre. Domestic flights use **Santos Dumont Airport** in the centre on Guanabara Bay. There are frequent buses between the two airports and into the centre, as well as taxis.

Rio's long-distance bus station, the **Rodoviária Novo Rio** (Avenida Francisco Bicalho 01 at Rodrigues Alves, Santo Cristo, T021-3213 1800, www.novorio.com.br) is just north of the city centre. Local buses link it with the centre and the airport; see Transport, page 99.

Getting around

Bus, *metrô* and taxi are the main ways to get around the city. Driving is not recommended.

Orientation

Rio squeezes between boulder mountains, the beaches of Guanabara bay – one of the world's biggest natural harbours – and the bottle-green Atlantic ocean. Tourists stay in the Zona Sul in the south of the city, and in Ipanema or Copacabana, which are both in the Atlantic Ocean beach neighbourhoods.

The centre lies to the north, separated by forest-covered hills with peaks sticking up like worn granite fingers and thumbs: Sugar Loaf, the Pico da Tijuca and Corcovado, Rio's most famous, crowned with a statue of Christ.

Santa Teresa (Rio's Montmatre), Lapa (the samba-driven nightlife capital), Maracanã (the famous football stadium and venue for the Olympic opening ceremony in August 2016) and the Sambodromo arena (where the carnival takes place) ring the centre.

Safety

Rio de Janeiro has a bad reputation for crime and violence. Most of this takes place in the favelas of northern Rio and the periphery – areas most tourists never stray near. Most visitors have trouble-free visits and many enjoying Rio's laid-back atmosphere and carefree feel wonder what the fuss is all about. In fact Rio is so easy on the eye with such a relaxed pace of life that it can be disarming. It's important to follow a few safety rules as follows.

- Be aware of your surrounds at all times. Most crime is targeted. Look out for who is watching you.
- Don't attract unwanted attention with bright jewellery, blingy brands and cameras around the neck. Keep jewellery in the safe, cameras in a bag and dress like a local in Havaiana flip-flops and casual T-shirts and shorts or suchlike.
- Ask your hotel about the local neighbour-hood. Are there any streets best avoided? Any times of day to be vigilant?
- Never visit a favela unaccompanied.
- Avoid empty alleys and streets after dark.
- Take cabs from a taxi rank or from outside the hotel.
- Don't use a satnav when driving in or out of Rio. They choose the shortest route. This could be through a dangerous area. Stick to the main roads.

When to go

Rio is good at any time of the year but bear in mind it's wet December to January (in winter), although warm with temperatures up to 33°C. Summer (April to October) is dry with blue skies. See also the weather chart on page 11.

Time required

Allow at least three days to explore the city; seven to 10 days for the city and state.

The central area of Rio (population 8 million) spreads back from Guanabara Bay in a jumbled grid of streets between Santos Dumont Airport and the Jesuit Mosteiro São Bento. It dates from 1567, but much of its architectural heritage has been laid waste by successive waves of government intent on wiping out the past in favour of dubious and grandiose visions of Order and Progress. Manueline follies and elaborate neoclassical façades huddle together under totalitarian blocks of flats and Le Corbusier-inspired concrete. All watch over a mass of cars and a bustle of people. It can all feel a bit hectic and bewildering. But don't give up. There is plenty to explore here and a wealth of air-conditioned havens in which to escape for respite and a coffee.

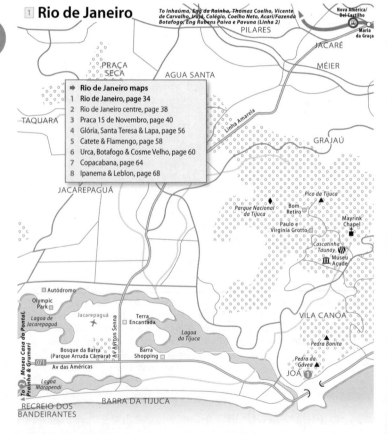

1 Rio de Janeiro

➡ **Rio de Janeiro maps**
1 Rio de Janeiro, page 34
2 Rio de Janeiro centre, page 38
3 Praca 15 de Novembro, page 40
4 Glória, Santa Teresa & Lapa, page 56
5 Catete & Flamengo, page 58
6 Urca, Botafogo & Cosme Velho, page 60
7 Copacabana, page 64
8 Ipanema & Leblon, page 68

Many of the historic buildings sit just south of the centre, near Santos Dumont Airport and, around **Praça 15 de Novembro**, from where Rio de Janeiro grew in its earliest days. Here you'll find most of the museums, some of the city's more beautiful little churches and colonial buildings such as the **Paço Imperial** and the **Palácio Tiradentes**. More colonial buildings lie at the centre's northern extremity around the Morro de São Bento. These include the finest baroque building in Rio, the **Mosteiro de São Bento**, and the city's most imposing church, **Nossa Senhora da Candelária**.

The city's main artery is the **Avenida Presidente Vargas**, 4.5 km long and more than 90 m wide, which divides these northern and southern sections. It begins at the waterfront, splits around the Candelária church, then crosses the Avenida Rio Branco in a magnificent straight stretch past the **Central do Brasil** railway station. Vargas is dissected by two important arterial streets. **Avenida Rio Branco**, nearest to the sea, was once lined with splendid ornate buildings, which were quite the equal of any in Buenos Aires,

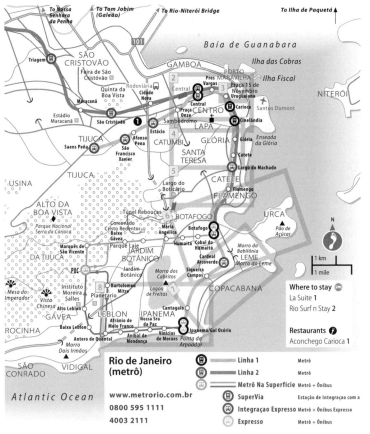

BACKGROUND
Rio de Janeiro

The coast of Rio de Janeiro was first settled about 5000 years ago by tribal peoples who arrived in South America either through the Bering Islands or possibly across the Pacific. When the Europeans arrived, the indigenous inhabitants belonged to the Tupi or Tupi-Guarani, Botocudos, Puri and Maxacali linguistic groups. Tragically, no indigenous people in this region survived the European incursions.

The Portuguese navigator, Gonçalo Coelho, landed at what is now Rio de Janeiro on 1 January 1502. Mistaking Baía de Guanabara (the name the local people used) to be the mouth of a great river, he called it the 'January River'. In 1555 the French occupied Lage Island and then Serigipe Island (now Villegagnon). Since the narrow channel was filled up, the island has now become a part of the mainland. Now called Ilha de Villegagnon, it's on the edge of Santos Dumont airport.

In 1559-1560, Mem de Sá, the governor of Brazil, invaded Rio with a huge army of indigenous Tabajara to attack the French. The Portuguese won and the Tabajara occupied villages around Cabritos and São João hills between Copacabana and Lagoa. The favela there, Tabajaras-Cabritos (see page 67), still bears their name. In 1567, the Portuguese formally founded the city of São Sebastião do Rio de Janeiro, named after the Portuguese prince who would soon assume the throne.

The new city grew rapidly and when King Sebastião divided Brazil into two provinces, Rio was chosen as capital of the south, with Salvador capital of the north. By the early 18th century Rio was becoming the country's leading city and after Independence, in 1834, it was declared capital of the empire.

King João and the entire Portuguese court fled to Brazil in 1808 in fear of Napoleon, abandoning Portugal. The ideas they brought with them from Europe began to transform Rio, which became a capital of the Empire. New formal gardens, stately *praças* and lavish palaces and mansions were built. Despite his fear of Napoleon,

but were razed to the ground in the early 20th century. However, a few remain around **Cinelândia**. **Avenida 31 Março**, further to the west beyond the railway station, leads to the **Sambódromo** and the Carnaval district. Some of the better modern architecture is to be found along Avenida República do Chile, including the conical 1960s **Catedral Metropolitana de São Sebastião**.

Praça 15 de Novembro and the imperial palaces
For Praça 15 de Novembro take the metrô *to Carioca in Cinelândia.*

Originally an open space at the foot of the Morro do Castelo – a hill which has now been flattened – the Praça 15 de Novembro (often called Praça Quinze) has always been one of the focal points in Rio de Janeiro. Today it has one of the greatest concentrations of historic buildings in the city. Having been through various phases of development, the area underwent major remodelling in the late 1990s. The last vestiges of the original harbour, at the seaward end of the *praça*, were restored. Avenida Alfredo

> **Tip...**
> Opening times for churches, museums and public buildings change frequently. All museums close during Carnaval.

King João invited an artistic mission from France to found academies of fine art and music in Rio. The city expanded geographically and grew in prosperity, with wealthy coffee barons building *chacaras* (country houses) in the hills around Tijuca and Santa Teresa. By the time Brazil became a republic in 1889, Rio was by far the most important city in the country.

The new republic was founded on French positivist principles, expressed by the national motto 'Order and Progress'. The past was discarded; sadly, much of colonial Rio was destroyed and replaced by poor versions of US office blocks lining broad new avenues. The disenfranchised poor Brazilian majority, many recently freed African-Brazilian slaves refusing work on the plantations, began to cluster on the hills in shanty towns, or favelas.

In 1960 the new president Juscelino Kubitschek declared that his country would leap 50 years in just five. JK shifted the nation's capital several thousand kilometres inland to the new purpose-built Jetson-age Brasília, sending the country into bankruptcy and Rio into decline. The commercial centre crumbled, the bright lights of Lapa and Cinelândia flickered and went dim and wealthy Cariocas left for the beaches around Ipanema and São Conrado.

Resurrection began in the 1990s, when a new mayor, Luiz Paulo Conde, embarked on a massive programme of regeneration, remodelling the bayside suburbs and reviving neglected districts. Lapa re-emerged as a nightlife centre and Rio began to find its cultural feet again.

The World Cup and the Olympics have stimulated further recent redevelopment. The *metrô* is being extended and the decrepit old docks rebranded as Porto Maravilha (meaning 'marvellous port'), with new museums (see page 43), malls and plans for the largest aquarium in Latin America. Many of favelas have been 'pacified', receiving police presence for the first time. But centuries of neglect have left a toll. Contemporary Rio has hundreds of favelas and a population chronically divided between the haves, who live in Cidade Maravilhosa, and the have-nots, who live in the Cidade de Deus slums.

Agache now goes through an underpass, creating an open space between the *praça* and the seafront and giving easy access to the ferry dock for Niterói. The area is well illuminated and clean and the municipality has started to stage shows, music and dancing in the *praça*. At weekends an antiques, crafts, stamp and coin fair (Feirarte II) is held 0900-1900.

The rather modest colonial former royal palace, **Paço Imperial** ⓘ *on the southeast corner of Praça 15 de Novembro, T021-2533 4407, www.pacoimperial.com.br, Tue-Sun 1200-1800*, is one of the centre's landmarks. It was built in 1743 as the residence of the governor of the Capitania and was made into the royal palace when the Portuguese court moved to Brazil. After independence it became the imperial palace. It fell into disuse in the mid-20th century to be resurrected as a temporary exhibition space and arts centre. There's often something interesting on display here, and two decent air-conditioned café-restaurants, the **Bistro** and **Atrium**, provide respite from the heat. Just north of the palace is the **Chafariz do Mestre Valentim** (or Chafariz do Pirâmide), a fountain designed by the famous sculptor.

Beside the Paço Imperial, across Rua da Assembléia, is the grand neoclassical **Palácio Tiradentes** ⓘ *T021-2588 1411, www.alerj.rj.gov.br, Mon-Sat 1000-1700, Sun and holidays 1200-1700, guided visits by appointment only, T021-2588 1251*. It was named in

② Rio de Janeiro centre

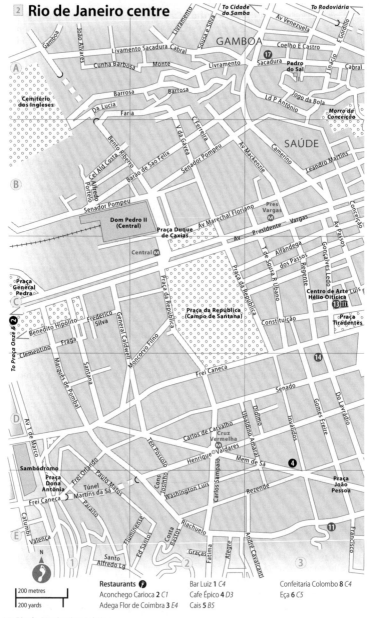

To Cidade do Samba
To Rodoviária

GAMBOA

SAÚDE

Cemitério dos Ingleses

Morro da Conceição

Pedro do Sal

Dom Pedro II (Central)

Praça Duque de Caxias

Central Ⓜ

Praça General Pedra

Praça da República (Campo de Santana)

Centro de Arte Luís Hélio Oiticica ⑬

Praça Tiradentes

⑭

Cruz Vermelha Ⓜ

Sambódromo

Praça Dona Antônia

Praça João Pessoa

❹

⑪

N

200 metres
200 yards

Restaurants ❼
Aconchego Carioca 2 C1
Adega Flor de Coimbra 3 E4

Bar Luiz 1 C4
Cafe Épico 4 D3
Cais 5 B5

Confeitaria Colombo 8 C4
Eça 6 C5

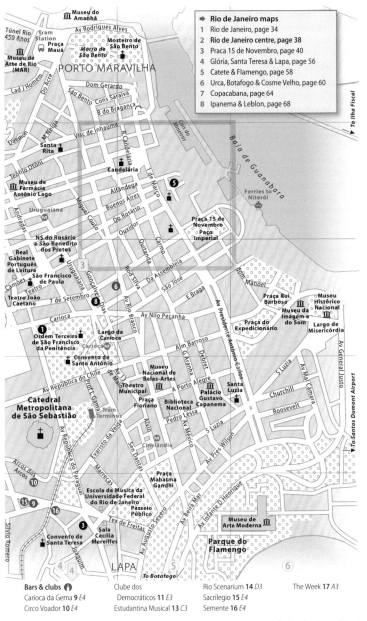

Bars & clubs
Carioca da Gema 9 *E4*
Circo Voador 10 *E4*
Clube dos Democráticos 11 *E3*
Estudantina Musical 13 *C3*
Rio Scenarium 14 *D3*
Sacrilegio 15 *E4*
Semente 16 *E4*
The Week 17 *A3*

honour of the former dentist (*tiradentes* means teeth puller), Joaquim José da Silva Xavier, who is often seen as the symbolic father of Brazilian independence, and who was held prisoner here and executed nearby. The building itself was constructed between 1922 and 1926 and is now the state legislative assembly. A **statue of Tiradentes** by Francisco de Andrade stands in front.

Largo da Misericórdia and the museums

There is a cluster of interesting little museums south of Praça XV on the way to Santos Dumont Airport that can be reached by the Largo da Misericórdia, which runs immediately south of the Palácio Tiradentes. At the end of the *largo* is the **Ladeira da Misericórdia**; the oldest street in Rio and now just a severed stump on the side of the grand Santa Casa da Misericórdia hospital. This hill was once crowned by a magnificent monastery and fort that watched out over the bay. Next door to the hospital, in a series of handsome buildings, is the **Museu Histórico Nacional** ⓘ *Praça Marechal Âncora, T021-3299 0324, www.museuhitoriconacional.com.br, Tue-Fri 1000-1730, Sat and Sun 1400-1800, US$2.25, free on Sun*. This is one of the city's more distinguished museums, with a collection of magnificent carriages, historical treasures, colonial sculpture and furniture, maps, paintings, arms and armour, silver and porcelain. It also retains a rampart from that first fort that crowned the former Morro do Castelo hill from the 1603 until the 20th century. The building was once the war arsenal of the empire, and was partly constructed in 1762 (this part is called the 'Casa do Trem').

➡ **Rio de Janeiro maps**
1 Rio de Janeiro, page 34
2 Rio de Janeiro centre, page 38
3 **Praça 15 de Novembro, page 40**
4 Glória, Santa Teresa & Lapa, page 56
5 Catete & Flamengo, page 58
6 Urca, Botafogo & Cosme Velho, page 60
7 Copacabana, page 64
8 Ipanema & Leblon, page 68

3 **Praça 15 de Novembro**

The **Museu da Imagem e do Som (MIS)** ① *at the moment split between 2 centres: R Visconde de Maranguape 15, Largo da Lapa, T021-2332 9508, and Praça Luiz Souza Dantas (aka Praça Rui Barbosa) 01, Praça XV, T021-2332 9068, Mon-Fri 1100-1700, www.mis.rj.gov.br, free, visits by appointment only*, is scheduled to move into a stunning purpose-built new building by New York architects Diller Scofidio + Renfro in Copacabana in late 2016. The collection comprises cinema images, photos of Rio and of Carioca musicians, and recordings of popular music, including early *choro* by artists including Jacob do Bandolim. There are booths for listening to music and a small cinema for watching the 16 mm and 35 mm film archive. The new museum will also house a collection of memorabilia related to Carmen Miranda and far more galleries devoted to Brazilian music.

Travessa do Comércio and the Carmelite churches

North of Praça XV, the **Travessa do Comércio** and its continuation to the left, the **Rua do Ouvidor**, are reached via the **Arco do Teles** directly across from the palace. The arch is all that remains of an 18th-century construction, now incorporated into a modern building, and the two streets give an idea of how most of Rio must have looked in the 19th century. Little bars and restaurants line the streets and are very lively after 1800. These include the **Arco Imperial**, where Carmen Miranda lived between 1925 and 1930 (her mother kept a boarding house). There are also some interesting bookshops and one of Brazil's prettiest little baroque churches, **Nossa Senhora da Lapa dos Mercadores** ① *R do Ouvidor 35, T021-2509 2239, Mon-Fri 0800-1400*. This began life as a street oratory erected in a blind alley by market vendors who traditionally petitioned Our Lady of Lapa for help in hard times; it became a church in 1750, was remodelled in 1869-1872 and has now been fully restored.

The busy thoroughfare of Rua 1 de Março cuts across the top of Praça XV and Rua Ouvidor and is littered with Carmelite churches, all of them worth a quick look. The most famous is at the northwestern corner of the *praça*: **Nossa Senhora do Carmo da Antiga Sé** ① *R 1 de Março at R 7 de Setembro 14, T021-2509 2239, Tue-Thu 0900-1700, Sat 1100-1700*, has one of the finest baroque interiors in Rio and occupies the site of the original founding Carmelite chapel, which stood here between 1590 and 1754. The current church dates from 1761. After the arrival of the Portuguese court in 1808 it became the designated Royal Chapel and subsequently the city's first cathedral – between 1900 and 1976. The crypt allegedly holds the remains of Pedro Alvares Cabral, the European discoverer of Brazil; a claim disputed by the town of Santarém in Portugal.

Just north of this church and right in front of the end of Rua Ouvidor is the **Igreja da Ordem Terceira do Monte do Carmo** ① *R 1 de Março s/n, Mon-Fri 0800-1400, Sat 0800-1200*. This was built in 1754, consecrated in 1770 and rebuilt in the 19th century. It has strikingly beautiful portals by Mestre Valentim, the son of a Portuguese nobleman and a slave girl. He also created the main altar of fine moulded silver, the throne and its chair and much else.

At the rear of the old cathedral and the Igreja da Ordem Terceira do Monte do Carmo, on Rua do Carmo, is the **Oratório de Nossa Senhora do Cabo da Boa Esperança**; one of the few remaining public oratories from the colonial period in Rio.

Candelária and around

To get to Candelária take the metrô to Uruguiana.

Rio's most imposing church lies on an island in a sea of traffic some 500 m north of Praça XV. The mock-Italianate **Igreja de Nossa Senhora da Candelária** ① *Praça Pio X, T021-2233 2324, Mon-Fri 0800-1600, Sat 0800-1200, Sun 0900-1300*, has long been the church of 'society Rio'. Celebrities still gather here in the marble interior for the city's most prestigious weddings. The church is modelled on the Basílica da Estrela in Portugal. The tiles in the dome are from Lisbon, the marble inside is Veronan and the heavy bronze doors were commissioned from France. All were shipped across at vast expense in the late 18th century, during an era when even though such materials were readily available in Brazil at similar quality and far lower prices, snob value demanded that they be imported. The church was built on the site of a chapel founded in 1610 by the Spaniard Antônio Martins Palma who arrived in Rio after surviving a terrible storm at sea. He erected the chapel in homage to Nuestra Señora de Candelária, the patron saint of his home, La Palma in the Canaries.

There are a number of cultural centres near the church. The **Centro Cultural Correios** ① *R Visconde de Itaboraí 20, T021-2253 1580, www.correios.com.br, Tue-Sun 1200-1900, free*, in a smart early 20th-century building with a little private park, is a good stop for an air-conditioned juice or coffee. It has a theatre, a 1000-sq-m concert hall and spaces for temporary exhibitions and cultural events, and a postage stamp fair on Saturdays.

Just opposite, with entrances on Avenida Presidente Vargas and Rua 1 de Março 66, is the **Centro Cultural Banco do Brasil (CCBB)** ① *R 1 de Março 66, T021-3808 2020, www. bb.com.br/cultura, Tue-Sun 1000-2100*, in a fine early 19th-century neoclassical building with a beautiful glass domed roof. The centre hosts many of the city's large and distinguished art shows, including some excellent photographic exhibitions. It also has an arts cinema, library, multimedia facilities and lunchtime concerts (around US$3). The restaurant is air conditioned and the food respectable.

At the corner of Rua Visconde de Itaboraí (No 253) and Avenida Presidente Vargas, just opposite Candelária, is the **Casa França-Brasil** ① *R Visconde de Itaboraí 78, T021-2253 5366, www. casafrancabrasil.com.br, Tue-Sun 1000-2000*, a Franco-Brazilian cultural centre designed by one of the key players in the 19th-century French cultural mission to Rio, Grandjean de Montigny. It holds temporary exhibitions exploring the long relationship between the two countries.

The newest of the cultural centres near Candelária is the **Espaço Cultural da Marinha** ① *Av Alfredo Agache, on the waterfront, T021-2104 6025, www.sdm.mar.mil.br/espaco.htm, Tue-Sun 1200-1700, free*. This former naval establishment, built on a jetty over the bay, now contains museums of underwater archaeology and navigation. *Galeota*, the boat used by the Portuguese royal family for sailing around the Baía de Guanabara, is kept here and a Second World War submarine and warship, the *Bauru* (not to be confused with the sandwich of the same name), is moored outside. The museum is very popular with Brazilian children and is crowded at weekends.

Just offshore, but connected to the mainland by a causeway to Ilha das Cobras, is the **Ilha Fiscal** ① *Av Alfredo Agache, T021-2233 9165, boats leave Thu-Sun at 1300, 1430 and 1600, closed 1 Jan, Carnaval, Holy Week and Christmas; when the sea is too rough transport is by van*. It was built as a customs house at the emperor's request, but he deemed it too beautiful, and said that it should be used only for official parties. Only one was ever held – a masked ball hosted by the viscount of Ouro Preto in honour of the crew of the Chilean warship, *The Admiral Cochrane*, five days before the republic began. It is now a museum, linked with the Espaço Cultural da Marinha. The island is passed by the ferry to Niterói.

Porto Maravilha museums

The **Praça Mauá**, which lies north of Avenida Presidente Vargas, marks the end of Centro and the beginning of the port zone, which is being completely reinvented and revitalized in preparation for the 2016 Olympics, under the Porto Maravilha programme (www.portomaravilha.com.br; check the website for the latest openings).

The myriad empty warehouses are being replaced by leisure areas, accommodation and a series of new museums and galleries. These include the **Museu de Arte do Rio** (**MAR**) ① *Praça Mauá, T021-3031 2741, www.museudeartedorio.org.br, Tue-Fri 1000-1700, US$2.50, free Tue*, which showcases artists responsible for the establishment of the Brazilian style (including Burle Marx, Castagneto, Dall'Ara, Di Cavalcanti, Facchinetti, Goeldi, Iberê Camargo, Ismael Nery and Lygia Clark) and those who are shaping Brazilian art and society today, through some of the city's most exciting temporary exhibitions, drawing on the relationship those artists have with Rio.

Immediately in front of MAR is the mesmerizing **Museu do Amanhã** (Museum of Tomorrow), a starship-shaped concrete wedge hovering over an artificial lake designed by Spanish neo-futurist Santiago Calatrava (of the Queen Sofía Palace of the Arts in Valencia), whose exhibition halls are due to open in time for the Olympics. They will be devoted to science and technology and are expected to be as state of the art as the architecture, which is best appreciated from the upper viewing deck of MAR.

Mosteiro de São Bento

R Gerardo 68, T021-2516 2286, www.osb.org.br, daily 0700-1730, free, guided tours Mon-Sat 0900-1600; modest dress, no shorts; taxi from the city centre US$6.

In stark contrast to the Porto Maravilha is the sober Brazilian baroque façade of the Mosteiro de São Bento, which sits above the Porto Maravilha on a promontory looking out over the bay. The church is widely publicized as a World Heritage Site, which it is not. But of all of the city's colonial buildings this is the most worth visiting, both for its magnificent interior and for its significance as the most important Benedictine monument outside Europe. The church began life in 1586 with a group of monks who arrived in Rio from Salvador and it grew to become the most powerful monastery in the city. It preserves a lavish gilt baroque interior but is very poorly lit (the church charges an absurd US$5 to put on all of the electric lights). However, in the gloom it is possible to make out that not an inch remains unadorned. The three doors sculpted by Father Domingos da Conceição, which give access to the nave, and the sculptures of St Benedict, St Escolastica and Our Lady of Monserrat are particularly remarkable. The last, which is also by Domingos de Conceição, has painted birds' eggs for eyes. The painting is as wonderful as the carving; particularly the panels in the Blessed Sacrament chapel by Inácio Ferreira Pinto and *O Salvador*, the masterpiece of Brazil's first painter, Frei Ricardo do Pilar, which hangs in the sacristy. The enormous candelabra are attributed to Mestre Valentim, Rio's most celebrated church artisan, and are made from solid silver especially imported from Peru and the mines of Potosí in Bolivia at a price higher than Brazil's own gold. The monastery's library (open to men only) preserves a number of priceless religious manuscripts alongside 200,000 other books.

São Bento can be reached either by a narrow road from Rua Dom Gerardo 68, or by a lift whose entrance is at Rua Dom Gerardo 40. Both routes lead to a *praça*

Tip...
Arrive an hour early to get a seat for the Latin Mass with plainsong on a Sunday at 1000. On other days, Mass is at 0715 and the monks often sing at vespers.

ON THE ROAD
The Rio Olympics

Rio knows how to throw a party – it's been hosting the world's biggest every year for half a century, and the 2016 Olympics will be above all about fun. Expect a riot of costume and colour, beginning with an opening ceremony which locals promise will upstage not only London but Carnaval itself. They'll be loads of ancillary events too, from samba dancing on the beaches to revelry in the clubs of revitalized centre, as the city takes three weeks off work, pours itself an ice-cold caipirinha and lets its hair down.

The games themselves take place between 5-21 August and with the Paralympics following between 7-18 September. Forty-two sports will be contested in four principal areas in the city. The opening ceremony will take place in Rio's famous Maracanã stadium and the athletics competitions in the adjacent Olympic stadium, both in the Maracanã neighbourhood. The other main events take place at the Olympic Park in Barra, 20 km south of Ipanema, and in Deodoro stadium some 20 km inland from Barra. Sailing, triathlon and a handful of other events will take place around Copacabana.

As this book went to press, building was far from finished, with work expected to carry on up to the wire. The planned metro extension (linking Maracanã with Barra and the Olympic Park) might not be completed in time for the games, so expect traffic congestion.

How do I get tickets?
You can only buy tickets through the official Rio 2016 agent Cosport (T0207-478 0673, www.cosport.com). Prices depend on availability so buy soon to get the cheaper deals.

---

with tall trees. Arriving in the lift is more magical as you are whisked from the heat and bustle of the dock area to an oasis of calm, which sets the mood beautifully for a wander around the monastery buildings. If you would rather walk, the monastery is a few minutes from Praça Mauá, turning left off Avenida Rio Branco; Rua Dom Gerardo 68 is behind the massive new RBI building.

Largo da Carioca and around
For Largo do Carioca take the metrô to Carioca in Cinelândia.

This higgledy-piggledy street of colonial churches, modern buildings and street stalls sits between Rua da Carioca and the Carioca *metrô* station about 1 km south of Praça XV along Rua da Assembléia. There is a variety of interesting sights here within a very small area.

The **Convento de Santo Antônio** ⓘ *T021-2262 0129, Mon, Wed, Thu, Fri 0730-1900, Tue 0630-2000, Sat 0730-1100 and 1530-1700, Sun 0900-1100, free*, the second oldest in Rio, sits on a little hill off the Largo da Carioca. You will often see single women here gathered to pray: there are many more women than men in Brazil and St Anthony is traditionally a provider of husbands. The church interior is baroque around the chancel, main altars and two lateral altars, which are devoted to St Anthony, St Francis and the Immaculate Conception respectively. The beautiful sacristy is decorated with *azulejos* (tiles) and adorned with paintings depicting scenes from St Anthony's life. Many members of the Brazilian imperial family are buried in the mausoleum.

Which will be the best events?

Athletics will be the highlight. Brazil didn't win any athletics medals in 2012 but former world pole vault champion Fabiana Murer – the face of Rio 2016 – is hoping to perform well in front of a home crowd. Look out for the cycling (in the Olympic Park), rowing (on the Lagoa near Copacabana), sailing (near Copacabana), judo and boxing (both in the Olympic Park).

Don't miss Brazil trying to right their 2014 FIFA World Cup™ woes at the Maracanã stadium and England (who play as Great Britain) trying to do the same in the Rugby Sevens in Deodoro, a new Olympic event for 2016.

Where should I stay?

Room prices are set to rise steeply from the week before the games with prices highest in Copacabana and Ipanema, the most stylish, beachside locations. Barra will be cheaper and is closer to the park. But the neighbourhood can feel sterile; it was built for commuters and the car. Be sure to book a room near the beach on Avenida Lúcio Costa. Windsor Hotels (www.windsorhoteis.com) have some of the better value, newer rooms. Other money-saving options include flat rental – through Rioflatrentals. com.br or airbnb.co.uk – and hostels, via websites like www.hostelbookers.com.

Can I still see the sights?

Rio will be packed during the games. To avoid the crowds be there for the opening party and one or two events, then hop on a plane north to the beaches of the Northeast, the Amazon or Iguaçu, returning to Rio to take in the sights when all has quietened down. Or combine a few days at the games with a bus or car trip south to the Costa Verde.

Separated from this church only by a fence of iron railings is one of Rio's least known and most beautiful baroque jewels: the little church of the **Ordem Terceira de São Francisco da Penitência** ① *T021-2262 0197, Mon-Fri 0900-1200 and 1300-1600, guided tours with access to the balcony and further rooms on Thu afternoon, US$2.50*, which was built between 1622 and 1738. Its splendid gilt interior is the masterpiece of one of the greatest woodcarvers of Latin American baroque, Francisco Xavier de Brito. Brito is largely credited with introducing baroque to Brazil and was probably Aleijadinho's teacher in Ouro Preto. The nave is breathtaking: covered in elaborately sculpted, swirling gilt, crowned by a magnificent reredos with a gory sculpture of Christ illuminated by a silvery shaft from a ceiling window light. The complex is offset by brightly coloured naïve paintings on side panels and the ceiling by Caetano da Costa Coelho depicting the glorification of St Francis. Behind the church is a tranquil catacomb-filled garden.

A couple of streets north, at the end of Rua do Ouvidor and dominating the square that bears its name, is the twin-towered **Igreja de São Francisco de Paula** ① *Largo São Francisco de Paula, Mon-Fri 0900-1300, free*, with some fine examples of Carioca art including carvings by another master sculptor, Mestre Valentim, as well as paintings by Vítor Meireles and murals by Manuel da Cunha.

Across the Largo de São Francisco is the **Igreja de Nossa Senhora do Rosário e São Benedito dos Pretos** ① *on the corner of R Uruguaiana 77 and Ouvidor, T021-2224 2900, Mon-Fri 0700-1700, Sat 0700-1300, free*. Since the 17th century this church has been at the centre of African Christian culture in Rio. During the 19th century it was the site of an elaborate festival that recreated scenes from the courtly life of the king of Congo. A king and queen were crowned and they danced through the nearby streets followed by long parades of courtiers in fancy dress; a precursor perhaps for Carnaval. It was here that the announcements for the final abolition of slavery were prepared. The church once had a fabulous gilt interior but this was sadly destroyed in a fire in 1967.

Next to the church is a small museum devoted to slavery in Brazil, whose collection of instruments of subjugation speaks starkly of life for black people in the last Western country to abolish the slave trade.

The **Real Gabinete Português de Leitura** ① *R Luís Camões 30, T021-2221 3138, www. realgabinete.com.br, Mon-Fri 0900-1800, free,* sits just to the north of Largo São Francisco de Paula on Rua Luís de Camões. This is one of the city's hidden architectural treasures and one of the best pieces of mock-Manueline architecture in Brazil. Manueline architecture is usually described as Portuguese Gothic and takes its name from King Manuel I who ruled Portugal between 1495 and 1521. It is unlike any other European Gothic style, drawing strongly on Islamic and nautical themes, a lavish fusion of Islamic ornamentalism and sculpted seaweeds, anchors, ropes and corals, typified by the Cristo monastery in Tomar and the Mosteiro dos Jerônimos in Lisbon. The modest exterior of the Real Gabinete, which was designed by Portuguese architect Rafael da Silva e Castro in 1880, was inspired by the façade of Jerônimos. It is decorated with statues of Camões, Henry the Navigator, Vasco da Gama and Pedro Álvares Cabral, who claimed Brazil for Portugal. More interesting, however, is the magnificent reading hall built around the oldest central steel structure in Rio. Towering arches decorated with Islamic flourish ascend via coiled wooden ropes to an elaborate painted ceiling with skylights from which a massive iron chandelier is suspended. There are some 120,000 books in the library's collection, many of them very rare. The magnificent but overpriced belle époque coffee house, **Confeitaria Colombo**, is a short walk to the east, at Rua Gonçalves Dias 32 (see Restaurants, page 83).

The streets around the Largo da Carioca – most notably Ruas da Alfândega, Uruguaiana, Buenos Aires and Senhos dos Passos – form the centre of one of Rio's best shopping areas: **Saara** (see page 94). Come here to buy clothes at a discount price, items from *candomblé* (the Brazilian-African spirit religion) and all manner of bric-a-brac.

Praça Tiradentes and the cathedral

One long block behind the Largo da Carioca and São Francisco de Paula is **Praça Tiradentes**, old and shady, with a **statue to Dom Pedro I** carved in 1862 by Luís Rochet. The emperor sits on horseback shouting his famous 1822 declaration of independence, the Grito de Ipiranga: 'Liberty or Death'.

The **Teatro João Caetano** sits on the northeastern corner of the *praça* and is named after a famous 19th-century actor. Prince Dom Pedro first showed the green and yellow Brazilian flag in the original building, which was an important venue for meetings discussing Brazilian independence. The current theatre was constructed in 1920 after the original had fallen into disrepair. Two canvases by one of the city's most celebrated artists, Emiliano Di Cavalcanti, hang on the second floor. The other buildings on the square are somewhat decrepit but are being restored for the Olympics.

Just north of the *praça*, in a handsome salmon pink colonial building, is the **Centro de Arte Hélio Oiticica** ① *R Luís de Camões 68, Mon-Fri 1000-1800,* named after another famous Carioca artist and now a smart contemporary art exhibition space with six galleries, a good art bookshop and an air-conditioned café. Important national and international artists exhibit here. Shops in nearby streets specialize in selling goods for *umbanda*, the Afro-Brazilian religion.

The **Catedral Metropolitana de São Sebastião** ⓘ *Av República do Chile, T021-2240 2669, www.catedral.com.br, daily 0700-1900, Mass Mon-Fri 1100, Sun 1000*, lies just south of the Praça Tiradentes and the Largo da Carioca; bordering Cinêlandia to the east and Lapa to the south. It is an oblate concrete cone fronted by a decorative ladder and replete with rich blue stained glass, which looks like a modernist Mayan temple. The design could be mistaken for a Niemeyer, but is in fact by another Brazilian Le Corbusier disciple, Edgar de Oliveira da Fonseca, with heavy modernist statues and panels by Humberto Cozzi. There is a small sacred art museum in the crypt, which has a handful of relics including Dom Pedro II's throne and the fonts used for the baptizing of imperial Brazilian babies. The *bonde* (tram) to Santa Teresa leaves from behind the cathedral, the entrance is on Rua Senador Dantas (see page 54). Soon after leaving the station the tram traverses the Arcos da Lapa offering wonderful views.

> **Tip...**
> It's best to visit the cathedral in the late afternoon when the sunlight streams through the immense monotone stained-glass windows.

One of the city's quirkier museums lies just a short walk from the cathedral. The **Museu de Farmácia Antônio Lago** ⓘ *R dos Andradas 96, 10th floor, T021-2263 0791, www.abf.org.br/museu.html, Mon-Fri 1430-1700 by appointment only via email abf@abf.org.br, US$1*, is a reproduction of a 17th-century Brazilian apothecary's shop, complete with Dr Jekyll cabinets and rows of dubious-looking herbal preparations in glass and porcelain vessels.

Northeast of the city centre
the birthplace of samba and the carnival

There are a handful of interesting attractions immediately northeast of the city centre beyond the new Porto Marvilha complex, most notably the famous Sambódromo where the carnival parades take place, Maracanã – Brazil's most famous football arena (and the site of the 2016 Olympic opening ceremony) – and the Feira de São Cristóvão market.

Gamboa and the Cidade de Samba

The neighbourhood of Gamboa has a rich and long African-Brazilian history which is connected to the birth of samba and carnival in Rio. In the early 20th century, after the Paraguayan war and the abolition of slavery, the neighbourhood was known as 'Little Africa' due to the high number of resident Bahian immigrants. With them, the African-Bahian rhythms of the *candomblé* religion were introduced into the Carioca community and the next generation spawned a host of famous local musicians that included Donga, Chico da Baiana and João de Baiana.

The streets and backyards of Gamboa became the birthplace of a new music: samba, born of Angolan *semba* rhythms fused with European singing styles and instruments. Donga and João da Baiana used to gather on the Pedra do Sal stairs close to the Praça Mauá to play and hold impromptu music and samba dance parties, which have since been resurrected every Monday night (see page 88). Later the dance was incorporated into an alternative Mardi Gras festival as a counterpart to the ballroom dances of the white elite. Street parade clubs were formed by another young Carioca, Hilário Jovino Ferreira.

Their structure was copied later by the much larger samba schools that still produce the Carnaval parades today.

In 2008 the city government inaugurated the **Cidade do Samba (Samba City)** ① *R Rivadávia Corréa 60, Gamboa, T021-2213 2503, http://cidadedosambarj.globo.com, Tue-Sat 1000-1900*, both to celebrate samba and to bring the administrative and production houses of the samba schools under one roof. The famous samba schools from the **Liga Independente das Escolas de Samba (LIESA)** now have a permanent carnival production centre of 14 workshops, each of them housed in a two-storey building. Visitors can watch floats and costumes being prepared or watch one of the year-round carnival-themed shows. A visit here is a wonderful experience and a real eye-opener, offering the chance to see how much painstaking work goes into creating the floats, costumes and dances of schools such as the **Primeira Estação de Mangueira** (see page 93), for one night of lavish display.

Rio's carnival is nailed, glued, stitched and sewn over an entire year. Much of the work is undertaken by **AMEBRAS** ① *www.amebras.org.br*, an association of stern older women who enrol, train and employ dozens of would-be artisans and dressmakers from the favelas. Thus carnival is an industry that revitalizes poor Rio. In the words of AMEBRAS president Célia Regina Domingues "there's no fooling about here – everything we do, from hat-making to foam-sculpting for the floats, is directed towards a profession, post-carnival. People leave our project with real skills." There is a gift shop at the Cidade do Samba where it is possible to buy Carnaval costumes and souvenirs, many by AMEBRAS, or you can request a visit through their website as part of a visit to the Cidade. The Cidade do Samba has weekly samba shows, tickets for which can be purchased at the booths near the main entrance.

Sambódromo and Cidade Nova

R Marquês de Sapucaí s/n, Metrô Central or Metrô Praça Onze, Cidade Nova, T021-2502 6996, www.rio-carnival.net. Mon-Fri 0900-1700. See also box, page 12.

Carnaval happens right next to Gamboa in the **Cidade Nova**. Oscar Niemeyer's 650-m stadium street, the **Sambódromo**, was purpose-built for the annual parades and is well worth a visit at any time.

Nearby, **Praça Onze** is today the terminus of the city's main thoroughfare, Avenida Presidente Vargas. But it was once a square and an established meeting place for *capoeristas* whose acrobatic martial art to the rhythm of the *berimbau* and hand clap inspired much Carnaval choreography. A replica of the head of a Nigerian prince from the British Museum, erected in honour of **Zumbi dos Palmares**, sits on Avenida Presidente Vargas itself. Zumbi was a Bantu prince who became the most successful black slave emancipator in the history of the Americas, founding a kingdom within Brazil in the 19th century. The **Centro de Memória do Carnaval** ① *Av Rio Branco 4, 2nd floor, T021-3213 5151, www.liesa.globo.com, visits by appointment only*, is a research centre and preserves one of the largest repositories of international and Brazilian carnival images, documents and publications in the world.

Maracanã stadium

Av Prof Eurico Rabelo, T021-2334 1705, www.maracanaonline.com.br, daily 0900-1700; independent visit Gate 15, 1-hr guided tours run hourly in Portuguese or English, daily 0900-1700, US$10.60, US$1 extra Sat-Sun. Take the metrô to Maracanã station on Linha 2, 1 stop beyond São Cristóvão. Bus Nos 238 and 239 from the centre, 434 and 464 from Glória, Flamengo and Botafogo, 455 from Copacabana, and 433 and 464 from Ipanema and Leblon all go to the stadium. Trips to football matches can be organized through www.bealocal.com. It is not advisable to drive in this part of Rio.

Whilst tour guides proclaim Maracanã the largest sports stadium in the world, in fact there are several larger stadiums, including Indianapolis in the USA and Strahov stadium in Prague. But Maracanã was the largest when it was first built and remains impressive, not least because it is

Tip...

Buy tickets from club websites the day before the match or at the gate; it's more expensive to buy tickets from agencies.

the hallowed temple to the most important religious practice in Brazil: the worship of football. This is where Pelé scored his 1000th goal in 1969. His feet, as well as those of Ronaldo and other Brazilian stars, are immortalized in concrete outside the stadium. The stadium hosted the largest crowd ever to see a football match in 1950 when Brazil lost to Uruguay in front of about 200,000 spectators, an event that shook the national psyche and which is known as the Maracanazo tragedy.

In 2012-2013, Maracanã was completely rebuilt and refurbished for the 2014 FIFA World Cup™, shrinking to some 80,000 seats. The project has been controversial, for whilst modest in its aims, it is expected to have cost an astounding US$400 million and includes the construction of 14,000 new parking spaces, 3000 of which are allocated inside Quinta da Boa Vista park.

Even if you're not a football fan, matches are worth going to for the spectators' samba bands and the adrenalin-charged atmosphere; try to catch a local or Rio-São Paulo derby, or an international game. There are four types of ticket: *Cadeira Especial* (special seats), the most expensive; *Arquibancada Branca* (white terraces), which give a good side view of the game; *Arquibancada Verde e Amarela* (green and yellow terraces), with a view from behind the goal; and *Cadeira Comum*. Prices vary according to the game.

Don't take valuables or wear a watch and take special care when entering and leaving the stadium. The rivalry between the local clubs Flamengo and Vasco da Gama is intense, often leading to violence, so it is advisable to avoid their encounters. If you buy a club shirt, don't be tempted to wear it on match day: if you find yourself in the wrong place, you could be in trouble.

Quinta da Boa Vista

Take the metrô to São Cristóvão and follow signs to Quinta da Boa Vista, a 5-min walk. Beware of muggings on weekdays; don't take valuables.

About 3 km west of Praça da República (beyond the Sambódromo) is the Quinta da Boa Vista, the emperor's private park from 1809 to 1889. The **Museu Nacional** ⓘ *T021-2562 6900, www.museunacional.ufrj.br, Tue-Sun 1000-1600, US$1.50*, is housed in the former imperial palace. It has an impressive collection of some 20 million objects but despite being the country's only national museum it is closed on a seemingly permanent basis due to lack of funds and huge debts.

Also in the park is the **Jardim Zoológico** ⓘ *Av Dom Pedro II, T021-3878 4200, Tue-Sun 0900-1630, US$1.50, young children free, students with ID half price.* The zoo is in the northeastern corner of the park. It has a collection of over 2000 animals, most of which are kept in modern, spacious enclosures, and there is an important captive breeding programme for golden-headed and golden lion tamarins, spectacled bears and yellow-throated capuchin monkeys. The aviary is impressive and children can enjoy a ride in a little train through the park.

Feira de São Cristóvão

T021-2580-6946, www.feiradesaocristovao.org.br. Tue-Fri 0900-1800, Sat 0900-1600. To get here, take bus No 474 or 441 from Copacabana or Ipanema or the metro São Cristóvão followed by the Metro-onibus Integracao Expressa No 209 bus from São Cristóvão metro to the Feira. A taxi from the southern beaches will cost around US$10.

Rio's tens of thousands of northeastern internal migrants keep their cultures alive in this big purpose-built arena. Here you will find scores of restaurants serving regional food from Bahia, Pernambuco, Ceará and beyond, shops proffering regional arts and crafts, folk medicines and foodstuffs, and venues where at night *Nordestinos* dance *forró* or listen to live music. Visitors are Rio's working classes – maids, porters and taxi drivers – so prices are low.

Nossa Senhora da Penha

Largo da Penha 19, T021-2290 0942, www.santuariodapenhario.com.br. Tue-Sun 1000-1600. Take the metrô *to Del Castilho. Leave the station to the left, walk down the passageway and catch microbus (*microônibus*) No 623 labelled 'Penha-Shopping Nova América 2' to the last stop. Get off at the shopping centre, in front of Rua dos Romeiros, and walk up that street to the Largo da Penha from where there are signposts to the church.*

The church of Nossa Senhora da Penha is one of the most important pilgrimage centres in the whole country, especially for black Brazilians. It sits on an enormous rock, into whose side 365 steps have been carved. Pilgrims ascend these on their knees during the festival month of October. The church in its present form dates from the early 20th century, but it was modelled on an early 18th-century chapel and a religious building has been on this site since the original hermitage was built in 1632. There are great views from the summit.

Cinelândia and Avenida Rio Branco

To get to Cinelândia take the metrô *to Carioca.*

The area around Praça Floriano was the liveliest part of the city in the 1920s and 1930s when Hollywood hit Brazil. All the best cinemas were situated here and their popularity became so great that the *praça* was named after them. Today Cinelândia remains lively, especially at the end of the week, owing to its proximity to the city's nightlife capital, Lapa. The 30-m-wide Avenida Rio Branco, which bisects Cinelândia, is the financial heart of the city. Lined by an untidy mishmash of modernist and art deco skyscrapers it was built at the turn of 20th century under the 'tear it down' regime of Mayor Pereira Passos. Rio once had long stately avenues that rivalled the best of Buenos Aires but only clusters have survived.

Beautifully renovated, the **Theatro Municipal** ⓘ *Praça Floriano, T021-2332 9191, www.theatromunicipal.rj.gov.br, Mon-Fri 1300-1700, bilingual guided tours by appointment T021-2299 1667,* is a splendid piece of French-inspired, lavish neoclassical pomp modelled on the Opéra Nacional de Paris. The tour is worth it to see front of house and backstage, the decorations and the machine rooms – a luxuriously ornate temple to an early 20th-century Carioca high society. On either side of the ostentatious colonnaded façade are rotundas, surmounted by cupolas. The muses of poetry and music watch over all, alongside an imperial eagle, wings outstretched and poised for flight. The interior is a mock-European fantasy of Carrara-marble columns, crystal chandeliers and gilt ceilings fronted by a vast sweeping, *Gone With the Wind* staircase. The stage is one of the largest in the world. The theatre was designed by Francisco de Oliveira Passos, son of the contemporary city mayor, who won an ostensibly open architectural competition together with French architect Albert Guilbert.

Opposite, on the other side of Avenida Rio Branco, is the refurbished **Museu Nacional de Belas-Artes** ① *Av Rio Branco 199, T021-2219 8474, www.mnba.gov.br, Tue-Fri 1000-1800, Sat and Sun 1200-1700, US$4, free on Sun*. Fine art in Rio and in Brazil was, as a whole, stimulated by the arrival in 1808 of the Portuguese royal family. In 1816 the Academia de Belas-Artes was founded by another Frenchman, Joaquim Lebreton. This building was constructed 1906-1908 to house the national gallery and contains the best collection of art in the country. This includes depictions of Brazil by European visitors such as Dutchman Frans Post and Frenchman Jean-Baptiste Debret, and the best of 20th-century Brazilian art by important names such as modernist and social realist Cândido Portinari, Emiliano Di Cavalcanti (famous for his iconographic images of black Cariocas at a time when racism was institutionalized in Rio), Tarsila do Amaral (founder of the first major school of Brazilian Art, *antropofagismo*, which strongly influenced *tropicália*) and the brutalist art deco sculptor Victor Brecheret. Another gallery contains further works by foreign artists and the temporary exhibition hall houses many of Rio de Janeiro's most important international exhibitions.

Another of Cinelândia's stately neoclassical buildings is the **Biblioteca Nacional** ① *Av Rio Branco 219/239, T021-3095 3879, www.bn.br, Mon-Fri 0900-2000, Sat 0900-1500, free*, an eclectic Carioca construction, this time with a touch of art nouveau. The library is fronted by a stately engaged portico supported by a Corinthian colonnade. Inside is a series of monumental staircases in Carrara marble. The stained glass in the windows is French. The first national library was brought to Brazil in 1808 by the Prince Regent, Dom João, from a collection in the Ajuda Palace in Lisbon. Today the library houses more than nine million items, including a first edition of the *Lusiad of Camões*, a 15th-century Moguncia Bible and Book of Hours, paintings donated by Pedro II, scores by Mozart and etchings by Dürer.

Nearby, in the former Ministry of Education and Health building, is the **Palácio Gustavo Capanema** ① *R da Imprensa 16, off the Esplanada do Castelo, at the junction of Av Graça Aranha and R Araújo Porto Alegre, just off Av Rio Branco, T021-2220 1490, by appointment only, Mon-Fri 0900-1800*. Dating back to 1937-1945, it was the first piece of modernist architecture in the Americas and was designed by an illustrious team of architects led by Lúcio Costa (under the guidance of Le Corbusier) and included a very young Oscar Niemeyer – working on his first project. Inside are impressive murals by Cândido Portinari, one of Brazil's most famous artists, as well as works by other well-known names. The gardens were laid out by Roberto Burle Marx who was responsible for many landscaping projects throughout Rio (including the Parque do Flamengo) and who worked with Costa and Niemeyer in Brasília.

At the turn of the millennium, Lapa – which lies just south of the cathedral on the edge of Cinelândia (see map, page 56; take the metrô to Carioca in Cinelândia)– was a no-go area. But it has undergone an unimagined renaissance and is now Rio's unofficial nightlife central – returning to a status it had in the belle époque before the dictatorship closed the area down for being too tawdry. This was once the Montmartre of Rio; the painter Di Cavalcanti wrote poetically of wandering its streets at night on his way home to Flamengo, past the little cafés and ballrooms and the rows of handsome townhouses. Like Monmartre it was busy with pickpockets and ne'er-do-wells and fringed with a seedy red light district walked by transvestites like the infamous 'Madame Sataan'. All has now returned. Nowhere in Rio is livelier at night: samba clubs, spit-and-sawdust alternative rock venues and Afro-Brazilian music centres pound out music; *cacacha* bars, *botecos* and buzzing restaurants rub shoulders with chic air-conditioned cafés serving gourmet coffee and microbrewery beer; and the streets throng with locals and foreign revellers, especially at weekends (see also Bars and clubs, page 88). Opera, jazz and world music play in the concert halls of the Escola de Música and the beautifully renovated Sala Cecilia Meirelles (see below) while the area's main thoroughfare, Rua do Lavradio, hosts one of the city's most interesting bric-a-brac and antiques markets on the last Saturday of every month.

The area's lively night scene and proximity to *metrô* stations, the Sambodromo, Porto Maravilha and Santa Teresa has stimulated new hotel investment. And with some smart four-star hotels, boutique places to stay and chic hostels, Lapa is now an attractive place to base yourself. The area can still be edgy though especially midweek, so be cautious with your wandering and avoid empty back alleys, or take a nightlife tour with a local guide like Kelly Tavares (see **Rio En Canto**, page 99).

Although the area is best seen on a cautious wander after 2100 on a Friday or Saturday, or during the Rua do Lavradio market, there are a few interesting sights. The most photographed are the **Arcos da Lapa**, built in 1744 as an aqueduct to carry water from Santa Teresa to the Chafariz da Carioca, with its 16 drinking fountains, in the centre of the city. The aqueduct's use was changed at the end of the 19th century, with the introduction of electric trams in Rio. Tracks were laid on top of the arches and the inaugural run was on 1 September 1896 for a tramline, one of the city's most delightful journeys; running from behind the Catedral de São Sebastião to Santa Teresa.

Bars huddle under their southern extremity on Avenida Mem de Sá, one of Rio's most popular nightlife streets. Street performers (and vagrants) often gather in the cobbled square between the *arcos* and the cathedral.

There are a number of moderately interesting buildings off this square. The eclectic baroque/neoclassical **Escola da Musica da Universidade Federal do Rio de Janeiro** ① *R do Passeio 98, only officially open for performances*, has one of the city's best concert halls. A stroll away is

Tip...
If you're staying in Lapa at the weekend, book a room on the upper floor away from the street because the party plays on until dawn.

the bizarre baroque façade of another prestigious classical concert hall, the **Sala Cecília Mereilles** ① *Largo da Lapa 47, http://salaceciliameireles.rj.gov.br.*

More picturesque are the mosaic-tiled **Ladeira do Santa Teresa** stairs, which wind their way steeply from the square and from the back of Rua Teotônio to Santa Teresa. These are much beloved of music video directors and fashion photographers who use them as a backdrop to carefully produced gritty urban scenes. The steps are tiled in red, gold and green and bordered by little houses, many of which are dishevelled and disreputable but wonderfully picturesque. Be vigilant here.

North of Avenida Mem de Sá is **Rua do Lavradio**. This was one of urban Rio's first residential streets and is lined with handsome 18th- and early 20th-century townhouses. These are now filled with samba clubs, cafés, bars and antiques shops. Any day is good for a browse and a wander, and on Saturdays at the end of the month there is a busy antiques market, live street tango, no cars and throngs of people from all sections of Carioca society. Some of the houses here were once grand. Number 84 once belonged to the marquis who gave the street its name. Further along is what was once Brazil's foremost Masonic lodge, the imposing **Palácio Maçônico Grande Oriente do Brasil**, which tellingly has had as its grand masters King Dom Pedro I and one of the country's most important republican politicians, José Bonifácio Andrada e Silva.

Central do Brasil railway station

Central do Brasil or **Dom Pedro II** railway station, as it is also known, once served much of the country but now serves only Rio. This brutal 1930s art deco temple to progress was one of the city's first modernist buildings and was made famous by the Walter Salles film *Central do Brasil* (Central Station). The film's thronging crowd scenes were set here. For similar shots come with your camera in the morning or evening and watch hundreds of thousands of people bustle in and out of trains leaving for the northern and western parts of Rio.

Santa Teresa

hilltop arty district with colonial buildings and sweeping views

A bus or tram ride from Rio's centre or Guanabara Bay suburbs to Santa Teresa is a magical experience – winding up the hilly streets lined with pretty colonial houses and lavish mansions towards the forested slopes of Tijuca National Park, and leaving impressive views of Guanabara Bay and the Sugar Loaf in your wake. As you reach the summit of Morro do Desterro hill, where Santa Teresa lies, you pass the Largo do Guimarães and the Largo das Neves, little *praças* of shops and restaurants that feel as if they belong clustered around a village green rather than in a large city.

Indeed, Santa Teresa feels almost like a town in itself rather than a neighbourhood, with a strong community identity forged by one of the highest concentrations of artists, writers and musicians in the city. They congregate in bars like **O Mineiro**, on the Largo do Guimarães, **Bar Gomes** and **Bar Porto das Neves**, on the Largo das Neves. At weekends the lively nightlife spills over into clubs in neighbouring Lapa which is only a five-minute taxi ride away.

A sense of separation is reflected not only in the suburb's geography, but also its history. In 1624, Antônio Gomes do Desterro chose the area both for its proximity to Rio and its isolation, and erected a hermitage dedicated to Nossa Senhora do Desterro. The

Essential Santa Teresa

Finding your feet

Bus Nos 434 and 464 run from Leblon (via Ipanema, Copacabana and the Guanabara Bay suburbs to Avenida Riachuelo in Lapa, a few hundred metres north of the arches) from where minibus No 014 Castelo (US$0.75) runs to the Largo do Guimarães. Taxis from Glória metro to Santa Teresa cost around US$4.

The famous yellow Santa Teresa trams are currently too infrequent to be used as a reliable form of transport. Their route runs from the Largo da Carioca (near the *metrô* station and the cathedral), passing over the Lapa viaduct and running along all the main streets in Santa Teresa (via the Largo do Guimarães and Largo das Neves), eventually reaching either Dois Irmãos or Paula Mattos at the far end of Santa Teresa (see page 104).

Safety

In recent years, Santa Teresa has had a reputation for crime but the area is much more heavily policed nowadays and you should encounter few problems. Nonetheless it's best to be vigilant with your camera at all times, and be particularly wary after dark. Steer clear of any steps that lead down the hill, on and around Rua Almirante Alexandrino or at the Tijuca end of Largo dos Guimarães.

Tip...

Santa Teresa is best explored on foot: wander the streets to admire the colonial buildings or stop for a beer in a little streetside café and marvel at the view.

---

name was changed from Morro do Desterro to Santa Teresa after the construction in 1750 of a convent of that name dedicated to the patroness of the order. The convent exists to this day, but it can only be seen from the outside.

Sights

The better colonial houses, most of which are private residences, include the **Casa de Valentim** (a castle-like house in Vista Alegre), the tiled **Chácara dos Viegas**, in Rua Monte Alegre, and the **Chalé Murtinho**. The latter was the house in which Dona Laurinda Santos Lobo held her famous artistic, political and intellectual salons at the turn of the 20th century. The house was in ruins until it was partially restored and turned into a cultural centre called **Parque das Ruínas** ⓘ *R Murtinho Nobre 41, daily 1000-1700*. It has superb views of the city, an exhibition space and an open-air stage (live music on Thursday).

Next door is the **Chácara do Céu**, or **Museu Castro Maya** ⓘ *R Murtinho Nobre 93, T021-3970 1126, www.museuscastromaya.com.br, Wed-Mon 1200-1700, US$1*, housed in the former home of the Carioca millionaire and art collector, Raymundo Ottoni de Castro Maya. It has a wide range of works by modern painters, including Modigliani and important Brazilian artists such as Di Cavalacanti. There are wonderful views out over Guanabara Bay. There are also superb views from the **Museu Casa de Benjamin Constant** ⓘ *R Monte Alegre 225, T021-2509 1248, Wed-Sun 1300-1700*, the former home of the Carioca military engineer and positivist philosopher who helped to found the Republic.

The city centre is separated from Copacabana and the other ocean beaches by a series of long white-sand coves that fringe Guanabara Bay and which are divided by towering rocks. The first of the coves is the Enseada da Glória, fronting the suburb of the same name and sitting next to Lapa and Santos Dumont Airport. Avenida Infante Dom Henrique, a broad avenue lined with an eclectic mix of grand houses and squat office blocks, leads from here to what was once the city's finest beach, Flamengo, a long stretch of sand separated from the rest of southern Rio by the Morro da Viúva (widow's peak). The suburb of Catete lies just behind Flamengo. These three areas were once the heart of recreational Rio; the posing-spots of choice for the belle époque middle and upper classes and perhaps the most coveted urban beaches in the world. These days the water is polluted and swimming ill-advised, but the suburbs are pleasant for a stroll.

The centrepiece of the three suburbs are the gardens of the Parque do Flamengo, on Avenida Infante Dom Henrique, reached from Metrô Glória, Catete, Largo de Machado or Flamengo. Bus No 119 from the centre or No 571 from Copacabana also serve the neighbourhoods, as does the *metrô*.

Glória and Flamengo

Before the pollution became too much, Burle Marx, Brazil's 20th-century Capability Brown, designed the **Parque do Flamengo**, a handsome stretch of waterfront to separate Avenida Infante Dom Henrique from the city's most glorious beach, and gave it ample shade with a range of tropical trees and stands of stately royal palms. The gardens stretch from Glória through to the Morro da Viúva at the far end of Flamengo; they were built on reclaimed land and opened in 1965 to mark the 400th anniversary of the city's founding. The lawns and promenade are favourite spots for smooching lovers, especially at sundown.

There are children's play areas and a handful of monuments and museums. These include the impressive postmodern **Monumento aos Mortos da Segunda Guerra Mundial** ① *Av Infante Dom Henrique, Tue-Sun 1000-1700 for the crypt museum; beach clothes and flip-flops not permitted*, the national war memorial to Brazil's dead in the Second World War. The gently curved slab is supported by two slender columns, representing two palms uplifted to heaven and guarded by soldiers from the adjacent barracks. In the crypt are the remains of the Brazilian soldiers killed in Italy in 1944-1945.

At the far northern end of the Parque do Flamengo is the **Museu de Arte Moderna** ① *Av Infante Dom Henrique 85, T021-2240 4944, www.mamrio.com.br, Tue-Fri 1200-1800, last entry 1730, Sat and Sun 1200-1900, last entry 1830, US$6*, another striking modernist building with the best collection of modern art in Brazil outside São Paulo. Works by many well-known Europeans sit alongside collections of Brazilian modern and contemporary art including drawings by Cândido Portinari and etchings of everyday work scenes by Gregório Gruber. Be cautious walking around the Parque do Flamengo early or late in the day and avoid it altogether after dark.

Tip...

On all Rio's beaches you should take a towel or mat to protect you against sandflies. In the water stay near groups of other swimmers; there is a strong undertow on many of the beaches, especially Copacabana.

The beautiful little church on the Glória hill, overlooking the Parque do Flamengo, is **Nossa Senhora da Glória do Outeiro** ① *T021-2225 2869, Tue-Fri 0900-1200 and 1300-1700, Sat and Sun 0900-1200, guided tours by appointment on the 1st Sun of each month.* Built 1735-1791, it was the favourite church of the imperial family and Dom Pedro II was

④ Glória, Santa Teresa & Lapa

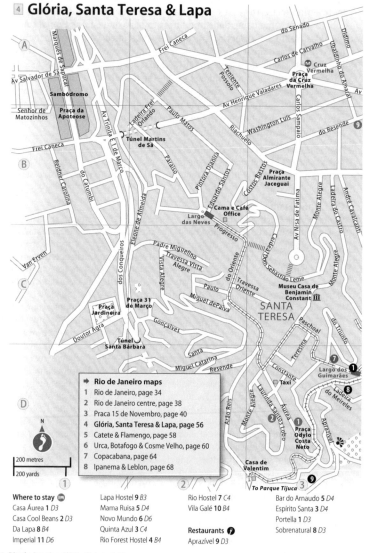

➡ **Rio de Janeiro maps**

1 Rio de Janeiro, page 34
2 Rio de Janeiro centre, page 38
3 Praca 15 de Novembro, page 40
4 Glória, Santa Teresa & Lapa, page 56
5 Catete & Flamengo, page 58
6 Urca, Botafogo & Cosme Velho, page 60
7 Copacabana, page 64
8 Ipanema & Leblon, page 68

200 metres
200 yards

Where to stay 🛏
Casa Áurea 1 *D3*
Casa Cool Beans 2 *D3*
Da Lapa 8 *B4*
Imperial 11 *D6*

Lapa Hostel 9 *B3*
Mama Ruisa 5 *D4*
Novo Mundo 6 *D6*
Quinta Azul 3 *C4*
Rio Forest Hostel 4 *B4*

Rio Hostel 7 *C4*
Vila Galé 10 *B4*

Restaurants 🍴
Aprazível 9 *D3*

Bar do Arnaudo 5 *D4*
Espírito Santa 3 *D4*
Portella 1 *D3*
Sobrenatural 8 *D3*

baptized here. The building is polygonal, with a single tower. It contains some excellent examples of the best *azulejos* (tiles) in Rio and its main wooden altar was carved by Mestre Valentim. Next door is the small **Museum of Religious Art** ① *T021-2556 6434, same hours as the church.*

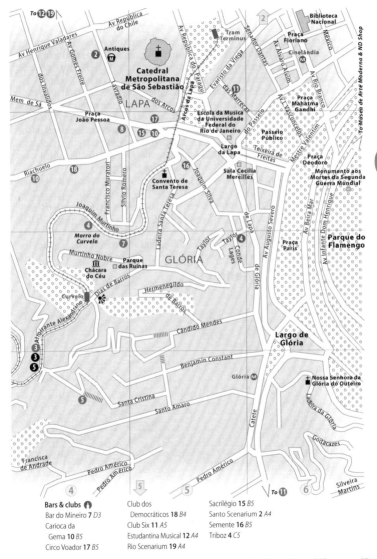

Bars & clubs ⊕
Bar do Mineiro **7** *D3*
Carioca da
 Gema **10** *B5*
Circo Voador **17** *B5*

Club dos
 Democráticos **18** *B4*
Club Six **11** *A5*
Estudantina Musical **12** *A4*
Rio Scenarium **19** *A4*

Sacrilégio **15** *B5*
Santo Scenarium **2** *A4*
Semente **16** *B5*
Triboz **4** *C5*

Catete

Behind Glória and Flamengo is the rather down-at-heel suburb of Catete, which is dotted with museums. The best of these is the **Museu da República** ⓘ *R do Catete 153, T021-3235 2650, www.museudarepublica.org.br, Tue-Fri 1000-1700, Sat, Sun and holidays 1400-1800, US$3, free Wed and Sun, under 10s and over 65s free, half price for students with ID,* the former palace of a coffee baron, the Barão de Nova Friburgo. The palace was built 1858-1866 and, in 1887, it was converted into the presidential seat, until the move to Brasília. The ground floor of this museum consists of the sumptuous rooms of the coffee baron's mansion. The first floor is devoted to the history of the Brazilian republic. You can also see the room where former president Getúlio Vargas shot himself. Behind the museum is the **Parque do Catete**, which contains many birds and monkeys and is a popular place for practising Tai Chi.

The **Museu do Folclore Edison Carneiro** ⓘ *R do Catete 181, T021-2285 0441, Tue-Fri 1100-1800, Sat and Sun 1500-1800, free,* houses a collection of amusing but poorly labelled small ceramic figures representing everyday life in Brazil, some of which are animated by electric motors. Many artists are represented and displays show the way of life in different parts of the country. There are also fine *candomblé* and *umbanda* costumes, religious objects, displays about Brazil's festivals and a small but excellent library, with helpful staff who can help find books on Brazilian culture, history and anthropology. Flash photography is prohibited.

The **Museu Carmen Miranda** ⓘ *Parque Brigadeiro Eduardo Gomes (Parque do Flamengo), Flamengo, T021-2334 4293, Tue-Fri 1100-1700, Sat and Sun 1300-1700, US$1,* has more than 3000 items related to the famous Portuguese singer forever associated with Rio, who emigrated to Brazil as a child and then moved to Hollywood. The collection includes some of her famous gowns, fruit-covered hats, jewellery and recordings. There are occasional showings of her films. Much of the content is due to move to the new Museu da Imagem e do Som in Copacabana (see page 41) in late 2016.

5 Catete & Flamengo

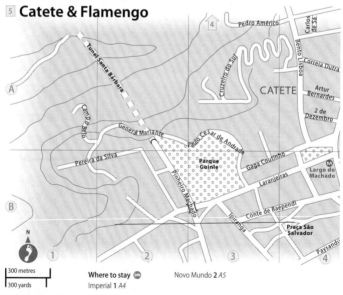

300 metres
300 yards

Where to stay 🛏
Imperial 1 *A4*

Novo Mundo 2 *A5*

Pão de Açúcar, or the Sugar Loaf, looms over the perfect wine-glass bay of Botafogo, the next cove after Flamengo. Huddled around the boulder's flanks is the suburb of Urca, home to a military barracks and the safest middle-class houses in Rio. Remnant forest, still home to marmosets and rare birds, shrouds the boulder's sides and a cable car straddles the distance between its summit, the Morro de Urca hill and the houses below, making one of the continent's most breathtaking views easily accessible. Urca and Botafogo have a few sights of interest and make convenient bases with decent accommodation and restaurant options, particularly in the lower price ranges.

Sugar Loaf mountain (Pão de Açúcar)

The western hemisphere's most famous monolith rises almost sheer from the dark sea to just under 400 m, towering over Botafogo beach and separating Guanabara Bay from the Atlantic Ocean. The views from the top, out over Copacabana, Ipanema and the mountains and forests of Corcovado and Tijuca, are as unforgettable as the view from New York's Empire State Building or Victoria Peak in Hong Kong. The **cable car** ⓘ *Av Pasteur 520, Praia Vermelha, Urca, T021-2461 2700, www.bondinho.com.br, daily 0800-1950, US$18 return, under 6s free, children 6-12 half*

> ⇒ **Rio de Janeiro maps**
> 1 Rio de Janeiro, page 34
> 2 Rio de Janeiro centre, page 38
> 3 Praca 15 de Novembro, page 40
> 4 Glória, Santa Teresa & Lapa, page 56
> 5 **Catete & Flamengo, page 58**
> 6 Urca, Botafogo & Cosme Velho, page 60
> 7 Copacabana, page 64
> 8 Ipanema & Leblon, page 68

Essential Sugar Loaf (Pão de Açúcar), Botafogo and Urca

Finding your feet

Botafogo has a *metrô* station. Buses that run between Copacabana and the centre stop in Botafogo, so take any bus marked 'Centro' from Copacabana or 'Copacabana' from the centre. Bus No 107 (from the centre, Catete or Flamengo) and No 511 from Copacabana (No 512 to return) take you to Urca; the cable car for the Sugar Loaf is on Praça General Tiburcio, next to the Rio de Janeiro federal university. The rides themselves go up in two stages, the first to the summit of Morro da Urca, the smaller rock that sits in front of the Sugar Loaf, and the second from there to the top of the Sugar Loaf itself.

When to go

Come early for the clearest air, best views and smallest crowds.

Time required

Allow at least two hours for your visit.

price, every 30 mins, last car down at 2100, runs to the top where there are extensive paths, plentiful shade and snack bars.

Paths up and around the Sugar Loaf There is more to the Sugar Loaf than the views from the top. The surrounding rocks hide secluded little beaches, such as **Praia da Urca**, as well as remnant forest and small colonial suburbs well worth exploring. The best place to begin is at **Praia Vermelha**, the beach to the south of the rock where there is a simple restaurant, the Círculo Militar da Praia Vermelha (no sign) with wonderful views. The paved walking track, **Pista Cláudio Coutinho** ① *daily 0700-1800*, runs from here along the waterfront around the foot of the rock. You'll see plenty of wildlife at dawn, especially marmosets and tanagers, along with various intrepid climbers scaling the granite. About 350 m from the beginning of the Pista Coutinho is a turning to the left for a path that winds its way up through the forest to the top of Morro de Urca, from where the cable car can be taken for US$7. You can save even more money by climbing the **Caminho da Costa**, a path to the summit of the Pão de Açúcar. Only one stretch of 10 m requires climbing gear; wait at the bottom of the path for a group going up. You can

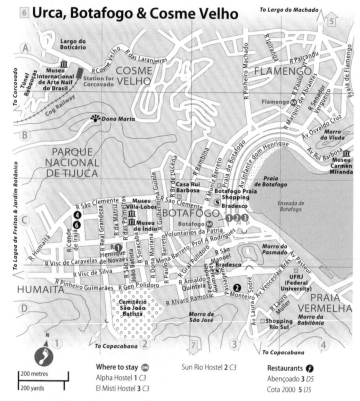

then descend to Morro de Urca by cable car for free and walk the rest of the way down. There are 35 rock-climbing routes up the boulder. The best months for climbing are April to August. See What to do, page 97.

Botafogo

The Funai-run **Museu do Índio** ① *R das Palmeiras 55, T021-3214 8702, www.museudoindio. org.br, Mon-Fri 0900-1730, Sat and Sun 1300-1700, US$1.50, free on Sun, 10-min walk from Botafogo metrô or bus No 571 from Catete*, preserves some 12,000 objects from more than 180 Brazilian indigenous groups, including basketry, ceramics, masks and weapons as well as 500,000 documents and 50,000 photographs. Very few are on display and the museum's few rooms are mostly devoted to information panels and short film shows. The garden includes a Guaraní *maloca* and there is a small, well-displayed handicraft shop and a library of ethnology.

The **Museu Villa-Lobos** ① *R Sorocaba 200, T021-2266 3845, www.museuvillalobos. org.br, Mon-Fri 1000-1700, free, lunchtime concert US$4-15,* is a block east of the Museu do Índio. Such was the fame and respect afforded to Latin America's most celebrated composer that the museum was founded just one year after his death in 1960. Inside the fine 19th-century building is a collection of his personal objects including instruments, scores, books and recordings. The museum has occasional concerts and temporary shows and supports a number of classical music projects throughout Brazil.

The **Dona Marta viewpoint**, which sits in the forest immediately above Botafogo and is connected by road to Corcovado, offers the best views of the Sugar Loaf in the city. Do not visit after dusk as robbers from the nearby favelas frequent the roads.

To Centre

Praia do Flamengo

Parque do Flamengo

Av Infante dom Henrique

Baía de Guanabara

Morro Cara do Cão

Praia da Urca

Av João Luís Alves

URCA

R Cândido Gaffree

Praia de Fora

Av Ramon Franco

R Mal Cantuária

Av Portugal

Morro de Urca

Cable Car

Pão de Açúcar

Praça Gen Tibúrcio

Pista Cláudio Coutinho

Praia Vermelha

Lasai *6 C1*
Miam Miam *2 D3*
Oui Oui *4 C1*

Bars & clubs 🎵
Bar Urca *7 C6*
Casa de Matriz *1 C2*

Few famous sights in the world live up to the high expectations overexposure has placed on them. The view from the feet of the Christ statue on Corcovado mountain is one of them. It is particularly impressive at dusk. Almost 1 km above the city and at the apex of one of the highest pinnacles in Tijuca forest stands O Redentor (Christ the Redeemer), lit in brilliant xenon at night, and with arms open to embrace the urban world's most breathtaking view.

At his feet to the west is a panoply of bays, fringed with white and backed by gleaming skyscrapers and, at night, the neon of myriad street lights. To the east as far as the eye can see lie long stretches of sand washed by green and white surf. In front and to the south, next to the vast ocean beaches, is the sparkle of Niterói watched over by low grey mountains and connected to Rio by a 10-km-long sinuous bridge that threads its way across the 10-km expanse of Guanabara Bay. As the light fades, the tropical forest at Christ's back comes to life in a chorus of cicadas and evening birdsong loud enough to drown even the chatter of 1000 tourists.

Mass is held on Sunday in a small chapel in the statue pedestal. There is a museum at the station of the cog railway with panels showing the history of the statue and the railway.

At the base of the mountain is the sleepy suburb of **Cosme Velho**, leafy and dotted with grand houses, museums and a little artist's corner called the Largo do Boticario. The two are linked by a 3.8-km-long railway, opened in 1884 by Emperor Dom Pedro II.

Cosme Velho and Laranjeiras

These twin residential neighbourhoods sit at the bottom of the mountain near the Corcovado train stop. They are leafy, tranquil and have streets of attractive belle époque houses.

The **Museu Internacional de Arte Naif do Brasil (MIAN)** ① *R Cosme Velho 561, on the same street as the station for Corcovado, T021-2205 8612, Tue-Fri 1000-1800, US$4*, is one of the most comprehensive museums of naïf and folk paintings in the world with a permanent collection of 8000 works by naïf artists from 130 countries. The museum also hosts several thematic and temporary exhibitions through the year. Parts of its collection are often on loan around the world. There is a coffee shop and a souvenir shop where you can buy paintings, books, postcards and T-shirts. Courses and workshops on painting and related subjects are also available.

The **Largo do Boticário** ① *R Cosme Velho 822*, is a pretty, shady little square close to the terminus for the Corcovado cog railway and surrounded by 19th-century buildings. It offers a glimpse of what the city looked like before all the concrete and highways. That the square exists at all is thanks to concerned residents who not only sought to preserve it but were also instrumental in rebuilding and refurbishing many of the buildings, using rubble from colonial buildings demolished in the city centre. Many of the doors once belonged to churches. The four houses that front the square are painted different colours (white, pale blue, caramel and pink), each with features picked out in decorative tiles, woodwork and stone. Many artists live here and can often be seen painting in the courtyard.

Essential Christ statue on Corcovado and around

Finding your feet

There are several ways to reach the top of Corcovado. The Trem do Corcovado cog railway and a road connect the city to the mountain from the suburb of Cosme Velho. Both are on the northern side of the Rebouças tunnel, which runs to and from the Lagoa. From the upper terminus of the **cog railway** or **Trem do Corcovado** (Rua Cosme Velho 513, T021-4063 3003, www.corcovado.com.br, daily every 30 minutes 0830-1830, 20-minute journey, US$16 return, in high season bookings are essential, through a travel agent or hotel concierge) there is a climb of 220 steps to the top or you can take the escalator, near which there is a café. To get to the cog railway station, take a taxi or bus to Cosme Velho and get off at the station.

Buses are as follows: from the centre or Glória/Flamengo bus No 180; from Copacabana bus Nos 583 or 584; from Botafogo or Ipanema/Leblon bus Nos 583 or 584; from Santa Teresa take the *micro-ônibus*.

Taxis, which wait in front of the station, also offer tours of Corcovado and Mirante Dona Marta and cost around US$22.

If going on foot, take bus No 206 from Praça Tiradentes (or No 407 from Largo do Machado) to Silvestre, where there is a station at which the train no longer stops. It is a steep 9-km walk from here to the top, along a shady road. Take the narrow street to the right of the station, go through the gate used by people who live beside the tracks and continue to the national park entrance. Walkers are charged entrance fees; even if you walk all the way you still have to pay for the van (US$8 Monday-Friday, US$10 at weekends). It is an illegal charge, but in a country with as high a level of corruption as Brazil they can get away with it. Allow a minimum of two hours (up to four hours depending on fitness).

By car, drive through Túnel Rebouças from Lagoa and then look out for the Corcovado signs before the beginning of the second tunnel and off to your right. Ignore the clamour of the touts at the beginning of the Corcovado road. They will try to convince you that the road is closed in order to take you on an alternative route and charge a hefty fee. If going by car to Corcovado, avoid going on weekends and public holidays – the slow traffic and long queues are overwhelming. Cars cannot go all the way to the parking outside the entrance, which is only for authorized cars and vans, instead you have to park halfway in a designated car park and then either walk or take a van (see above). You have to pay for the van whether you take it or walk. Avoid returning after dark; it is not safe. Parking space near the Trem do Corcovado is very limited.

Tours

Almost all hotels, and even hostels, offer organized coach trips to Corcovado, which usually take in Sugar Loaf and Maracanã as well. These offer a fairly brief stop on the mountain and times of day are not always the best for light. Helicopter tours are available, though these leave from the Sugar Loaf, the Dona Marta Mirante or the Lagoa. See also Tour operators, page 98.

Tip...

If travelling by train, take the earliest one possible for the best light and smallest crowds.

a splendid sweeping crescent of fine sand

Copacabana, which is called Leme at its northern end, epitomizes picture-book Rio: a broad sandy beach stretching for almost 8 km, washed by a bottle-green Atlantic and watched over by the Morro do Leme – another of Rio's beautiful forest-covered hills. Behind it is a wide neon- and argon-lit avenue lined with high-rises, the odd grand hotel and various bars, restaurants and clubs. The tanned and toned flock all around in skimpy bikinis, tiny *sungas* (swimming trunks) and colourful beach wraps, playing volleyball on the sand and jogging along the wavy black and white dragon's tooth pavements, while others busk, play capoeira and sell their wares.

Until the turn of the 21st century, Copacabana and Leme were a little tawdry. New beach cafés, paving, a clampdown on the unpleasant street-walking, and targeted policing have

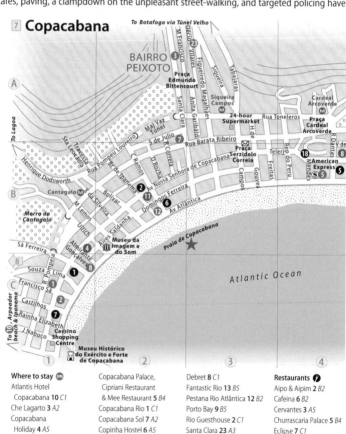

Where to stay

Atlantis Hotel
  Copacabana **10** *C1*
Che Lagarto **3** *A2*
Copacabana
  Holiday **4** *A5*

Copacabana Palace,
  Cipriani Restaurant
  & Mee Restaurant **5** *B4*
Copacabana Rio **1** *C1*
Copacabana Sol **7** *A2*
Copinha Hostel **6** *A5*

Debret **8** *C1*
Fantastic Rio **13** *B5*
Pestana Rio Atlântica **12** *B2*
Porto Bay **9** *B5*
Rio Guesthouse **2** *C1*
Santa Clara **23** *A3*

Restaurants

Aipo & Aipim **2** *B2*
Cafeina **6** *B2*
Cervantes **3** *A5*
Churrascaria Palace **5** *B4*
Eclipse **7** *C1*

made the beach far safer. While the water can be dirty when the currents wash shoreward, Copacabana and Leme are now as pleasant places to relax in the sun as neighbouring Ipanema. And they're a good deal cheaper.

Sights

The best way to enjoy the area is to wander along the dragon-tooth paved promenade, perhaps stopping to enjoy a coconut at one of the numerous beachfront snack bars, and noting the different crowd at each one. Everyone looks at everyone else in Rio so don't be afraid to do the same.

It's impossible to tell by walking along the 4.5-km stretch of unbroken sand but Copacabana is in reality two beaches – Copacabana is strictly speaking the beach running west of the Tunel Novo (new

➡ **Rio de Janeiro maps**
1 Rio de Janeiro, page 34
2 Rio de Janeiro centre, page 38
3 Praca 15 de Novembro, page 40
4 Glória, Santa Teresa & Lapa, page 56
5 Catete & Flamengo, page 58
6 Urca, Botafogo & Cosme Velho, page 60
7 **Copacabana, page 64**
8 Ipanema & Leblon, page 68

La Fiorentina **10** *B6*
No Mangue **1** *C1*
Traiteurs de France **18** *B4*

Bottle's Bar **8** *B4*
Clandestino **19** *A5*
Deck **11** *B2*

Bars & clubs 🎵
Bip Bip **4** *B1*

Essential Copacabana and Leme

Finding your feet

Buses are plentiful and cost US$2.70; Nos 119, 154, 413, 415, 455 and 474 run between the city centre and Avenida Nossa Senhora de Copacabana. If you are going to the centre from Copacabana, look for 'Castelo', 'Praça XV', 'E Ferro' or 'Praça Mauá' on the sign by the front door. 'Aterro' means the expressway between Botafogo and downtown Rio (not open on Sunday). From the centre to Copacabana is easier as all buses in that direction are clearly marked. The 'Aterro' bus takes 15 minutes. Numerous buses and minivans run between Copacabana and Ipanema; the two beaches are connected by Rua Francisco Otaviano or Rua Joaquim Nabuco, immediately west of the Forte de Copacabana.

Copacabana has *metrô* stations a few blocks inland from the beach at Cardeal Arcoverde, Siqueira Campos and Cantagalo. Copacabana *metrô* is linked to Lapa, the centre and Ipanema.

Tip...
It's possible to swim in the sea off Copacabana and Leme beaches when the current is heading out from the shore. At other times check on water quality with the lifeguards and the lifeguard stations (*postos*) lining the beach.

ON THE ROAD

Rio's sun worshippers

Ipanema and Copacabana are the most famous beaches in the world and there can surely be no people more devoted to lazing in the sun than Cariocas. But it wasn't always so. In the 19th century Brazilians would only go near sea water if they had been ordered to do so by a doctor. Even then it would only be for a quick dip at the beginning or the end of the day when the sun was weak. A tan was regarded as unhealthy and a sign of being lower class; to actually sit in the sun was a serious breach of social propriety.

All this began to change when the famous French actress Sarah Bernhardt came to Rio in 1886 to star in *Frou Frou* and *The Lady of the Camelias* at the São Pedro theatre. During her time off she caused a scandal, appalling the great and the good by travelling to then distant Copacabana, throwing on a swimsuit, sunbathing and even swimming in the sea. By the turn of the 20th century others had begun to follow suit, and by 1917 going to the beach had become sufficiently fashionable that the city established strict rules and regulations to govern sun worship. People were permitted to bathe only between 0500-0800 and 1700-1900, had to wear appropriate dress and be quiet and discreet; failure to do so resulted in five years in prison. Official attitudes only began to change in the 1920s with the building of the Copacabana Palace and the arrival of more foreigners who ignored Rio's prudishness and convinced Cariocas to begin to enjoy the beach.

Modern Rio is still far less permissive than southern France. Every year a handful of Europeans going topless on Rio's beaches are arrested by the police for public indecency.

tunnel) and Avenida Princesa Isabel. To the east of this the beach is known as Leme. Both beaches are capped by forts.

At the western end is the the **Forte de Copacabana and Museu Histórico do Exército (Army Museum)** ① *Av Atlântica at Francisco Otaviano, Posto 6, T021-2521 1032, www.fortedecopacabana.com, Tue-Sun and bank holidays 1000-1800, US$3*, built at the turn of the 19th century and inaugurated at the outbreak of the First World War in 1914 when (with its massive 305 mm, 190 mm and 75 mm German Krupp canons on a rotating head), it was South America's most formidable gun emplacement. In 1987, the Coastal Artillery Batteries were abolished, and the fort is now devoted to an army museum charting the history of the Portuguese colony and subsequently the Brazilian army in the country's limited conflicts, and in the creation of the Republic. There are a few items of interest, notably military artefacts and panels (in Portuguese) on campaigns such as the one fought at Canudos against Antônio Conselheiro. There's a small restaurant too and a branch of the **Confeitaria Colombo** (without the illustrious art deco of the branch in the centre; see page 83), and there are good views out over the beaches from the bulwarks.

Copacabana/Leme beach's other fort is older and far more interesting, primarily because of the superb views it has from the battlements and from the trail leading up to them from the army base at the end of Leme beach. The **Forte Duque de Caxias** ① *Praça Almirante Júlio de Noronha s/n, Leme, T021-3223 5076, cep.ensino.eb.br, Tue-Sun and bank holidays 0930-1830, US$1.50*, was built in the late 18th century by the second Rio de Janeiro-based governor general of Brazil, Luís de Almeida Portugal, in anticipation of a possible attempt to invade Rio de Janeiro by the Spanish. It was modernized when Copacabana fort was built and fitted with similarly massive German guns. The walk up to the fort, along a forest-lined cobbled road with sweeping views of the Urca, Guanabara Bay, Niterói and Copacabana, is one of the loveliest short walks in southern Rio.

In 2016 Copacabana is set to become the home to one of Latin America's most exciting new museums, the striking new, state-of-the-art Music and Visual Arts Museum: the **Museu da Imagem e do Som do Rio** (see page 41). The building is by New York studio Diller Scofidio + Renfro, who built the Boston ICA and the new MoMA expansion in New York, and is a zig-zag of compressed and folded concrete platforms built to echo the lines and waves of Copacabana's famous dragon's tooth pavements.

Tabajaras-Cabritos favela

The Tabajaras-Cabritos favela, swathing the São João and Cabritos hills behind Copacabana, is a lively, creative community attracting increasing numbers of emerging artists and musicians. It also has some of the finest views in the city reachable on a day hike, organized by **CEESC**; see page 97. It's breathtaking, both physically and metaphorically; a head-spinning, steep scramble up the side of the hill to a huge flat rock, the **Pedra do Marroca**, set in one of the city's smallest and prettiest protected areas. On the way up you'll see the Sugar Loaf sitting between the ocean and Guanabara Bay, Christ high on Corcovado and, as you reach the Pedra do Marroco itself, the long sweep of Ipanema beach stretching between the hulking Dois Irmãos mountains and backed by the heart-shaped Rodrigo de Freitas lagoon. Look out for capuchin monkeys, toucans and kitten-sized marmosets along the trail.

Ipanema and Leblon

Rio's most fashionable and cool stretches of sand

Like Copacabana and Leme, Ipanema and Leblon are essentially one long curving beach enclosed by the monolithic Dois Irmãos rocks at the western end and the Arpoador rocks to the east. And, like Copacabana and Leme, they have few sights beyond the sand, the landscape and the beautiful people. If Copacabana is samba, then Ipanema and Leblon are bossa nova: wealthy, pricey, predominantly white, and sealed off from the realities of Rio in a neat little fairy-tale strip of streets, watched over by twinkling lights high up on the flanks of the Morro Dois Irmãos. They look so romantic that it is easy to forget that they come from one of the city's largest favelas.

Essential Ipanema and Leblon

Finding your feet

General Osório *metrô* station lies at the Copacabana end of Ipanema. By late 2016 new metro stations are due to open further along the beach, including in Leblon on a route which will run to Barra da Tijuca via Gavea in 2017. In the meantime, express 'Metrô Na Superfície' buses run from Ipanema/General Osório to Gávea along the beachfront Rua Visconde de Pirajá in Ipanema and Avenida Ataulfo de Paiva in Leblon. Minivans run between the centre and/or Leme and Leblon, along the seafront roads. Bus destinations are clearly marked but, as a rule of thumb, any buses heading east along the seafront go to Copacabana or, if going west, to Barra da Tijuca; those going inland will pass by the Lagoa or Gávea.

Costly, closeted and cosseted though they may be, these are the beach suburbs in which to base yourself whilst in Rio if you're in the money. Almost all the city's best restaurants and high-end shops are here (and in the suburbs of Gávea and Lagoa, which lie behind). The streets are fairly clean and usually walked by nothing more dangerous than a small white poodle, the sea is good for swimming and the only beach hotels of any character lie in here.

Sights

Like Copacabana, Ipanema and Leblon are places for people-watching. A few hours wandering around Ipanema/Leblon followed by a half-day wandering Copacabana/Leme can be most interesting. The crowds are quite different. While Copacabana attracts a real cross-section of Rio society, Ipanema and Leblon are predominantly haunts of the fashionable peacocks who strut along the beachfront promenade, especially around **Posto Nove**.

Beyond the people and the breathtaking landscape, there is little to see here but plenty to do, especially for avid consumers. Shopping is best on and around Rua Visconde de

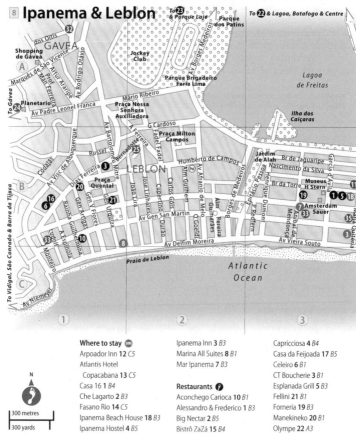

8 Ipanema & Leblon

Where to stay	Ipanema Inn 3 B3	Capricciosa 4 B4
Arpoador Inn 12 C5	Marina All Suites 8 B1	Casa da Feijoada 17 B5
Atlantis Hotel	Mar Ipanema 7 B3	Celeiro 6 B1
Copacabana 13 C5		CT Boucherie 3 B1
Casa 16 1 B4	**Restaurants**	Esplanada Grill 5 B3
Che Lagarto 2 B3	Aconchego Carioca 10 B1	Fellini 21 B3
Fasano Rio 14 C5	Alessandro & Frederico 1 B3	Forneria 19 B3
Ipanema Beach House 18 B5	Big Nectar 2 B5	Manekineko 20 B1
Ipanema Hostel 4 B5	Bistrô ZaZá 15 B4	Olympe 22 A3

N

300 metres
300 yards

Piraja and Rua Garcia D'Avila, where you'll find famous Rio brands like Lenny, Salinas, Blue Man and Oh Boy (see Shopping, page 94), and at the **Feira Hippy** (see Markets, page 95), where you will find everything from high-quality Brazilian designer swimwear to seed bracelets and T-shirts with pictures of Bob Marley.

Those seeking culture but unwilling to leave the beach should head for the **Casa de Cultura Laura Alvim** ① *Av Vieira Souto 176, T021-7104 3603, www.casadelaura.com.br*, comprising an arts cinema, art galleries (temporary exhibitions), workshop spaces and a bookshop. If it is pouring with rain you could watch diamonds being cut and set at the **Museus H Stern** ① *R Garcia D'Avila 113, T021-2106 0000*, or **Amsterdam Sauer** ① *R Garcia D'Avila 105, T021-2512 1132*, or hang out in the **Garota de Ipanema**, the bar where the *Girl from Ipanema* was written in the late 1950s (see Bars and clubs, page 90).

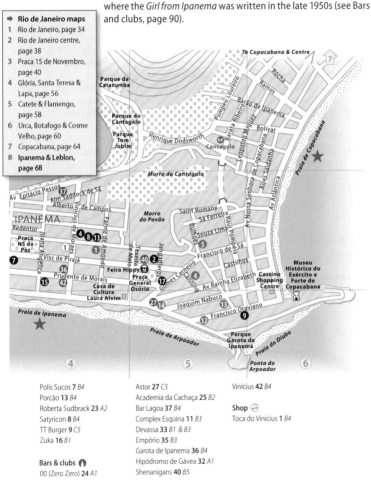

Polis Sucos **7** *B4*
Porção **13** *B4*
Roberta Sudbrack **23** *A2*
Satyricon **8** *B4*
TT Burger **9** *C5*
Zuka **16** *B1*

Bars & clubs 🍸
00 (Zero Zero) **24** *A1*

Astor **27** *C5*
Academia da Cachaça **25** *B2*
Bar Lagoa **37** *B4*
Complex Esquina **11** *B3*
Devassa **33** *B1 & B3*
Empório **35** *B3*
Garota de Ipanema **36** *B4*
Hipódromo de Gávea **32** *A1*
Shenanigans **40** *B5*

Vinícius **42** *B4*

Shop 🛍
Toca do Vinicius **1** *B4*

Just inland from Ipanema and Leblon, nestled under the forested slopes of Corcovado and the Tijuca National Park and spread around the picturesque saltwater lagoon of Lagoa Rodrigo de Freitas, are these three mainly residential suburbs, with a few sights of interest. Gávea tends to attract the young and wealthy, while the 30-somethings dine in the restaurants in Lagoa overlooking the lagoon and go out to clubs in Leblon or to the exclusive Jockey Club.

Lagoa de Freitas

This lake is another of Rio de Janeiro's unfeasibly beautiful natural sights and has long been admired. Darwin and German naturalists Spix and Martius mention it in their accounts. It is best seen in the early evening when thick golden sunlight bathes the rainforest-clad slopes of the **Serra da Carioca**, which rise high above it to reach their spectacular pinnacle with the distant xenon-white statue of Christ.

Like Copacabana and Guanabara Bay, it could be even more beautiful if only it were looked after a little better. The canal that links the lake to the sea is far too narrow to allow for sufficient exchange of water; pollution makes it unsafe for swimming and occasional summer algal blooms have led to mass fish deaths.

The lake is surrounded by a series of parks. Immediately next to it is the **Parque Tom Jobim** and contiguous are **Brigadeiro Faria Lima**, **Parque do Cantagalo** and **Parque das Taboas**. All have extensive leisure areas popular with roller skaters and volleyball players. There are live shows and *forró* dancing in the **Parque dos Patins** and kiosks serve a variety of food from Arabic to Japanese. Nearby is the **Parque Carlos Lacerda** ⓘ *Av Epitacio Pessoa, daily 0800-1900*, an open-air art gallery with sculptures by local artists in a landscaped park shaded by ornamental trees.

Jardim Botânico

R Jardim Botânico 1008, T021-3874 1808, www.jbrj.gov.br, daily 0800-1700, US$2.50.

These extensive 137-ha botanical gardens protect 9000 rare vascular plants and are home to 140 species of bird, and butterflies including the brilliant blue morphos. There are stately stands of 40-m-high royal palms, large tropical ficus and ceiba trees and pau brasil, from which the country gets its name. Giant Amazonian Victoria regia lilies cover many of the ponds and there are views up to Corcovado through the trees.

The gardens were founded in 1808 by the king, Dom Joao VI, as a nursery for European plants and new specimens from throughout the world. When the electric tram line arrived in this part of the city, housing and industries soon followed, but the gardens, then as now, remained a haven of peace.

There is a herbarium, an aquarium and a library as well as the **Museu Botânico**, housing exhibitions on the conservation of Brazilian flora, and the **Casa dos Pilões**, the first gun-powder factory in Brazil. A newish pavilion contains sculptures by Mestre Valentim. Many improvements were carried out before the 1992 Earth Summit, including a new *orquidario*, an enlarged bookshop and a smart café. Birdwatchers can expect to see rarities including the social flycatcher, great and boat-billed kiskadees, cattle tyrants, sayaca, palm and seven-coloured (green-headed) tanagers as well as over 20 different kinds of hummingbird, roadside hawks, laughing falcons and various toucans and parakeets. There are marmosets in the trees.

Less than 1 km from the gardens is the little-visited **Parque Laje** ⓘ *R Jardim Botânico 414, daily 0900-1700, free,* which is more jungle-like than the Jardim Botânico and has a series of small grottoes, an old tower and lakes, as well as the **Escola de Artes Visuais** (visual arts school) housed in a large colonial house in the grounds.

The **Planetário** ⓘ *R Padre Leonel Franco 240, Gávea, www.rio.rj.gov.br/planetario, by appointment, free,* has a sculpture of the Earth and Moon by Mário Agostinelli. On Wednesday evenings at dusk, in clear weather, astronomers give guided observations of the stars. At weekends there are shows for children at 1630, 1800 and 1930. There are occasional *chorinho* concerts on Thursday or Friday.

Rough paths lead to the summit of the flat-topped **Pedra da Gávea** and to magnificent views. Hang-gliders fly to the beach at São Conrado from the **Pedra Bonita** behind the Pedra da Gávea; see What to do, page 97.

São Conrado, Barra da Tijuca and beyond

one of the city's most exclusive residential suburbs

The next beach along from Leblon – reached by a winding road which hugs the cliffs along the coast – is the upscale residential district of São Conrado, watched over by the giant Rocinha and Vidigal favelas. Beyond is even more exclusive Joatinga (with a beach enclosed by a private condominium) where Pele lives, and beyond that, some 15 km from Ipanema, is Barra da Tijuca, or Barra as it is known to locals, which is one of the city's principal middle-class residential areas.

Essential São Conrado, Barra da Tijuca and beyond

Finding your feet

A new metro station is due to open at the northeastern end of Barra in early 2017. Buses from the city centre to Barra are Nos 175 and 176; from Botafogo, Glória or Flamengo take No 179; from Leme Nos 591 or 592; and from Copacabana via Leblon No 523 (45 minutes to one hour). A taxi from the centre costs US\$20 (US\$30 after 2400) or US\$12 from Ipanema. A comfortable bus, **Pegasus**, goes along the coast from the Castelo bus terminal to Barra da Tijuca and continues to Campo Grande or Santa Cruz; or take the free 'Barra Shopping' bus. Bus No 700 from Praça São Conrado runs the full length of the beach to Recreio dos Bandeirantes.

ON THE ROAD

Favelas

Brazil's reputation as a violent country comes almost exclusively from the gun fights against the police and the inter-gang wars which take place in the slums of the big cities. Such slums are known as favelas in Portuguese. And while tourists rarely encounter violence in Brazil, residents of many of the country's favelas face it on a near daily basis – as shockingly portrayed in the multi award-winning film, *Cidade de Deus* (City of God). The film was no exaggeration: Brazil's favela-driven crime statistics speak for themselves. Most murders in Brazil take place in the favelas and involve fights with the police or between rival drug gangs, like the Comando Vermelho and the ADA (Amigos de Amigos) in Rio.

In 2008 in an effort to curb the violence in Rio, the police moved into a number of city's favelas, most of them in the Zona Sul which is situated around the touristy areas of Ipanema and Copacabana. They installed armed pacification units (Unidades de Polícia Pacificadora or UPPs) and regular patrols in areas which had never been policed before. While there have been protracted problems in some of the larger favelas like the Complexo Alemao (which erupted into violence in mid-2015) other favelas like Tabajaras-Cabritos, Vidigal and Santa Marta have seen a dramatic reduction in crime, followed by an increase in local enterprise, investment and infrastructure. This reduction in crime was felt throughout the city. Between the UPP programme's start and 2012, Rio saw a steep decline in homicides and robberies all over the city. Inside favelas with UPPs, homicide rates were actually halved.

There are currently some 37 UPPs in Rio, operating in fewer than half of the city's 750-plus favelas, either with the tolerance or in the absence of groups like the Comando Vermelho or ADA. The other communities remain in the hands of the drug gangs or armed militia.

It's not all good news though. For while crime has decreased in Rio and in the favelas, it has increased elsewhere in Brazil, fuelled by a growth in the crack trade and the emigration of Rio drug runners to outlying cities.

These neighbourhoods were planned and built for the car. Walking distances are long and the neighbourhoods feels characterless and lacking in intimacy compared to the rest of Rio.

Sights

Barra da Tijuca is a rapidly developing district, modelled on Miami, which is focused on a 20-km sandy beach renowned for its surfing, especially at its far westernmost end: **Recreio dos Bandeirantes**. There are countless bars and restaurants, concentrated at both ends, as well as campsites, motels and hotels, built in increasing number in anticipation of the 2016 Olympics, many of whose events will take place at the new Olympic Park behind the suburb. Budget accommodation in Barra tends to be self-catering.

The beaches beyond Barra and Recreio, at (Praia do) **Pontal**, **Prainha** and **Grumari**, are some of the best in Rio, with fluffy white sand, fresh, clean pounding surf and pretty little chic shack restaurants. They are very busy at weekends and are most easily visited on

Visiting a favela

Tourists thinking of visiting a favela face a few key questions.

Why is it interesting to go?

Favelas are close-knit communities, each with a different and unique set of people, often drawn from a different part of Brazil. Tabajaras, for instance, was founded by North Eastern Amerindians in the 16th century and then grew from an indigenous village. The Morro da Providencia was established by refugee soldiers from the great Canudos war and Gamboa by Afro-Brazilians from Bahia who invented samba here, on the steps of Pedra do Sal. Carnival, Brazilian football, samba and the gregarious spirit of Rio were not born on the asphalt of Ipanema – they come from the alleys and trails of the favelas. These are vibrant, creative places where suffering stands alongside joy and misery alongside triumphs of the human spirit. Properly undertaken, a favela visit is *never* a poor people safari.

What is there to see?

With their stunning views, lively creativity and strong community spirit, favelas like Vidigal, Santa Marta and Tabajaras-Cabritos have so much to offer. A trail walk to the Pedra do Maroca or the peak of the Morro dos Dois Irmãos is one of Rio's greatest experiences, as is a funk party in Rio das Pedras or a samba dance in Santa Marta.

Is it safe?

A visit to a favela is never 100% safe. But you are extremely unlikely to encounter any problems if you visit in the right way with the right people. I have been visiting favelas in Rio for 20 years. I've never had a problem and I have had many wonderful experiences. The benefits have far outweighed the risks but the risks are always there – even if they are small.

Who should I go with?

Only go with people you can trust. We can vouch for those we include in our guidebook. If in any other doubt ask the local tourist board or the concierge in your hotel or hostel.

Can I go alone?

Never. A favela is a community. Everyone knows everyone. Think of it like someone's home. You would never walk in uninvited, especially if the homeowner had a gun. Don't do so in a favela. Not only is it disrespectful, it is downright dangerous.

a tour (see page 98). For the best views of Prainha beach, head to the viewpoint in the **Parque Natural Municipal da Prainha**.

The **Bosque da Barra/Parque Arruda Câmara** ⓘ *junction of Av das Américas and Av Ayrton Senna, daily 0700-1700*, preserves the vegetation of the sandbanks that existed on this part of the coast before the city took over. The **Autódromo** (motor-racing track) is behind Barra and the Lagoa de Jacarepaguá, in the district of the same name. The Brazilian Grand Prix was held here during the 1980s before returning to Interlagos, São Paulo.

A bit further out is the **Museu Casa do Pontal** ⓘ *Estrada do Pontal 3295, Recreio dos Bandeirantes, T021-2490 3278, www.museucasadopontal.com.br, Tue-Sun 0930-1700*. Located in a little wood near Pontal beach, this is one of the finest collections of Brazilian folk art in the country. There are over 5000 works by more than 200 artists from 24 different Brazilian states, accumulated French designer Jacques van de Beuque over a 40-year period. Recommended.

Further west are the **Barra de Guaratiba** and **Pedra de Guaratiba** beaches, backed by extensive mangroves and lagoons and, finally, those at **Sepetiba**, after which the road heads further south west towards **Ilha Grande** and **Paraty** and **São Paulo state**.

Sítio Roberto Burle Marx ⓘ *Estrada da Barra de Guaratiba 2019, Barra de Guaratiba, T021-2410 1171, daily 0930-1330, by appointment only*, was, from 1949 to 1994, the home of the great Roberto Burle Marx (1909-1994), the world-famous landscape designer and artist. His projects achieved a rare harmony between nature, architecture and man-made landscapes. He created many schemes in Brazil and abroad; in Rio alone his work includes the Parque do Flamengo, the pavements of the Avenida Atlântica in Copacabana, Praça Júlio de Noronha in Leme, the remodelling of Largo da Carioca, the gardens of the Museu Nacional de Belas Artes and the Biblioteca Nacional, and the complex at the Santa Teresa tram station near the Catedral Metropolitana.

Covering 350,000 sq m, the estate contains an estimated 3500 species of plant, mostly Brazilian. It is run now by the **Instituto do Patrimônio Histórico e Artístico Nacional (IPHAN)** and one of its main aims is to produce seedlings of the plants in its collection. Also on view are Burle Marx's collection of paintings, ceramics, sculptures and other objets d'art, plus examples of his own designs and paintings. The library houses 2500 volumes on botany, architecture and landscape design.

The 12,500-ha **Parque Estadual da Pedra Branca** ⓘ *www.inea.rj.gov.br/unidades/pqpedra_branca.asp, Tue-Sun 0800-1700, free*, which lies inland of western Rio, is the largest stretch of urban forest in Rio (a claim often erroneously made for Parque Nacional da Tijuca) and the second largest in the world after the Serra da Cantareira in São Paulo (which, unlike Pedra Branca, is not flanked entirely by urban areas). The park focuses on the 1025-m-high Pedra Branca and preserves numerous important Mata Atlântica species. Visits can be arranged through the **Amigos do Parque** ⓘ *www.parquepedrabranca.com*.

Parque Nacional da Tijuca
one of the largest areas of urban rainforest in the world

Corcovado is situated within Tijuca National Park, a haven for city-weary Cariocas, as well as for some 200 species of bird, numerous small mammals and primates and hundreds of species of endangered Atlantic coast rainforest plants. There is plenty of shade and the views from the various vantage points are almost as impressive as those from Corcovado.

The vegetation in the Parque Nacional da Tijuca is not primary; most is natural regrowth and planned reforestation. It is a testament to what humans can do to regenerate lost forest. The first Europeans to arrive in the area cut down trees for use in construction and as firewood. The lower areas were cleared to make way for sugar plantations. When coffee was introduced to Rio de Janeiro in 1760 further swathes were cut down for *fazendas*. But the deforestation destroyed Rio's watershed and in 1861, in one of the world's first conservation projects, the imperial government decided that Tijuca should become a rainforest preserve. The enormous task of reforesting the entire area was given to an army major, Manuel Gomes Archer, who took saplings from other areas of Atlantic forest and replanted Tijuca with native trees and a selection of exotics in fewer than 13 years. The names of the six slaves who did the actual manual work is not known. Reforestation was continued by Tomas de Gama. In 1961 Tijuca was joined to several other patches of remnant forest to form a national park of 3300 ha.

The park

One of the best walks is to the **Pico da Tijuca** (1022 m). Views from the top are wonderful and the walk offers the chance to see plenty of animals. Allow two to three hours. To get to the trailhead enter the park at **Alto da Boa Vista** and follow the signposts (maps are displayed) to **Bom Retiro**, a good picnic place (1½ hours' walk). At Bom Retiro the road ends and it is another hour's walk up a fair footpath to the summit (take the path from the right of the Bom Retiro drinking fountain, not the more obvious steps from the left). The last part consists of steps carved out of the solid rock. There are several sheer drops at the summit which are masked by bushes – be wary. The route is shady for almost its entire length. The main path to Bom Retiro passes the **Cascatinha Taunay** (a 30-m waterfall) and the **Mayrink Chapel** (1860). Panels painted in the Chapel by Cândido Portinari have been replaced by copies and the originals will probably be installed in the Museu de Arte Moderna. Beyond the chapel is the wonderful little restaurant **Os Esquilos** set in the forest, which dates from 1945 and is a popular lunch spot on weekends. Come early to avoid crowds. Allow at least five hours for the walk.

Other viewpoints include the **Paulo e Virginia Grotto**, the **Vista do Almirante**, the **Mesa do Imperador** and the **Vista Chinesa** (420 m), a Chinese-style pavilion with a view of the Lagoa Rodrigo de Freitas, Ipanema and Leblon. **Museu Açude** ⓘ *Estrada do Açude 764, Alto da Boa Vista, T021-2492 2119, www.museuscastromaya.com.br, Thu-Sun 1100-1700, Sun brunch with live music 1230-1700*, is in the former home of tycoon Castro Maia with some impressive murals and *azulejos* (tiles).

Essential Parque Nacional da Tijuca

Finding your feet

To get to the park entrance, take bus No 221 from Praça 15 de Novembro, No 233 ('Barra da Tijuca') or No 234 from the *rodoviária* or No 454 from Copacabana to Alto da Boa Vista.

Getting around

There is no public transport within the park and the best way to explore is by trail, tour, bicycle or car. If hiking in the park other than on the main paths, a guide may be useful if you do not want to get lost. Contact the **Sindicato de Guías**, T021-267 4582. See also Hiking, page 97.

Opening hours

Daily 0600-2100.

Tip...

Bring your swimming gear because the forest has a number of natural springs, many of which have been diverted through bamboo channels to form natural showers.

ON THE ROAD

Rio's top 10 views and how to see them

Perhaps more than any other metropolis, Rio is a city of wonderful views. Every beach, every peak and every street corner has a view. Most are breathtaking. Here's a top 10, in no particular order.

Prainha beach and Praia do Pontal, Barra, from the viewpoints in the Parque Natural Municipal da Prainha (see page 72)
How: With Rio Connexion Tours (see page 99)
When: Early morning or late afternoon

Corcovado, from the Sugar Loaf
How: Take the cable car (see page 59)
When: Late afternoon and early evening

Ipanema, Lagoa and the Christ statue from Pedra do Maroca mountain
How: With CEESC (see page 96)
When: Sunset or dawn

Ipanema, Lagoa and Pedra da Gávea from Morro dos Dois Irmãos
How: With Ana Lima of Trilha Dois Irmãos (see page 98)
When: Early morning

Rio Skyline, from Parque da Cidade in Niterói
How: With Alex Feliciano (see page 98)
When: Anytime

Rio Skyline and Baía da Guanabara from Pico da Tijuca
How: With Rio Hiking (see page 98)
When: Late afternoon

Sugar Loaf and Botafogo Bay from Favela Santa Marta
How: With a Favela Santa Marta tour (see page 97)
When: Anytime

Rio, Guanabara Bay and Niterói from the Christ statue
How: Trem do Corcovado (see page 63)
When: Anytime

Copacabana and Sugar Loaf from the Forte Duque de Caxias do Leme
How: Walk the trail – Tuesday-Sunday 0930-1630 (see page 66)
When: Anytime

Rio centre and Guanabara Bay from Aprazível Restaurant
How: Book for dinner (see page 84)
When: Sunset and evening meal

Tourist information

Embratur
*R Uruguaiana 174, 8th floor, Centro,
T021-2509 6017, www.visitbrasil.com.*
Provides information on the whole country.

Rio Convention and Visitors Bureau
*R Visconde de Pirajá 547, suite 610,
Ipanema, T021-2259 6165,
www.rioconventionbureau.com.br.*
A private sector organization offering
information and assistance in English.

Riotur
*Praça Pio X, 119, 9th floor, Centro, T021-
2271 7000, www.rioguiaoficial.com.br.*
The city's government tourist office. There
are also booths or offices in **Copacabana**
(Centro Integrado de Informação ao Turista,
Av Princesa Isabel 183, T021-2541 7522,
Mon-Fri 0900-1800, Sat 0900-1700),
Copacabana beach (Av Atlantica at Hilário
de Gouveia, T021-2541 4421, daily 0900-
2000), **Ipanema** (Visconde de Pirajá, daily
0800-1900) and **Leblon** (Praça Cazuza s/n
at Av Ataulfo de Paiva, daily 0800-1800).
The helpful staff speak English, French and
German and can provide good city maps
and a very useful free brochure.

There are further information stands in
Lapa (Av Mem de Sa s/n), **Sugar Loaf** (Praça
General Tiburico, Urca, daily 0800-2000),
Barra (Av do Pepê at Olegário Maciel, daily
0900-1800) and at the **international airport**
and **Novo Rio bus station**.

Turisrio
*R da Ajuda 5, 6th floor, Centro, T021-2215 0011,
www.turisrio.rj.gov.br. Mon-Fri 0900-1800.*
The state tourism organization.

Where to stay

The best places to stay in Rio are
Copacabana/Leme, Ipanema/Leblon and
Santa Teresa – depending whether you
want to be on the beach (Copacabana and
Ipanema) or within easy access of nightlife,
the Sambódromo and the centre. Ipanema
is probably the safest area in the city.

Those looking for hotels with charm and
personality will find Rio unremarkable.
With a few notable exceptions, those in the
higher and mid-range bracket are a mix
of anonymous business chain towers and
fading leftovers from the 1970s, complete
with period decor. The best of the hotel
chains is **Windsor** (www.windsorhoteis.com),
with a range of good options throughout Rio
from Barra to the centre and with a number
of excellent hotels in Copacabana (the
Windsor Leme is a favourite). We don't list
them all below because there are too many,
not due to a lack of quality.

City centre hotels at the lower end of the
market can be tawdry, so if you need to stay
here opt to pay more or stay in the beaches
and take the metro. Guesthouses and B&Bs
are a far better option even for those on
a medium budget. Homestays through
hiddenpousadasbrazil.com or **Cama e Café**
are popular and offer a good way to become
more integrated with locals. Backpackers
are well catered for. Searches on sites such
as www.hostels.com or www.hostelworld.
com will yield almost 50 hostel options and
numbers are increasing every month. There
are far too many for us to list them all here,
so we have only included our favourites.

Accommodation prices increase
significantly over New Year and Carnaval,
when they are among the most expensive in
the world, soaring above equivalents in New
York or London. Reserve well in advance.

New hotels for Rio

The 2014 FIFA World Cup™ showed that Rio was desperately short of quality hotel rooms. The years leading up to 2020 promise to change that, with new ventures announced or in the pipeline from a string of hotel investors, from the bold and brash to the stylish and boutique. Alongside a spate of chain hotels from the likes of **Marriot, Hilton, Mercure and Windsor**, here are a few of the more interesting rooms set or rumoured to open. Check out their websites for the latest news.

Chic São Paulo boutique hotel **Emiliano** (www.emiliano.com.br) plan to open a new Copacabana branch in 2016.

Rio's best boutique hotel, French-owned **La Suite**, will see a sister hotel open in the new centre by 2017, packed with panache: **Le Paris** (www.bydussol.com) will sit in a gorgeous, fully refurbished belle époque townhouse off Praça Tiradentes.

Donald Trump expands his blingy tower empire into South America with a 38-floor **Trump Towers Rio** (www.trumptowersrio.com), due to open in 2016 in the Porto Maravilha area.

Oscar Niemeyer's iconic cylindrical **Hotel Nacional**, perched over the beach in São Conrado and set in gardens landscaped by Burle Marx, is being refurbished with a 1960s retrofit by US-based **VOA** (www.voa.com), in collaboration with the architect's nephew, João Niemeyer. It is expected to open in late 2016.

Hotel Gloria, Rio's other great grand dame hotel, was ranked with **Copacabana Palace** in its 20th-century heyday, with a guest list which included Albert Einstein. After a disastrous investment from fallen Brazilian billionaire Eike Batista it is rumoured to be being resurrected as Rio's first **Four Seasons**.

Self-catering apartments

Self-catering apartments are a popular and good-value form of accommodation in Rio, available at all price levels. In Flamengo furnished apartments for short-term lets, accommodating up to 6, cost from US$200 per month. In Copacabana, Ipanema and Leblon prices start at about US$205 a day (US$400-500 a month) for a simple studio and up to US$2500 a month for a luxurious residence sleeping 4-6. Heading south past Barra da Tijuca, virtually all the accommodation available is self-catering. Renting a small flat, or sharing a larger one, can be much better value than a hotel room.

Blocks consisting entirely of short-let apartments can attract thieves, so check the (usually excellent) security arrangements. Residential buildings are called 'prédio familial'. Higher floors ('alto andar') are quieter.

See websites such as www.alugue temporada.com.br, www.riotemporada.net and www.vivareal.com.br for more details. 'Apart-Hotels' are also listed in the *Guia 4 Rodas* and **Riotur**'s booklet. Agents and private owners advertise under 'Apartamentos – Temporada' in publications like *Balcão* (twice weekly), *O Globo* or *Jornal do Brasil* (daily); advertisements are classified by district and size of apartment: 'vagas e quartos' means shared accommodation; 'conjugado' (or 'conj') is a studio with limited cooking facilities; '3 quartos' is a 3-bedroom flat. There should always be a written agreement when renting.

Homestays and guesthouses

Many visitors choose to stay in family guesthouses or through homestay schemes. The former are listed in the text below; the latter are available through international schemes like www.airbnb.com (paid) or www.couchsurfing.org (free), though value-for-money/quality can be hard to come by. More reliable are locally run operators. These include:

$$$$-$$$ Hidden Pousadas Brazil
www.hiddenpousadasbrazil.com.
Great accommodation options in carefully selected small mid- to upper-end hotels and homes throughout Rio and beyond. These include lovely properties in Leblon, Ipanema, Copacabana and Santa Teresa.

$$$$-$$ Cama e Café and Rio Homestay
R Laurinda Santos Lobo 124, Santa Teresa, T021-2225 4366, T021-9638 4850 (mob 24 hrs), www.camaecafe.com and www. riohomestay.com.
One of the best accommodation options in Rio with a range of more than 50 homestay deals in Santa Teresa, Cosme Velho and Ipanema from the simple to the luxurious.

$ Favela Experience
www.favelaexperience.com.
Offer homestays in favelas and tours with locally based tour operators. Stays in a favela should be undertaken with caution. Be sure to check and double-check on security.

Lapa *map p56*
This popular nightlife area neighbouring Santa Teresa, Glória and the centre has seen a handful of attractive new hotels and hostels open in the last few years.

$$$$-$$$ Vila Galé
R Riachuelo 124, T021-2460 4500, www.vilagale.com.
Smart modern rooms with wooden floors, muted colours and faux 18th-century furnishings gathered around a courtyard in a handsome belle époque townhouse in the heart of all the Lapa action. Ask for a room furthest from the street if staying on a weekend night.

$$$ Da Lapa
R do lavradio 200, T021-2252 4237, www.dalapahotel.com.
This upmarket hostel-meets-low key boutique hotel offers modish, minimalist shared rooms and suites in Lapa's busiest nightlife street. Opt for the suites if you don't want to be woken in the early hours by returning revellers. Tastefully decorated shared areas include a big courtyard and raw-brick lounge area with sumptuous sofas and anodyne modern art.

$$ Lapa Hostel
R do Resende 43, T021-2507 2869, www.lapahostelrio.com.
This place offers hospital-white rooms and corridors, a big shared kitchen, computers and TVs and decent beds in dorms and doubles (which get hot during the day). Attracts a party crowd. In a quiet street in the heart of Lapa but take care at night.

Santa Teresa *map p56*

$$$$ Mama Ruisa
R Santa Cristina 132, T021-2242 1281, www.mamaruisa.com.
French-run boutique hotel with carefully casual public spaces and 4 simply decorated, elegant hard wood and whitewash rooms decorated in a modern French colonial style and named in homage to French artistic icons.

$$$ Casa Cool Beans
R Laurinda Santos Lobo 136, T021-2262 0552, with another branch in Ipanema, www.casacoolbeans.com.
Situated in a large Santa Teresa town house on a quiet backstreet, decorated with art and graffiti by local artists, with a small pool, spacious wood-floored rooms and a generous breakfast.

$$$ Quinta Azul
R Almirante Alexandrino 256, T021-3253 1021, www.quintaazul.com.
Cosy little boutique hotel with sweeping views from the upper rooms. Well situated. Small pool.

$$ Casa Áurea
R Áurea 80, T021-2242 5830,
www.casaaurea.com.br.
Tranquil, friendly, arty hostel and boutique hotel in a colonial house in a Santa Teresa backstreet. All rooms vary in shape, size and colour and they and the public spaces, which include a large garden patio, are decorated with tasteful art and craftwork.

$$ Rio Forest Hostel
R Joaquim Murtinho 517, T021-3563 1021,
www.rioforesthostel.com.br.
Bright, airy hostel with dorms and rooms with a view. Decent showers, friendly and welcoming staff and Wi-Fi throughout. Be sure to get to breakfast early if the hostel is fully booked to ensure a table.

$$ Rio Hostel
R Joaquim Murtinho 351, T021-3852 0827,
www.riohostel.com.
One of Rio's best small hostels. Clinging to the side of a hill, it has spectacular views of the centre and is on the doorstep of the city's best nightlife. Also with a branch in Ipanema.

Glória, Catete and Flamengo *map p58*
Primarily residential areas between the centre and Copacabana, with good bus and *metrô* connections. Glória, Catete and Flamengo lie next to a park landscaped by Burle Marx and a beautiful beach lapped by a filthy sea.

$$$$ Novo Mundo
Praia Flamengo 20, Catete, T021-2105 7000,
www.hotelnovomundo.com.br.
The 4-star price belies this art deco dame's 3-star fittings (plastic shower curtains, tiny gym), but the views of the Sugar Loaf from the bay-facing rooms and the proximity to the centre and Santos Dumont Airport make this a good business choice.

$$ Imperial
R do Catete 186, Catete, T021-2112 6000,
www.imperialhotel.com.br.
One of the city's very first grand hotels, built in the late 19th century. Rooms are divided

between the old building and the newer annex. The latter has modern US-style motel rooms.

Botafogo and Urca *map p60*

$$ Alpha Hostel
R Praia de Botafogo 462, casa 3,
T021-2286 7799, www.alphahostel.com.
Small-scale hostel in a pretty little townhouse with pocket-sized but well-kept a/c rooms.

$$ El Misti Hostel
Praia de Botafogo 462, casa 9, Botafogo,
T021-2226 0991, www.elmistihostel.com.
A converted colonial house with 6 dorms, shared bathrooms, kitchen and internet, capoeira classes and tour service. Popular with party-goers.

$$ Sun Rio Hostel
R Praia de Botafogo 462, casa 5, Botafogo,
next door to El Misti, T021-2226 0461,
www.sunriohostel.com.br.
A/c dorms, doubles and en suites, all very well kept and clean. Shared kitchen, internet, bike rental and tours organized. Friendly owner Daniela is very welcoming.

Copacabana and Leme *map p64*
Many hotels charge about 30% more for a sea view, but some town-side upper rooms have good views of the mountains. The **Windsor** group (www.windsorhoteis.com, see page 77) have a number of hotels on the beach.

$$$$ Copacabana Palace
Av Atlântica 1702, T021-2548 7070,
www.copacabanapalace.com.br.
Made famous by Ginger Rogers and Fred Astaire, who filmed *Flying down to Rio* here. Rooms are quiet, spacious and comfortable, with superb beds, effortless service, and conservative and faux European decor. The hotel has a **Cipriani** restaurant (sister to the restaurants in Venice, New York and other cities) and a new Asian-Brazilian fusion restaurant, **Mee**, which was awarded

a Michelin star in 2015. Both are open to non-guests.

$$$$ Copacabana Rio
Av N S de Copacabana 1256, T021-2267 9900, www.copacabanariohotel.com.br.
Quiet, efficiently run 1970s tower with simple but well-maintained standard 3-star rooms.

$$$$ Pestana Rio Atlântica
Av Atlântica 2964, T021-2548 6332, www.pestana.com.
Spacious bright rooms and a rooftop pool and terrace with sweeping views.

$$$$ Porto Bay
Av Atlântica 1500, T021-2546 8000, www.portobay.com.
Freshly renovated for the Olympics this beachside tower in the centre of Copacabana has excellent views from the rooftop pool area, a small gym and a pleasant lobby lounge bar with leather sofas and decent caipirinhas.

$$$ Atlantis Copacabana
Av Bulhões de Carvalho 61, T021-2521 1142, www.atlantishotel.com.br.
Equally close to Ipanema and Copacabana, this Arpoador hotel sits in a quiet, safe street very close to the beach. Small rooftop pool, sauna and Wi-Fi.

$$$ Copacabana Sol
R Santa Clara 141, T021-2549 4577, www.copacabanasolhotel.com.br.
Tiled, a/c rooms with cable TV, Wi-Fi, safes and en suite bathrooms with marble commodes and showers. Good value.

$$$ Debret
Av Atlântica 3564, T021-2522 0132, www.debret.com.
Bright, spacious, modern seafront rooms in pastel colours; others are a little dark. Free Wi-Fi. Separate restaurant.

$$$ Rio Guesthouse
R Francisco Sa 5, T021-2521 8568, www.martarioguesthouse.com.
Modest but comfortable a/c rooms in the top floor apartment of a tall building overlooking the beach. Superb views. The owner Marta is welcoming and helpful.

$$$ Santa Clara
R Décio Vilares 316, Metrô Siqueira Campos, T021-2256 2650, www.hotelsantaclara.com.br.
Bright, newly refurbished rooms a few blocks back from the beach. Well maintained, discreet and good value, at the lower end of this price range.

$$ Che Lagarto Copacabana
R Barata Ribeiro 111, T021-3209 0348, www.chelagarto.com.
Very popular and well-run hostel with spacious, clean dorms and doubles, a lovely pool and bar on the terrace and one of the best ranges of tours in Rio, including surf classes. Excellent English spoken. Taken over by the Argentine chain in 2012.

$$ Copinha Hostel
R Felipe de Oliveira 11, T021-2275 8520, www.copinhahostel.com.br.
Clean, well-run little lemon-yellow hostel with a range of a/c dorms and doubles in white tile and with en suites. 24-hr reception, kitchen, cable TV and transport services.

Self-catering apartments

Copacabana Holiday
R Barata Ribeiro 90A, T021-2542 1525, www.copacabanaholiday.com.br.
Recommended, well-equipped small apartments from US$450 per month, minimum 30-day let.

Fantastic Rio
Av Atlântica 974, apt 501, Leme, T021-3507 7491, http://fantasticrio.br.tripod.com.
All types of furnished accommodation from US$20 per day. Good service, contact Peter Corr.

Ipanema and Leblon *map p68*

$$$$ Fasano Rio
Av Vieira Souto 80, Ipanema, T021-3202 4000, www.fasano.com.br.
This pricey Philippe Starck-designed luxury hotel is in the most luxurious, modish hotel in Ipanema. Standard rooms are a little boxy. If you can, opt to upgrade. The bright and airy **Fasano Al Mare** restaurant serving decent light Mediterranean seafood has the best beachside lunch in the city and the Brit-rock themed bar is one of Rio's most popular high-end drinking spots, There's a sumptuous rooftop terrace and poolside bar (come for sunset), and limousine service for airport transfers.

$$$$ Marina All Suites
Av Delfim Moreira 696, Ipanema, T021-2294 1794, www.hoteismarina.com.br.
A rather faded-looking luxury boutique with 41 old-fashioned looking 1990s designer suites set in a beachfront tower. Decent bar and restaurant.

$$$ Arpoador Inn
Francisco Otaviano 177, Ipanema, T021-2523 0060, www.arpoadorinn.com.br.
One of the best deals on the seafront. Well maintained, with off-season special offers.

$$$ Ipanema Inn
Maria Quitéria 27, behind Caesar Park, Ipanema, T021-2523 6092, www.ipanemainn.com.br.
A popular package tour and small business hotel less than 100 m from the beach. Good value and location.

$$$ Mar Ipanema
R Visconde de Pirajá 539, Ipanema, T021-3875 9190, www.maripanema.com.
Simple, smart, modern rooms a block from the beach. The front rooms can be noisy.

$$ Casa 16
R Barão da Torre 175, casa 16, Ipanema, T021-2247 1384, www.casa16 ipanema.com.
This French-owned B&B in 2 townhouses sits on a street filled with hostels, 3 blocks from the beach. It offers good long-stay rates and the small rooms with en suites are decorated in wood and tile and fan-cooled.

$$ Che Lagarto
R Barão de Jaguaripe 208, Ipanema, T021-2247 4582, www.chelagarto.com.
Bright red, bustling party hostel with young staff and a terrace with views of Corcovado. Dorms and doubles.

$$ Ipanema Beach House
R Barão da Torre 485, Ipanema, T021-3203 3693, www.ipanemahouse.com.
Great little hostel with very friendly staff, pool, internet, outdoor bar, continental breakfast, a range of dorms and doubles, 24-hr check-in.

$$ Ipanema Hostel
R Canning, casa 1, Ipanema, T021-2287 2928, www.riohostelipanema.com.
Sister hostel to the friendly and welcoming **Rio Hostel** in Santa Teresa with a range of small rooms and dorms, a tour operator, internet and a lively crowd.

Gávea

$$$$ La Maison
R Sergio Porto 58, T021-3205 3585, www.bydussol.com.
Rio's only other decent boutique hotel, also run by the French owners of **La Suite** (see below), sits in a period town house on a quiet backstreet in this residential suburb. The bright spacious rooms are tastefully decorated in primary colours and there are wonderful views of Corcovado from the open-sided breakfast area and the little pool. The beach is a taxi ride away.

São Conrado, Barra da Tijuca and beyond *map p34*
Barra da Tijuca offers a spectacular setting and is close to the Olympic park. Traffic between Barra, Ipanema/Copacabana and the centre is very heavy between 0700 and 1000 and 1700 and 2000. Alongside international big names which include the

Hilton and **Sheraton** (who have a lovely beach-view property in Barra), **Windsor** hotels (see page 77) offer the best options in the area beyond those we list below.

$$$$ La Suite
R Jackson de Figueiredo, 501, Joá, T021-2484 1962, www.bydussol.com.
Rio's only boutique hotel of distinction with 8 individually themed and exquisitely designed rooms perched like an eyrie over an exclusive beach in Joatinga, immediately south of São Conrado. The rooms, the excellent restaurant and the pool offer magical views and Pelé is a neighbour.

$$ Rio Surf n Stay
R Raimundo Veras 1140, Recreio dos Bandeirantes, T021-3418 1133, www.riosurfnstay.com.
Hostel and surf camp with double rooms, 6-bed dorms and camping. Free Wi-Fi. Surfing lessons and equipment rental are available.

Restaurants

The rise of Brazil on the international gastronomic scene has seen a great improvement in Rio's restaurants. Roberta Sudbrack (see page 87) was listed as one of Latin America's best by San Pellegrino and in 2015 a handful of Rio restaurants were awarded Michelin stars. Rio's restaurants are more expensive than anywhere else in the country. Expect to pay at least US$20 per person in the better restaurants. At the cheaper end of the spectrum, Rio lacks that almost ubiquitous Brazilian institution, the corner bakery. Cariocas generally wolf down their breakfast and snacks on foot at streetside bars. But there are plenty of per kilo eateries and stand-up juice booths serving fruit juices made from as many as 25 different fruits from orange to *açai* and carrot to *cupuaçu*, all of which are wonderful.

Central Rio and Lapa *maps p38 and p40*
Restaurants in the business district are generally only open for weekday lunch. Many *lanchonetes* in this area offer good cheap meals. The **Travessa do Comércio** has many extemporaneous street restaurants after 1800, especially on Fri, and is always buzzing with life. **R Miguel Couto** (opposite Santa Rita church) is called the 'Beco das Sardinhas' because on Wed and Fri in particular it is full of people eating sardines and drinking beer.

There are several Arabic restaurants on **Av Senhor dos Passos**, which are also open Sat and Sun. In addition to those listed there are plenty of cafés and bars serving food, especially in Lapa around **R Lavradio**, which stay open in the evenings.

$$$$-$$$ Confeitaria Colombo
R Gonçalves Dias 32 (near Carioca metrô station), Centro, T021-2505 1500, www.confeitariacolombo.com.br. Open afternoons only during the week.
The only remaining belle époque Portuguese coffee house in Rio, serving a range of café food, cakes, pastries and light lunches which though excellent are absurdly expensive. The *feijoada colonial* on Sat is accompanied by live *choro*.

$$$ Adega Flor de Coimbra
R Teotônio Regadas 34, Lapa, T021-2224 4582, www.adegaflordecoimbra.com.br.
Chope and reliable Portuguese food, including excellent *bacalhau* and sardines in olive oil. Once the haunt of Carioca painter Cândido Portinari and Rio's left-wing intelligentsia.

$$$ Cais
www.caisgourmet.com.br.
A grand old-dame dining room dating from 1878 and retro-renovated with a beautiful belle époque exterior hiding a modish open-plan dining room lined with raw brick and illuminated with art nouveau chandeliers. Light Mediterranean food. The surrounding area is busy with after-work cafés and *botecos*, especially on Thu and Fri.

$$$ Eça
Av Rio Branco 128, T021-2524 2300,
www.hstern.com.br/eca.
Rio city centre's best business lunch from
Frederic de Maeyer, a classically trained chef
who once cooked in the Michelin-starred
L'Escalier du Palais Royale in Brussels.

$$ Bar Luiz
R da Carioca 39, Centro, T021-2262 6900,
www.barluiz.com.br.
For 117 years this little bar in one of the few
remaining colonial houses in the city centre
has been at the heart of Rio life. Almost every
Carioca you can name from Di Cavalcanti and
Tom Jobim to Ronaldo and Chico Buarque
has at one time or another formed part of the
lively throng which gathers here on weekday
evenings and most particularly on Fri and Sat
to drink the famous *chope* and eat tapas.

$$ Café Épico
R Mem de Sá, Centro, T021-2411 2243,
www.cafeepico.com.br.
Gourmet coffee, artisan beer, *petiscos*, cakes
and tarts served in chic a/c surrounds.

Santa Teresa *map p56*

$$$ Aprazível
R Aprazível 62, T021-2508 9174,
www.aprazivel.com.br.
Decent but unspectacular Brazilian dishes
and seafood with one of the best restaurant
views in the city: tables are outdoors in a
tropical garden overlooking Guanabara Bay.

$$$ Espírito Santa
R Almte Alexandrino 264, T021-2507 4840,
www.espiritosanta.com.br. Lunch only Tue,
Wed and Sun; closed Mon.
Upstairs is a chic boho restaurant with a
view serving sumptuous Amazon food by
Natacha Fink.

$$$ Sobrenatural
R Almte Alexandrino 432, T021-2224 103,
www.restaurantesobrenatural.com.br.
Simple, elegant seafood served by
sexagenarian career waiters in bow

ties. The huge dining room is always lively
with chatter.

$$ Bar do Arnaudo
Largo do Guimarães, R Almte
Alexandrino 316, T021-2252 7246.
A modest-looking restaurant decorated
with handicrafts but serving generous
portions of wonderful northeast Brazilian
cooking. Try the *carne do sol* (sun-dried beef,
or jerky) with *feijão de corda* (brown beans
and herbs), or the *queijo coalho* (a country
cheese, grilled). The **Bar do Mineiro** (see
Bars and clubs, page 88) down the street
attracts a similar arty crowd and is well-
known for its *feijoada*, said to be second
only to the **Academia da Cachaca**.

$$ Portella
R Paschoal Carlos Magno 139/141,
Largo do Guimarães, T021-2507 5181,
www.portellabar.com.br.
São Paulo-style corner restaurant-bar with
good *picanha* steaks, award-winning *petiscos*
(bar snacks). Try the *portadella* with flaky
pastry stuffed with catupiry cream cheese
and pistachio. Ice-cold *chopp*. Live music
most weekend nights.

Botafogo and Urca *map p60*
There are many cheap and mid-range options
in the **Botafogo Praia** shopping centre.

$$$ Abençoado
Morro de Urca s/n, T021-2275 8925,
www.abencoadorio.com.br.
There can be few restaurants anywhere in
the world with a better view than this: over
the bay to Corcovado and the Christ on
one side and the pearly Atlantic beaches of
Copacabana, Ipanema and distant Niterói
on the other. Eating is alfresco from a menu
of Brazilian comfort food given a gourmet
twist. Plates include *angu* (corn meal with
Santa Catarina prawns and field mushrooms)
or *escondidinho* (jerk meat with cheese
gratin served on a bed of pureed *aipim*,
or cassava). The accompanying caipirinhas
are the best in Rio.

$$$ Cota 2000
Morro de Urca s/n, T021-2543 8200,
www.cota200restaurante.com.br.
Daily and for evening bookings Sun-Tue.
This newly opened gourmet Brazilian
restaurant sits next to **Abencoado**, but unlike
that restaurant it specializes in dinner, with
the same privileged view. Book for an early
dinner with sunset cocktails; the restaurant
closes at 2000 in time for the last cable car
down at 2100.

$$$ Lasai
R Conde de Irajá 191, Botafogo,
T021-3449 1834, www.lasai.com.br.
Michelin-starred cooking from newcomer
Rafa Costa e Silva, who learnt his chops at
Mugaritz in Spain. His inspired European-
Brazilian fusion cooking is as beautifully
presented as it is inventive. There are
2 degustation menus only – one short,
one long. Reservations essential.

$$$ Miam Miam
General Goes Monteiro 34, Botafogo,
T021-2244 0125, www.miammiam.com.br.
Closed Mon.
The most fashionable of Rio's alternative
fashion set sip caipirinhas here. Decoration
is retro chic with 1950s and 1960s lounge
furniture from the **Hully Gully** antique
shop in Copacabana's Siqueira Campos
mall and cartoons in homage to cult 1970s
Carioca cartoonist, Carlos Zéfiro. Food is
light Mediterranean.

$$$ Oui Oui
R Conde de Irajá, 85, T021-2527 3539,
www.restauranteouioui.com.br.
Art deco lounge bar serving the *petiscos*
(small plates of contemporary Brazilian food
served tapas style and ordered in pairs).

Copacabana *map p64*
There are stand-up bars selling snacks
all around Copacabana and Ipanema.
There are plenty of open-air restaurants
along **Av Atlântica**, none of which can be
recommended for anything but the view.

$$$ Cipriani & Mee
Copacabana Palace (see page 80).
The best hotel restaurants for formal dining,
with a chef from the **Hotel Cipriani** in Venice
(and very good seafood and Italian fare)
in the former and an inventive, Michelin-
starred menu of modern Japanese and
Thai dishes in the latter, served in warm
minimalist surrounds.

$$$ La Fiorentina
Atlântica 458a, T021-2543 8395,
www.lafiorentina.com.br.
The Italian has been a Copa institution
for over half a century and is famous for
its *espaguete com frutos do mar* (seafood
spaghetti), served in a light prawn marinade.

$$$ No Mangue
R Sá Ferreira 25 ljB, T021-2521 3237,
www.nomangue.com.br.
Copa's best northeast Brazilian and seafood
restaurant offering sumptuous *moquecas*
(fish stews), *bobó de camarão* (shrimp and
cassava stew) and *petiscos* like crab or prawn
pasty and squid in garlic oil.

$$$-$$ Churrascaria Palace
R Rodolfo Dantas 16B, T021-2541 5898,
www.churrascariapalace.com.br.
Copa's answer to **Porcão** or **Esplanada Grill**
with 20 different kinds of barbecued meat
served at your table with buffet salads
to accompany.

$$-$ Aipo and Aipim
Av Nossa Senhora de Copacabana 391b
and 920 in Copacabana, and R Visconde
de Pirajá 145 in Ipanema, T021-2267 8313,
www.aipoeaipim.com.br.
Plentiful tasty food sold by weight at this
popular chain. Branches in Copacabana
and throughout Rio.

$$-$ Eclipse
Av NS de Copacabana 1309, T021-2287 1788,
www.bareclipse.com.br.
Spruce, well-run and very popular 24-hr
restaurant offering good-value *prato feito*
lunches and a generous range of meats,

pastas, snacks and sandwiches served in the cool interior or on streetside tables.

$ Cafeina
R Constante Ramos 44, T021-2547 8651, www.cafeina.biz.
Very popular breakfast spot with good coffee, tasty pastries and other snacks and ice cold juices.

$ Cervantes
Barata Ribeiro 07-B at Prado Júnior 335B, T021 2275 6147, www.restaurantecervantes. com.br. Open 1200-0500.
Stand-up bar and said to serve the best late-night toasted sandwiches and street food in town. A local institution.

Ipanema and Leblon *map p68*

$$$ Alessandro & Frederico
R Garcia D'Ávila 151, Ipanema, T021-2522 5414, www.alessandroefrederico.com.br.
Upmarket café with decent café latte and breakfasts.

$$$ Bistrô ZaZá
R Joana Angélica 40, Ipanema, T021-2247 9101, www.zazabistro.com.br.
Hippy chic pseudo-Moroccan/French restaurant that attracts a mix of tourist and bohemian Zona Sul Cariocas.

$$$ Capricciosa
R Vinícius de Moraes 134, Ipanema, T021-2523 3394, www.capricciosa.com.br.
The best pizzeria chain in town. At this branch, a lynchpin in the TV and fashion scene, the famous and wealthy gather to gossip. Queues can be long.

$$$ CT Boucherie
R Dias Ferreira 636, Leblon, T021-2529 2329, www.ctboucherie.com.br.
Claude Troisgros of **Olympe** (see below) expands his restaurant empire onto Leblon's gastronomic centre with this elegant, unpretentious meat restaurant. The focus is on the superb cuts of meat, accompanied by sauces and delectable sides – honed to bring out the taste of the cuts of choice, and

including English-inspired and tropically flavoured passion fruit infused pureed apple.

$$$ Esplanada Grill
R Barão da Torre 600, Ipanema, T021-2239 6028, www.esplanadagrill.com.br.
The formal atmosphere and stiff penguin-suited staff aren't as much fun as the whirligig waiters at **Porcão** (see below) but the meat can't be beat. Come here if you crave steak. There are no finer cuts in Rio.

$$$ Forneria
R Aníbal de Mendonça 112, Ipanema, T021-2540 8045, www.restauranteforneria.com.br.
Paulistano restauranteur Rogerio Fasano's elegant eating-space in Rio serves supreme burgers in pizza dough and cooked in a wood-fired oven, and other superior bar snacks. Usually full with an elegant after-beach crowd.

$$$ Manekineko
R Dias Ferreira 410, Leblon, T021-2540 7641, www.manekineko.com.br.
Rio's best Japanese chain with a large menu of superb traditional dishes and Japanese, European and South American fusion. The intimate dining area, comprising a corridor of low-lit booths, is always packed.

$$$ Porcão
Barão de Torre 218, Ipanema, T021-3202 9158, www.porcao.com.br.
One of the city's best *churrascarias* serving all manner of meat in unlimited quantities for a set price.

$$$ Satyricon
R Barão da Torre 192, Ipanema, T021-2521 0627, www.satyricon.com.br.
The best seafood in Rio. Lively crowd in a large dining room which precludes intimacy. A favourite with businessmen, politicians and Ronaldo. Avoid Sat when there is a buffet.

$$$ Zuka
R Dias Ferreira 233B, Leblon, T021-3205 7154, www.zuka.com.br.
Eclectic fusion of everything – French and Japanese, American fast food and Italian –

all presented on huge rectangular plates and in a carefully designed modern space.

$$$-$$ TT Burgers
R Francisco Otaviano 67, Arpoador, T021-2227 1192.
This hugely popular upmarket streetside burger bar sitting behind the **Arpoador** in a modish row of surf shops, bars (the best is **Informalizinho**) and cafés is said to serve the best burgers in Rio. It is owned and run by the son of Michelin-starred chef Claude Troigros.

$$ Aconchego Carioca
Rua Rainha Guilhermina 48, T21-2294 2913.
Katia Barbosa's *petiscos* (Portuguese tapas) are some of the best in the city. Try the *bolinhos de feijoada*. There is another branch west of the centre at R Barão de Iguatemi, 379.

$$ Big Nectar
R Teixeira de Melo 34, T021-2522 3949.
One of the largest range of juices in Rio including uniquely South American and Brazilian fruits such as *seriguela*, *mangaba*, *umbu* and *cupuaçu*.

$$ Casa da Feijoada
Prudente de Morais 10, Ipanema, T021-2247 2776.
Serves excellent *feijoada* all week. Generous portions.

$$ Celeiro
R Dias Ferreira 199, Leblon, T021-2274 7843, www.celeiroculinaria.com.br.
Superior salads and buffet food, which has been consistently voted the best in the city by the magazine *Veja*.

$$ Fellini
R General Urquiza 104, Leblon, T021-2511 3600, www.fellini.com.br.
The best pay-by-weight restaurant in the city with a large range of delicious Brazilian and international dishes, salads and quiches. Plenty of options for vegetarians. Funky website.

$$ Polis Sucos
R Maria Quitéria 70a, T021-2247 2518.
A favourite Carioca pre- and post-beach pit-stop offering a huge range of tropical juices and snacks such as *açaí na tigela* (mushed *açaí* berries with *guarana* syrup).

Gávea, Lagoa and Jardim Botânico
map p68
Gávea is the heartland of trendy 20-something Rio. The neighbourhoods of Jardim Botânico and Lagoa appear at first sight to offer unlimited exciting upmarket dining opportunities, but the restaurants are mostly mutton dressed up as lamb. They look great, cost loads and serve dreadful food. The following are the few exceptions.

$$$ Olympe
R Custódio Serrão 62, Lagoa, T021-2539 4542, www.claudetroisgros.com.br.
The Troisgros family were founders of nouvelle cuisine and run a 3 Michelin-star restaurant in Roanne. Claude Troisgros' cooking fuses tropical ingredients with French techniques, exemplified by the roasted quail filled with *farofa* and served with raisins, pearl onions and a sweet and sour *jabuticaba* sauce. The restaurant is Michelin-starred.

$$$ Roberta Sudbrack
R Lineu de Paula Machado 916, Jardim Botânico, T021-3874 0139, www.robertasudbrack.com.br.
Roberta was the private chef for President Henrique Cardoso and cooked for all the visiting international dignitaries who dined with him during his term of office. She is celebrated for her European-Brazilian fusion cooking has a string of awards including *Veja*'s coveted chef-of-the-year, a listing in the San Pellgrino best in the world and a Michelin star.

Bars and clubs

Rio nightlife is young and vivacious. Lapa remains the focus, and the neighbourhood's ongoing popularity has now spilled over into neighbouring Glória and parts of the city centre, producing a nightlife scene which covers an extensive area on pretty much any night of the week but especially from Thu to Sat. It's well worth taking a wander, though be careful (or consider taking a nightlife tour, see page 96), as pockets of the region are still down-at-heel and seedy. Ruas Mem de Sá (around the arches) and Lavradio and a little alley known as the Beco do Rato remain the heartland of Lapa nightlife and the whole neighbourhood throbs to live music and DJ mixes, from samba and *forró* to techno, alternative rock and hip-hop.

Similarly busy, even on Sun and Mon, is Baixa Gávea, where beautiful 20-somethings gather around Praça Santos Dumont to drink beer and chew the fat. But there are only bars here, no dance or live music clubs.

Wherever you are in Rio, there's a bar or *botequim* (Rio's equivalent of a tapas spot) near you. Beer costs around US$1.50 for a large bottle, but up to US$7 in the plusher venues, where you are often given a card that includes 2 drinks and a token entrance fee. A cover of US$2-5 may be charged made for live music, or there might be a minimum consumption charge of around US$2, sometimes both. Snack food is always available.

Copacabana, **Ipanema** and **Leblon** have many beach *barracas*, several open all night. The seafront bars on Av Atlântica are great for people-watching, but avoid those towards **Leme** which ply a different trade.

Clubs on and around Rio's beaches are generally either fake Europe, eg **Melt** or fake US, eg **Nuth** and **00**. Santa Teresa feels more Carioca, with bohemian *boteco* bars and is a good place to begin a weekend night before heading down the hill to Lapa. See also Samba schools, page 93.

Central Rio, Lapa, Glória and Santa Teresa *maps p38 and p56*

Lapa, Santa Teresa (and increasingly, the city centre and Glória), have Rio's most interesting, bohemian nightlife and shouldn't be missed if you are in Rio over a weekend. It is easy to walk between the Santa Teresa and Lapa but ill-advised either along the streets or up the Selaron mosaic staircase. For safety's sake, take a cab. On Mon there is live samba and/or Afro-Brazilian funk on the Pedra do Sal staircase in Gamboa just to the north of the centre and where samba was born. Don't come unaccompanied; take a cab and bring a local or come on a bespoke tour (see page 98).

Bar do Mineiro
R Paschoal Carlos Magno 99, 100 m from Largo dos Guimarães, Santa Teresa, T021-2221 9227.
Rustic *boteco* opening right onto the street and with hundreds of black-and-white photos of Brazilian musicians displayed on the white-tiled walls. Attracts a busy, arty young crowd and serves a famous *feijoada*.

Carioca da Gema
Av Mem de Sá 79, Centro, near Rio Scenarium, T021-2221 0043, www.barcariocadagema. com.br.
One of the longest established samba clubs and daytime cafés in Lapa, with the cream of the live bands and, if you arrive early, sit-down tables. Great little pre-show pizza restaurant upstairs.

Circo Voador
See Live music, page 91.
Together with **Fundição Progresso** (www. fundicaoprogresso.com.br) next door, this the best venue in central Rio for emerging and established alternative local samba, roots fusion and funk bands. Acts like Seu Jorge began here.

Club Six
R das Marrecas 38, Lapa, T021 2510 3230, www.clubsix.com.br.
Huge pounding European/NYC club with everything from hip-hop to ambient house.

Clube dos Democráticos
R do Riachuelo 91.
A grungy old dance hall where transvestites gossip on the stairs and bands play *gafieira* or dance hall samba.

Estudantina Musical
3 piso, Praça Tiradentes 79, T021-2232 1149, www.estudantinamusical.com.br. Closed Mon-Wed.
This is one of central Rio's most famous old school *gafieira* halls. It's at its busiest and liveliest on Tue when it hosts Rio's most popular *forró* night and Thu when hundreds gather to dance samba to some of the best big samba bands in the city. Less touristy than Lapa.

Rio Scenarium
R do Lavradio 20, Lapa, T021-3147 9005, www.rioscenarium.com.br.
3-storey samba and dance club in a beguilingly spacious colonial house used as a movie prop storage facility by *TV Globo*. Overflowing with Brazilian exuberance and people of all ages dancing furiously, to samba and assorted Euro and Lusitanian club sounds, and the bizarre backdrop of a 19th-century apothecary's shop or mannequins wearing 1920s outfits. Arrive after 2300.

Sacrilégio
Av Mem de Sá 81, Lapa, next door to Carioca da Gema, T021-3970 1461, www.sacrilegio.com.br.
Samba, *chorinho*, *pagode* and occasional theatre. Close to many other bars.

Santo Scenarium
R do Lavradio 36, Lapa, T021-3147 9007, www.santoscenarium.com.br.
The bossa nova counterpart to the famous live samba club, attracting a similar mix of foreign tourists and locals and with middle-of-the-road musicians and bands taking the stage Thu-Sun. Come before 2100 for a table. Food available.

Semente
R Evaristo da Veiga 149, Lapa, T021-2507 5188. Mon-Sat from 2200, US$6 cover, minimum consumption US$7.
Popular for samba, *choro* and salsa. Book at weekends. Great atmosphere. Recommended.

Triboz
R Conde de Lages 19, Glória, T021-2210 0366, www.triboz-rio.com.
Nominally this is Rio's Australian-Brazilian cultural centre. In reality it's a sit-down jazz café serving food and playing jazz fusion and jazzy bossa nova. It's busiest on weekend nights.

The Week
R Sacadura Cabral 154, Zona Portuária, T021-2253 1020, www.theweek.com.br.
One of the most popular dance clubs in the city, with a mostly gay crowd, state-of-the-art dance spaces, and New York house and Eurotrash tunes.

Botafogo and Urca *map p60*

Bar Urca
R Cândido Gafree 205, Urca, T021-21 2295 8744, www.barurca.com.br.
The most popular of a string of little Portuguese-style street bars, attracting a post-Sugar Loaf sunset view crowd and serving cold beer and snacks. The **Garota da Urca** bar just down the road and overlooking Urca beach serves excellent *casquinha do siri* and is more upmarket.

Casa da Matriz
R Henrique de Novaes 107, Botafogo, T021-2226 9691, on Facebook: grupomatriz.
Great grungy club with a bar, Atari room, small cinema and 2 dance floors. Full of Rio students.

Copacabana, Ipanema and Leblon *map p64*
Copacabana and Leme are popular spots for live music, with frequent, free open-air concerts on the beach and a string of

traditional little samba and bossa nova bars in the back streets like **Bip Bip** and the **Bottle's Bar** (see below). On New Year's Eve the whole suburb becomes a huge party venue and bands play along the entire length of the beach. Ipanema and Leblon are quieter, more sterile and more up-market. Look out for the **Belmonte** chain of *boteco* bars – with branches all over Rio serving ice-cold draught *chope* and quality *petisco* bar snacks.

Academia da Cachaça
R Conde de Bernadotte 26-G, Leblon, T021-2529 2680, with another branch at Av Armando Lombardi 800, Barra da Tijuca, www.academiadacachaca.com.br.
The best *cachacas* and caipirinhas in the city (try the delicious *pitanga* caipirinha), and some of Rio's best *feijoadas* and bar snacks. Good on Fri.

Alto Vidigal Favela Party
R Armando de Almeida Lima 2, Arvrao, Vidigal, T021-99596 0338, www.mirantedoarvrao.com.br.
The high-society invasion of Vidigal favela continues with this Sat night dance party on the expansive dance area of the **Arvrão** hostel in Vidigal. Contact the hostel for information on the free VW vans which run to the party, usually from the **Belmonte** bar in Ipanema.

Astor
Av Vieira Souto 110, Ipanema, T021-2523 0085, www.barastor.com.br.
Pleasant place to watch the sunset with a cold glass of *chope* beer in hand.

Bip Bip
Loja D-R, Almirante Gonçalves 50, Copacabana, T021-2267 9656, facebook: Bip Bip.
This little streetside bar in earshot of the waves has been serving cold *chope* and playing fine music for nearly 50 years. Come for *choro* on Mon and Tue, bossa nova on Wed and samba every other day of the week. Some of the city's best musicians play here.

Bottle's Bar
R Duvivier 37, Beco das Garrafas, Copacabana, T021-2543 2962.
Resurrected live bossa nova music bar on the legendary Beco das Garrafas alley where the style was born in the 1950s. It showcases live acts most nights.

Complex Esquina
R Maria Quitéria 111, Ipanema, T021-3256 9375, www.thecomplex.com.br.
Decent comfort food, great cocktails and caipirinhas (including *pitanga* and ginger and basil) and anodyne US music. Modish middle-class Ipanema 20- and 30-something crowd.

Deck
Pestana Copacabana, Av Atlântica 2964, Copacabana, T021-2548 6332.
Bangkok sky bar it isn't … but what this rooftop bar lacks in Asian sophistication it makes up for with wonderful Copacabana views, drinks at prices which should shame those at **Fasano** and a sprinkling of loungey sofa seats.

Devassa
R Rainha Guilhermina 48, Leblon, and an alternative menu at Ipanema branch, Av Visconde de Pirajá 539, www.devassa. com.br/cervejaria.php.
A 2-floor pub-bar-restaurant that is always heaving with the Ipanema middle class. Brews its own beer.

Empório
R Maria Quitéria 37, Ipanema, T021-3813 2526.
Street bar that attracts the hordes. Mon is the busiest night.

Garota de Ipanema
R Vinícius de Moraes 49, Ipanema.
Where the song *Girl from Ipanema* was written. Now packed with foreigners on the package Rio circuit listening to bossa. For the real thing head to **Toca do Vinícius** on a Sun lunchtime (see page 92).

ON THE ROAD

SESC cultural centres

Little known to visitors but beloved of cultured Brazilians are the SESC centres. These are spaces devoted to arts in general, with fine art and photographic exhibitions, theatre, film and, in the Espaço SESC in Copacabana, live music. Many of the better Brazilian jazz, alternative and bossa nova bands and artists play here.

There are several SESC centres in Rio and the excellent website www.sescrj.com.br (in Portuguese only but easy to follow) has information on forthcoming concerts.

Espaço SESC, R Domingos Ferreira 160, Copacabana, T021-2547 0156.
SESC Copacabana, R Domingos Ferreira 160, T021-2548 1088.
SESC Niterói, R Padre Anchieta 56, Niterói, T021-2719 9119.
SESC Tijuca, R Barão de Mesquita 539, Barra da Tijuca, T021-3238 2139.

Shenanigans
R Visconde de Pirajá 112, Ipanema, T021-2267 5860, www.shenanigans.com.br.
Obligatory mock-Irish bar with Guinness and Newcastle Brown. Not a place to mix with the locals.

Vinícius
R Vinícius de Moraes 39, Ipanema, www.viniciusbar.com.br.
Mirror image of the **Garota de Ipanema** with slightly better acts and food.

Gávea, Lagoa and Jardim Botânico
map p68

00 (Zero Zero)
Av Padre Leonel Franca 240, Gávea, T021-2540 8041, www.00site.com.br.
Mock-LA bar/restaurant/club with a small outdoor area. Currently the trendiest club in Rio for Brazil's equivalent of 'sloanes' or 'valley girls'. Gay night on Sun.

Bar Lagoa
Av Epitácio Pessoa 1674, Lagoa, T021-2523 1135, www.barlagoa.com.br.
Attracts an older arty crowd on weekdays.

Hipódromo da Gávea
Praça Santos Dumont 108, Gávea, T021-2274 9720.
On weekend and Thu nights this restaurant bar, and its neighbours, fill with young middle-class Cariocas who talk and flirt over beer and bar snacks. The crowds from all bars spill out onto Praça Santos Dumont square. Very few tourists make it here.

Barra da Tijuca

Nuth
R Armando Lombardi 999, www.nuth.com.br.
Barra's slickest club; very mock-Miami and frequented by a mixed crowd of rich-kid surfers, footballers and women with surgically enhanced beauty.

Entertainment

Cinema
There are cinemas serving subtitled Hollywood fare and major Brazilian releases on the top floor of almost all the malls.

Live music
Cariocas congregate in Lapa between Thu and Sat for live club music. There are free concerts throughout the summer along the Copacabana and Ipanema beaches, in Botafogo and at the parks: mostly samba, reggae, rock and MPB (Brazilian pop). There is no advance schedule; information is given in the local press. Rio's famous jazz, in all its forms, is performed in lots of enjoyable venues too, see www.samba-choro.com.br for more information.

Centro Cultural Carioca, *R do Teatro 37, T021-2242 9642, www.centroculturalcarioca.com.br. Open 1830-late.* This restored old house with wraparound balconies and exposed brick walls is a dance school and music venue that attracts a lovely mix of people. Professional dancers perform with musicians; after a few tunes the audience joins in. Thu is impossibly crowded; Sat is calmer. Bar food available. US$10 cover charge. Highly recommended.

Circo Voador, *R dos Arcos, Lapa, T021-2533 0354, www.circovoador.com.br.* Lapa's recuperation began with this little concert hall under the arches. Some of the city's best smaller acts still play here – including Seu Jorge who first found fame playing with *Farofa Carioca* at the Circo.

Toca do Vinícius, *R Vinícius de Moraes 129C, Ipanema, www.tocadovinicius.com.br.* Rio's leading bossa nova and *choro* record shop has concerts from some of the finest performers every Sun lunchtime.

Theatre

There are about 40 theatres in Rio, presenting a variety of classical and modern performances in Portuguese. For information check on the website www.rioecultura.com.br.

Carnaval *See also box, page 12.*
Tickets Sambódromo, *R Marquês de Sapucaí s/n, Cidade Nova. http://carnaval.rioguiaoficial. com.br and www.rioguiaoficial.com.br. The nearest tube is Praça Onze.*

The Sambódromo parades start at 1900 and last about 12 hrs. Gates open at 1800. There are *cadeiras* (seats) at ground level, *arquibancadas* (terraces) and *camarotes* (boxes). The best boxes are reserved for tourists and VIPs and are very expensive or by invitation only. Seats are closest to the parade, but you may have to fight your way to the front. Sectors 4, 7 and 11 are the best spots (they house the judging points); 6 and 13 are least favoured (being at the end when dancers might be tired) but have more space. The terraces, while uncomfortable, house the most fervent fans and are tightly packed; this is the best place to soak up the atmosphere but it's too crowded to take pictures. Tickets start at US$90 for *arquibancadas* and are sold at travel agencies as well as the Maracanã stadium box office (see page 49). Travel agency: **Carnaval Turismo** (Av Nossa Senhora de Copacabana 583, T021-2548 4232, www.carnavalinrio.com.br). Tickets should be bought as far as possible in advance; they are usually sold out before Carnaval weekend but touts outside can often sell you tickets at inflated prices. Samba schools have an allocation of tickets which members sometimes sell, if you are offered one of these check the date. Tickets for the champions' parade on the Sat following Carnaval are much cheaper. Many tour companies offer Rio trips including Carnaval, but tickets are at inflated prices.

Sleeping and security

Be sure to reserve accommodation well in advance. Virtually all hotels raise their prices during Carnaval, although it is usually possible to find a reasonably priced room. Your property should be safe inside the Sambódromo, but the crowds outside can attract pickpockets; as ever, don't brandish your camera, and only take the money you need for fares and refreshments (food and drink are sold in the Sambódromo). It gets hot, so wear shorts and a T-shirt.

Taking part

Most samba schools will accept a number of foreigners and you will be charged from US$175 up to US$435 for your costume depending on which school of samba you choose. This money helps to fund poorer members of the school. You should be in Rio for at least 2 weeks before Carnaval. It is essential to attend fittings and rehearsals on time, to show respect for your section leaders and to enter into the competitive spirit of the event. For those with the energy and the dedication, it will be an unforgettable experience.

Rehearsals
Ensaios are held at the schools' *quadras* from Oct onwards and are well worth seeing. It is wise to go by taxi, as most schools are based in poorer districts.

Carnaval shows
Tour agents sell tickets for glitzy samba shows, which are nothing like the real thing. When buying a Carnaval DVD, make sure the format is compatible (NTSC for USA or most of Europe; PAL for the UK, region 4).

Samba school addresses and parties
Samba schools hold parties throughout the year, especially at the weekends. These are well worth visiting. See websites for details.
Acadêmicos de Salgueiro, *R Silva Teles 104, Andaraí, T021-2238 5564, www.salgueiro.com.br.*
Beija Flor de Nilópolis, *Pracinha Wallace Paes Leme 1025, Nilópolis, T021-2791 2866, www.beija-flor.com.br.*
Imperatriz Leopoldinense, *R Prof Lacê 235, Ramos, T021-2560 8037, www.imperatriz leopoldinense.com.br.*
Mocidade Independente de Padre Miguel, *R Coronel Tamarindo 38, Padre Miguel, T021-3332 5823, www.mocidade independente.com.br.*
Portela, *R Clara Nunes 81, Madureira, T021-2489 6440, www.gresportela.com.br.*
Primeira Estação de Mangueira, *R Visconde de Niterói 1072, Mangueira, T021-2567 4637, www.mangueira.com.br.*
Unidos da Viradouro, *Av do Contorno 16, Niterói, T021-2516 1301, www.gresuviradouro. com.br.*
Vila Isabel, *Boulevard 28 de Setembro, Vila Isabel, T021-2578 0077, www.gresunidosde vilaisabel.com.br.*

Transport
Taxis to the Sambódromo are negotiable and will find your gate, the nearest *metrô* is

Praça Onze and this can be an enjoyable ride in the company of costumed samba school members. You can follow the participants to the *concentração*, the assembly and formation on Av Presidente Vargas, and mingle with them while they queue to enter the Sambódromo. Ask if you can take photos.

Useful information
Carnaval week comprises an enormous range of official and unofficial contests and events, which reach a peak on the Tue. **Riotur**'s guide booklet and website gives concise information on these in English. The entertainment sections of newspapers and magazines such as *O Globo, Jornal do Brasil, Manchete* and *Veja Rio* are worth checking. Felipe Ferreira's guide to the Rio Carnaval, *Liga Independente das Escolas de Samba do Rio de Janeiro*, www.liesa.com.br, has good explanations of the competition, rules, the schools, a map and other practical details.

Other festivals
20 Jan The **festival of São Sebastião**, patron saint of Rio, is celebrated by an evening procession, leaving Capuchinhos church in Tijuca and arriving at the cathedral of São Sebastião. On the same evening, an *umbanda* festival is celebrated at the *Caboclo* monument in Santa Teresa.
Jun The **Festas Juninas** are celebrated throughout Brazil. In Rio they start with the **Festival of Santo Antônio** on 13 Jun, when the main event is a Mass, followed by celebrations at the Convento do Santo Antônio and the Largo da Carioca. All over the state, the **Festival of São João** is a major event, marked by huge bonfires on the night of 23-24 Jun. It is traditional to dance the *quadrilha* and drink *quentão, cachaça* and sugar, spiced with ginger and cinnamon, served hot. The Festas Juninas close with the **Festival of São Pedro** on 29 Jun. Being the patron saint of fishermen, his feast is normally accompanied by processions of boats.

Oct This is the month of the feast of **Nossa Senhora da Penha** (see page 50).

30 Dec Less hectic than Carnaval, but very atmospheric, is the **Festival of Yemanjá** when devotees of the *orixá* of the sea dress in white and gather at night on Copacabana, Ipanema and Leblon beaches, singing and dancing around open fires and making offerings. The elected Queen of the Sea is rowed along the seashore. At midnight small boats are launched as offerings to Yemanjá. The religious event is dwarfed, however, by a massive New Year's Eve party, called **Reveillon** at Copacabana. The beach is packed as thousands of revellers enjoy free outdoor concerts by big-name pop stars, topped with a lavish midnight firework display. It is most crowded in front of the Copacabana Palace Hotel. Another good place to see the fireworks is at the far end of the beach in front of R Princesa Isabel, famous for its fireworks waterfall at about 0010. Many followers of Yemanjá now make offerings on 29 or 30 Dec and at Barra da Tijuca or Recreio dos Bandeirantes to avoid the crowds and noise of Reveillon.

Shopping

Arts and crafts

La Vereda, *R Almirante Alexandrino 428, Santa Teresa, T021-2507 0317, www.la vereda.art.br.* Colourful arty little boutique filled with crafts, from illuminated favela models to textiles, toys and paintings.

Novo Desenho (**ND**), *Av Infante Dom Henrique 85, Glória (next to MAM), T021-2524 2290, www.novodesenho.com.br.* This pocket-sized boutique stocks a range of homeware and furniture from some of Brazil's best small artisan designers. These include established names such as Sergio Rodrigues (whose Mole chair is in MoMA New York's permanent collection) and Mendes-Hirth alongside up-and-coming designers like Morito Ebine, whose chairs are built entirely of Brazilian wood with hardwood pins instead of screws.

Many of the items are small enough to fit in a suitcase.

Universo das Velas, *R dos Andrades 4, T021-2221 2474. Candomblé* and *umbanda* regalia including candles, incense, Orixa statues and books.

Fashion

Fashion is one of the best buys in Brazil, with a wealth of Brazilian designers selling clothes of the same quality as European or US famous names at a fraction of the price. Rio is the best place in the world for buying high-fashion bikinis. The best shops in Ipanema are in the **Forum de Ipanema** arcade, R Visconde de Pirajá 351 (where you will find many of the best beachwear brands), **Garcia D'Ávila** and **R Nascimento Silva**, which runs off it. The latter areas are home to some of the best Brazilian designers, together with international big-name stalwarts like Louis Vuitton and Cartier, and Brazil's classiest jeweller, Antonio Bernardo. Most of the international names, together with all the big Brazilian names are also housed in the **São Conrado Fashion Mall**.

There are some little shops on **Aires Saldanha** (Copacabana, 1 block back from beach), which are good for bikinis and cheaper than in the shopping centres. For the best-value shopping in the city head for **SAARA** (www.saararario.com.br), a complex of some 600 shops in the centre covering several blocks between R Alfandega, R dos Andradas, Praça da Republica and R Buenos Aires where you will find bargain-basement clothing, costume jewellery, toys, perfume and sundry items including *candomblé* and carnival regalia and exceptional Afro-Brazilian and indigenous wigs and braids made from human hair and sourced by French fashion houses.

Blue Man, *R Visconde de Pirajá, 351, lojas C & D, T021-2247 4905, also at São Conrado Fashion Mall.* Tiny, bright bikinis beloved of those with perfect bodies.

Bum Bum, *R Visconde de Pirajá 351, Ipanema, T021-2287 9951, www.bumbum.com.br.*

Together with **Lenny and Salinas**, one of the most internationally renowned bikini designers, tiny and beautifully cut.

Carlos Tufvesson, *R Nascimento Silva 304, Ipanema, T021-2523 9200, www.carlos tufvesson.com*. Sensual evening wear in high-quality fabric.

Casa Turuna, *R Senhor dos Passos 77, T021-2509 3908, www.casaturuna.com.br*. The place to buy your Carnaval costumes in or out of carnival season, together with samba skirts, masks and general pageantry. Open since 1915.

Lenny, *R Visconde de Pirajá, 351, Ipanema, T021-2287 9951, lennyniemeyer.com, and in the São Conrado Fashion Mall*. Lenny Niemeyer is widely regarded as Brazil's most sophisticated bikini designer.

Oh Boy! *R Visconde de Pirajá 550, Ipanema, T021-3875 7231, www.ohboy.com.br*. Brightly coloured beach and casual wear for teens and 20-somethings. Very à la mode with big spreads in recent editions of Brazilian *Vogue*.

Osklen, *R Maria Quitéria 85, Ipanema, T021-2227 2911, www.osklen.com*. Elegant, casual-chic men's wear from a label which has been described as Brazil's answer to Ralph Lauren.

Salinas, *R Visconde de Pirajá 547 & 351, lj 20 Ipanema, T021-2274 0644, and fashion mall, T021-2422 0677*. Very highly regarded Brazilian bikinis: small, exquisitely made with great attention to detail and using only the best fabrics, in a variety of contemporary styles from hand crochet and beading to reversibles in multiple colour combinations.

Football souvenirs

Loja Flá, *Av Nossa Senhora de Copacabana 219C, T021-2295 5057, www.lojafla.com.br*. All things related to Brazil's favourite team, Flamengo, from rare and limited edition kit to, balls, boots, DVDs and memorabilia.

Jewellery

Only buy precious and semi-precious stones from reputable dealers. There are several good jewellery shops at the Leme end of Av NS de Copacabana and branches of big

international Brazilian names **Stern** and **Amsterdam Sauer** in Ipanema.

Antônio Bernado, *R Garcia d'Ávila 121, Ipanema, T021-2512 7204, and in the São Conrado Fashion Mall*. Brazil's foremost jeweller who has been making beautifully understated pieces with contemporary designs for nearly 30 years. Internationally well known but available only in Brazil.

Markets

The **northeastern market** takes place at the Centro Luiz Gonzaga de Tradições Nordestinas, Campo de São Cristóvão, www. feiradesaocristovao.org.br, with music and magic, on Fri from 1800, Sat 0800-2200 and Sun 0800-1200 (bus No 472 or 474 from Copacabana or centre). There's a Sat **antiques market** on the waterfront near Praça 15 de Novembro, open 1000-1700. Also on Praça 15 de Novembro is **Feirarte II**, Thu and Fri 0800-1800. **Feirarte I** is an open-air handicrafts market (everyone calls it the **Feira Hippy**) at Praça Gen Osório, Ipanema, www.feirahippieipanema.com, Sun 0700-1900; touristy but fun, with items from all over Brazil. **Babilônia Feira Hype** is held every other weekend at the Jockey Club 1400-2300. This lively and popular market has lots of stalls selling clothes and crafts, as well as massage and live music and dance performances. A **stamp and coin market** is held on Sun in the Passeio Público. There are **markets** on Wed 0700-1300 on R Domingos Ferreira and on Thu, same hours, on Praça do Lido, both Copacabana. Praça do Lido also has a **Feir Arte** on weekends 0800-1800. There is an **artesania market** nightly by the Othon Hotel, near R Miguel Lemos: one part for paintings, one part for everything else. There's a **Sunday market** on R da Glória, selling colourful, cheap fruit, vegetables and flowers; and an early morning **food market**, open 0600-1100, R Min Viveiros de Castro, Ipanema. An excellent **food and household goods markets** take place at various places in the city and suburbs (see newspapers for times and places). **Feira do Livro** is a book market that moves around various locations (Largo do Machado, Cinelândia, Nossa Senhora da Paz, Ipanema), selling books at 20% discount.

Music

Arlequim Música, *Paço Imperial, Praça XV de Novembro 48, loja 1, T021-2220 8471, www.arlequim.com.br. Mon-Fri 1000-2000 Sat 1000-1800.* A good selection of high-quality Brazilian music and film.

Bossa Nova e Companhia, *R Duvivier 37a, Copacabana, T021-2295 8096, www. bossanovaecompanhia.com.br.* This long-established music shop, with its chic dragon's-tooth paving, has a little music museum in the basement and the best selection of bossa nova, *chorinho* and Brazilian jazz in the city. The shop is next to the Beco das Garrafas alley, where Tom Jobim and João Gilberto first played together, **Toca do Vinícius**, *R Vinícius de Moraes 129C, Ipanema, T021-2247 5227, www.tocadovinicius. com.br.* Specializes in bossa nova books, CDs and souvenirs, doubles as a performance space.

Shopping centres

Rio Sul, *at the Botafogo end of Túnel Novo, www.riosul.com.br.*

Shopping Leblon, *Av Afrânio de Melo Franco 290, www.shoppingleblon.com.br.* The most fashionable mall in the Zona Sul. After the **São Conrado Fashion Mall**, it's the best one-stop shopping mall for Rio's most sought-after labels, less than 5 mins' walk from the beach.

Shopping Village Mall, *Av das Americas 3900, Barra da Tijuca, T021-3252 2999, www. shoppingvillagemall.com.br.* This vast mega-shopping mall opened in 2012 to much fanfare. It's packed with big name Brazilian and international brands, including the first **Apple** store in the country.

Other shopping centres, which have a wide variety of shops and services, include: **São Conrado Fashion Mall** (Estrada da Gavea 899, T021-2111 4444,

www.scfashionmall.com.br); **Shopping Cidade Copacabana** (R Siqueira Campos, www.shoppingcidadecopacabana.com.br); **Shopping Botafogo Praia** (Praia de Botafogo 400, T021-3171 9559, www. botafogopraiashopping.com.br); **Norte Shopping** (Todos os Santos); **Plaza Shopping** (Niterói); and **Barra** (in Barra da Tijuca).

What to do

Boat trips

Several companies offer trips to **Ilha de Paquetá**, and day cruises, including lunch, to **Jaguanum Island**, and a sundown cruise around **Guanabara Bay**.

Moreno Urca, *Quadrado de Urca, T021-9316 6733, www.morenourca.blogspot.com.* Great low-key boat tours of the bay and Atlantic in a fisherman's wooden boat, calling at some of the less-visited sights such as Adam and Eve beach in Jurujuba, the Cagarras islands (for snorkelling) and the Forte São João. Book ahead in high season as it's a little boat. Bring sun protection.

Saveiros Tour, *Av Infante Dom Henrique s/n lojas 13 and 14, T021-2225 6064, www.saveiros. com.br.* Tours in sailing schooners around the bay and down the coast, Mon-Fri 0900-1730, Sat and Sun 0900-1200. Also 'Baía da Guanabara Histórica' historical tours.

Driving tours, personal driver-guides and motorbike tours

Andre Albuquerque, *T021-7811 2737/2427 3629, andralbuquerque@yahoo.com.br.* Private driver tours of Rio from a genuine 'Carioca da Gema' (born and bred local). Friendly, reliable, helpful with English-speaking guides on request.

CEESC RIO, *T021-99369 2844, ceesc.com.br.* Rio's traffic jams are world-beatingly awful. Avoid tedious hours in tour buses riding pillion on a bespoke motorbike tour from US$60 pp for a half-day sightseeing.

Madson Araujo, *T021-9395 3537, www.tour guiderio.com.* Bespoke personal tours of the Rio city sights and trips into Rio de Janeiro state

Otávio Monteiro, *T021-8835 1160 or T021-7841 4799, om2brasil@hotmail.com*. Good-value driver and personal tours will go anywhere in Rio or the state. Reliable, good English.

Rio Connexion Tours, *T021-99715 9794, www.rioconnexiontours.com*. First-class driver-guided tours of Rio de Janeiro city and state, including less-visited areas like the southern beaches around Prainha and Grumari. Nightlife tours, music and general sightseeing. Good English and personable company. Ask for Rodrigo.

Roz Brazil, *T024-9257 0236, www.rozbrazil. com*. Some of the best tours around Petrópolis, Teresópolis and the Serra dos Órgãos with British Brazilian Rosa Thompson, who has been living in the area for decades. Pick-ups from Rio.

Favela tours

Be A Local, *T021-9643 0366, www.bealocal. com*. Good favela tours with walking trips around Rocinha and money going towards community projects; trips to *baile funk* parties at weekends and to football matches.

Favela Santa Marta, *T021-9177 9459, www. favelasantamartatour.blogspot.co.uk*. Visits with locals to the beautifully situated Santa Marta favela – with stunning views of Corcovado and Sugar Loaf – and insights into local community life.

Favela Tour, *Estr das Canoas 722, bl 2, apt 125, São Conrado, T021-3322 2727, T99989 0074 (mob), www.favelatour.com.br*. Safe, interesting guided tours of Rio's favelas in English, French, Spanish, Italian, German and Swedish (3 hrs). For the best attention and price call Marcelo Armstrong direct rather than through a hotel desk. Also offers eco-tours and river rafting.

Tabritur, *T021-99369 2844*. Tours of the Cabritos-Tabajaras favela straddling Copacabana, Ipanema and Lagoa. Can include a hike up Cabritos mountain for incredible views over the city. Profits go to the local community. One of the few projects owned and managed by people from the favela itself and not outsiders.

Football coaching

Pelé da Praia, *R Garcia D'Avila, Ipanema, T021-9702 5794, Facebook: pele da praia*. Football and volleyball coaching from a real Carioca character who has been working on Ipanema beach for many years.

Hang-gliding and paragliding

Delta Flight, *T021-3322 5750, T021-9693 8800, www.deltaflight.com.br*. Hang-gliding rides above Rio from Pedra Bonita mountain with instructors licensed by the **Brazilian Hang-gliding Association**.

Just Fly, *T021-2268 0565, T021-9985 7540 (mob), www.justfly.com.br*. Tandem flights with Paulo Celani (licensed by the **Brazilian Hang-gliding Association**) (5% discount for Footprint readers: present this book at time of reservation).

Pedro Beltrao, *T021-7822 4206, pedrobeltrao77@gmail.com*. One of the best and safest pilots in Brazil, with more than 20 years of experience; competitive rates. Can organize flights throughout Rio state. Highly recommended.

Ruy Marra, *T021-3322 2286, www.riosuperfly. com.br, or find him at the beach*. Paragliding from Leblon beach.

Helicopter flights

Helisight, *R Visconde de Pirajá 580, loja 107, Térreo, Ipanema, T021-2511 2141, www. helisight.com.br. Daily from 0900*. Helicopter sightseeing tours. Prices from US$90 per person for 6-7 mins from Morro de Urca or the Lagoa over Sugar Loaf and Corcovado, to US$300 per person for 30 mins over the city.

Hiking and climbing

CEESC, *T021-99369 2844, www.ceesc.com.br*. The only company to choose for hikes up the Morro do Cabritos, which has some of the best views in Rio from a patch of pristine Mata Atlântica forest. No climbing is involved but it's steep and you will need a head for heights. Also offer the Morro dos Dois Irmaos above Ipanema and Pedra da Gávea.

Clube Excursionista Carioca, *R Hilário Gouveia 71, room 206, T021-2255 1348, www.carioca.org.br.* Recommended for enthusiasts, meets Wed and Fri.

Diogo Monnerat, *T021-7712 7489, diogo.monnerat@gmail.com.* Hiking and climbing tours in Sugar Loaf and Tijuca National Park, from beginners to experienced climbers.

Rio Hiking, *T021-2552 9204 and T021-9721 0594, www.riohiking.com.br.* Hiking tours around Rio city and state, including the Pedra da Gávea, Tijuca Park, Itatiaia and the Serra dos Órgãos and various city tours, including Santa Teresa.

Trilha Dois Irmãos, *T021-99759 9023, www.trilhadoisirmaso.com.br.* Hikes to the top of the Dois Irmãos hills overlooking Ipanema and Leblon. With guides from the local Vidigal favela community.

Language courses

IGI Instituto Globus de Idiomas, *R do Catete 310, sala 303/305, www.institutoglobus.com.br.* Individual lessons cost US$26 per hr, cheaper for groups, helpful staff. Recommended.

Instituto Brasil-Estados Unidos, *Av N Sra de Copacabana 690, 5th floor, www.ibeu.org.br.* This school offers an 8-week course, with 3 classes a week, for US$150, and a 5-week intensive course for US$260. There's a good English library at same address.

Parachuting

Several people offer tandem jumps; check that they are accredited with the **Associação Brasileira de Vôo Livre** (www.abvl.com.br).

Barra Jumping, *Aeroporto de Jacarepaguá, Av Ayrton Senna 2541, T021-3151 3602, www.barrajumping.com.br.* Tandem jumping (*vôo duplo*).

Surfing

See also **Rio Surf n Stay** (page 83) and **Rio Hiking** (above) for surf lessons on Barra, Grumari and Prainha.

Nomad Surfers, *www.nomadsurfers.com.* Runs a surf camp in Recreio dos Bandeirantes,

a stroll from Macumba beach, with simple backpacker accommodation. They offer beginners surf instruction (with attractive packages including a 7-night intensive surf school), surf board rental and surf safaris.

Surf schools include: **Associação Brasileira de Surf Profissional** (R Serzedelo Correia 15, room 804, Copacabana, T021-2235 3972, www.abrasp.com); **Confederação de Bodyboard do Estado do Rio de Janeiro** (R Barata Ribeiro 348/701, Copacabana, T022-2771 1802, T021-9219 3038, www.cbrasb.com.br); **Federação de Surf do Estado do Rio de Janeiro** (T021-7884 4226, www.feserj.com.br); **Organização dos Surfistas Profissionais do Rio de Janeiro** (R Visconde de Pirajá 580, shop 213, Ipanema).

Tour operators and guides

See also Be a Local (page 97) and CEESC (page 96).

Alex Feliciano, *T021-99479 4529, alexfeliciano@gmail.com.* First-class historical tours of the centre, trips to the forts in Rio and Niterói (for superb views) and general Rio tours. Excellent English.

Cultural Rio, *R Santa Clara 110/904, Copacabana, T021-3322 4872 or T021-9911 3829 (mob), www.culturalrio.com.br.* Tours escorted personally by Professor Carlos Roquette, English and French spoken, almost 200 options available.

Exotic Tours, *T021-2179 6972, www.exotic tours.com.br.* Rejane Reis runs unusual trips throughout Rio, such as *candomblé*, rafting or hikes up to the Pedra da Gávea. Cultural and favela tours. Good English spoken.

Fábio Sombra, *T021-9729 5455 (mob), fabiosombra@hotmail.com.* Offers private and tailor-made guided tours focusing on the cultural aspects of Rio and Brazil.

Gilmar Lopes Walking tours, *T021-99369 2844, gilmar.lopes@talk21.com.* Fascinating walking and public transport tours of Rio telling the story of the city from the point of view of the communities and not the wealthy aristocrats and churchmen, and showing the places where Cariocas love to shop, visit and drink a cold beer.

Guanatur Turismo, *R Dias da Rocha 16A, Copacabana, T021-2548 3275, www.guanatur turismo.com.br.* Sells long-distance bus tickets.

Jungle Me, *T021-4105 7533, www.jungleme. com.br.* Hikes in Rio off the beaten track, including the 3 peaks in Tijuca National Park (an 8-hr circuit), wild beaches and Pedra Bonita.

Rio Adventures, *T021-96479 7414, rioadventures.com.* All manner of adventure tours in and around Rio from rafting, zip-lining and canoeing to biking and rock climbing.

Rio by Jeep, *T021-3322 5750, T021-9693 8800, www.riobyjeep.com.* 5-hr tours in open or closed jeeps with local guides showing Rio from 3 perspectives: gorgeous beaches, historical downtown and Tijuca National Park. Contact Ricardo Hamond.

Rio Connexions, *T021-99715 9794, www. rioconnexiontours.com.* Upscale bespoke driver-guide tours of Rio state with an inventive range of options for hikes, favela visits, beach trips and music tours.

Rio EnCantos, *T021-98378 1895, www. rioencantos.com.* Excellent nightlife, music and walking tours of the city centre and favela communities with Lapa local Kelly Tavares.

Rio Turismo Radical, *www.rioturismoradical. com.br.* A broad menu of light adventure activities including rafting on the Rio Paraibuna, hiking, hang-gliding and scuba-diving off Arraial do Cabo.

Rio Xtreme, *T021-8806 0235.* A broad range of excursions from city tours to the key sights and nightlife excursions to hikes to the Pedra da Gávea, Itatiaia National Park and Ilha Grande.

Trilha a Pé, *T021-0408 0179, www.trilhaape. com.br.* Custom-made hiking trips, kayaking, surfing and light adventure tours in and around Rio.

Volleyball classes

For more general information and other schools see www.voleirio.com.br.

Escola de Vôlei Bernardinho, *R das Laranjeiras 346, T021-3079 1235, www.escola devoleibernardinho.com.br.* Professional volleyball coaching for groups and individuals.

Escola de Vôlei da Leticia, *Ipanema beach, between R Farme de Amoedo and R Vinicius de Moraes, T021-9841 3833, escoladevoleidaleticia@ig.com.br, facebook: Escola-de-Volei-Letícia.* Classes for adults and children in Portuguese, Mon-Fri morning and afternoon. Run by Letícia Pessoa who has been working on Ipanema since 1995.

Escola de Vôlei do Renato, *Copacabana beach, in front of R Hilário de Gouvea, T021-9544 4524, http://voleirenatofranca.blogspot. co.uk. Adults Mon-Fri 1900-2100, adult and 8-12 year olds Mon-Fri 0730-0930.* Run by Renato França who has been working on the beach for 12 years.

Whitewater rafting

See Tour operators, above, for trips on the Paraibuna and Macaé rivers (both around 2 hrs from Rio).

Transport

Air

Aeroporto Internacional Tom Jobim, Ilha do Governador, 15 km north of the city centre, www.aeroportogaleao.net (also known as Galeão), receives international and domestic flights. It has been expanded for the 2016 Olympics, doubling the number of gates and expanding the international terminal by adding a new departure hall which was not fully ready when this book went to press.

There are *câmbios* in the departure hall and on the first floor of international arrivals. The **Banco do Brasil** on the 3rd floor (open 24 hrs) has better rates of exchange. There are also ATMs for major Brazilian banks. Duty-free shops comprise mostly the predictable international brands with little of interest from Brazil beyond over-priced souvenirs. There are **Riotur** information booths in the domestic arrivals hall of **Terminal 1**, T021-3398 4077, daily 0600-2300, and in the international arrivals hall in **Terminal 2**, T021-3398 2245, daily 0600-2400, which provide maps and can book accommodation.

Santos Dumont Airport, in the city centre on Guanabara Bay, www.aeroportosantosdumont.net, sits on a little peninsula next to the island where the first French colony was situated. It too has been renovated for the Olympics and is used for Rio–São Paulo shuttle flights (see below), a handful of other domestic routes (including flights to Porto Seguro with *Azul*), private planes or air taxis. There are banks in the terminal, and a handful of souvenir shops and cafés. Toilets are very poorly signposted.

Taxis can be booked from within the airports or picked up at the stands outside the terminals. A taxi which is pre-booked through desks in the airport – the *taxi especial* – is safer than the metered taxis outside. For the airport-based taxis you pay a fixed rate before the journey; they are very reliable but also more expensive. Fixed-rate taxis charge around US$25-30 from Jobim to Copacabana or Ipanema and US$15 to the city centre or Santa Teresa (about half as much from Santos Dumont); buy a ticket at the counter. Fixed-price taxis have clearly marked booths selling tickets. Staff will direct you to the taxi rank.

Aerotaxi cabs, T021-2467 1500, are available outside both terminals at Tom Jobim Airport and cost US$15 (plus US$0.75 per item of luggage) to the centre. Other special taxis run by the meter starting at R$5.70 (US$1.60), adding R$2.46 (US$0.66) per km. Beware of pirate taxis, which are unlicensed.

There are frequent buses between the 2 airports, the *rodoviária* (interstate bus station) and the city; the best is the a/c **Real Auto**, T0800-886 1000, www.realautoonibus.com.br, or *frescão* which leaves from outside arrivals on the 1st floor of terminals 1 and 2 at Tom Jobim (aka Galeão) and run 0500-2400, US$3.50.

There are 4 routes between the international airport and Rio's city centre and beaches run by **Real Autos**. Linha 2018 to the southern beaches (Copacabana, Ipanema) via the *rodoviária* (long-distance bus station, see under Bus, Long distance, below), daily 0530-2340 every 30-40 mins, US$4. Linha 2101 to Santos Dumont domestic airport via the Linha Vermelha urban highway, daily 0650-1810, every hour or so but sporadic, US$3.50. Linha 2145 to Santos Dumont via the *rodoviária* and Av Presidente Vargas in the city centre, daily 0530-2330, every 45-60 mins, US$3.50. Linha 2918 to the city centre via the Linha Amerala urban highway, daily 0530-2300, every hour, US$4.

Ordinary city buses also run from the airport to various locations in Rio, from the first floor of both terminals. These are far less secure and are not recommended.

There is a shuttle flight between **Santos Dumont Airport** and **São Paulo** (Congonhas Airport, US$150 single, US$250 return). The shuttle operates every 30 mins throughout the day 0630-2230. Sit on the right-hand side for views to São Paulo, the other side coming back; book flights in advance.

Bicycle

There are cycle paths all along Rio's beaches – including from late 2016 all the way to Barra – and the number of Carioca cyclists is on the increase. Some hostels have bicycles for rent. Check the cycle path map on this link: www.ta.org.br/site2/index.htm. Note that the cycle path is a relatively new space in Rio that people are learning to respect – you might find pedestrians, dogs and skaters on it. Early in the morning it's quieter. Make sure you lock the bikes well. Be careful on the roads themselves: Carioca drivers are generally disrespectful of other road users, and especially of cyclists.

ITAU sponsor an unreliable public bike service which requires online registration. More reliable bikes can be rented from **Velobike** (T021-3442 4315, R Francisco

Otaviano 20C, Arpoador or R Gustavo Sampaio 802, Leme) in the Arpoador or Copacabana, for around US$10 per hr.

Bus
Local
There are good services to all parts of the city, but buses are very crowded and not for the aged or infirm during rush hours. Buses have turnstiles which are awkward if you are carrying luggage. Hang on tight as drivers live out Grand Prix fantasies. At busy times allow about 45 mins to get from Copacabana to the centre by bus.

The fare for municipal buses – whether a/c (*frescão*) or non-a/c (*quentão*) – is US$1. Suburban buses cost up to US$3, depending on the distance.

Bus stops are often not marked. The route is written on the side of the bus, but it's hard to see until the bus has actually pulled up at the stop. Buses are usually marked with the destination and any going south of the centre will call at Copacabana and generally Ipanema/Leblon.

Private companies, including **Real**, **Pegaso** and **Anatur**, operate a/c *frescão* buses, which can be flagged down practically anywhere. They run from all points in Rio Sul to the city centre, *rodoviária* and the airports.

The fare for municipal buses – whether a/c (*frescão*) or non-a/c (*quentão*) is US$1. Suburban buses cost up to US$3.

City Rio is an a/c tourist bus service with security guards, which runs between all the major parts of the city. Bus stops, marked by grey poles, are found where there are concentrations of hotels. Good maps show the places of interest close to each bus stop. Timetables change frequently; ask at hotels for the latest information.

Minivans (R$2.50/US$0.70 per journey) run from Av Rio Branco in the centre as far south as Barra da Tijuca and have the destination written on the window. These vans also run along the seafront from Leme to Rocinha and can be hailed from the kerb.

Long distance
Rio's interstate bus station, the **Rodoviária Novo Rio**, Av Francisco Bicalho 01 at Rodrigues Alves, Santo Cristo, T021-3213 1800, www.novorio.com.br, is just north of the city centre and can be reached by various buses: No 326, Bancários–Castelo, from the centre and the airport; No 136, Rodoviária–Copacabana via Glória, Flamengo, and Botafogo; No127, Rodoviária–Copacabana (via Tunel do Pasmado); No 172, Rodoviária–Leblon (via Joquei and Jardim Botânico); No 128, Rodoviária–Leblon (via Copacabana and Ipanema); No 170, Rodoviária–Gávea (via Glória, Botafogo, Jardim Botânico). The local bus station is next to the Rodoviária. The area around the bus stations is not safe after dark and you should beware of thieves at any time. Take a taxi to or from the nearest *metrô* station (Estácio or Praça Onze) or to your hotel; taxis can be booked at the booth on the ground floor. A taxi to Flamengo costs approximately US$8.

Riotur, T021-2263 4857, daily 0700-1900, has an information booth in the bus station that can help with orientation, hotel reservations and point you to the taxi bookings stand. Left luggage costs US$3. There are *câmbios* (cash only) and ATMs.

Buses run from Rio to every state capital and many smaller cities in all parts of the country from Belém in the far north to Porto Alegre and the Uruguay border in the far south. There are departures to major destinations, such as São Paulo, more than every hour. It is advisable to book in advance in high season and weekends. Travel agencies throughout the city sell tickets as do many hostels. Otherwise turn up at least 90 mins before your bus leaves to buy a ticket. Timetables, companies and platform information and the most up to date prices are available on www.novorio.com.br; type your destination into the box provided.

Most street travel agents and hostels sell *passagens de onibus* (interstate bus tickets), or will direct you to a company that does so. Agencies include **Dantur Passagens e**

Turismo, Av Rio Branco 156, subsolo loja 134, Metrô Carioca, T021-2262 3424/3624, www.dantur.com.br; **Guanatur**, R Dias da Rocha 16A, Copacabana, T021-2235 3275, www.guanaturturismo.com.br; **Paxtur Passagens**, R República do Líbano 61 loja L, Center, T021-3852 2277; and an agency at R Visconde de Pirajá 303, loja 114, Ipanema, T021-2523 1000. They charge about US$3 for bookings.

Within Rio state

To **Niterói**, No 761D Gávea–Charitas (via Jardim Botânico and Botafogo); 751D Galeão–Charitas and 741D Leme–Charitas (via Copacabana, Botafogo, Lapa and Santos Dumont Airport), US$2. Frescões Gávea–Charitas, Galeão–Charitas; all run between Rio and Niterói.

To **Búzios**, buses leave almost every hour 0600-2130 daily from Rio's *rodoviária* (US$17, 2½ hrs). Go to the **1001** counter, T021-4004 5001 for tickets or buy online at www.autoviacao1001.com.br/en. Buying the ticket in advance is recommended in high season and on major holidays. You can also take any bus from Rio to the town of **Cabo Frio** (these are more frequent), from there take the Viação Salineira bus, it runs every 30 mins, US$3, from where it's 30 mins to Búzios and vice versa.

To **Petrópolis**, buses leave the *rodoviária* every 15 mins throughout the day (US$6.50) and every hour on Sun; buy tickets from **Única & Fácil** counter, www.unica-facil.com.br. The journey takes 1½ hrs. Sit on the left-hand side for the best views and bring travel sickness pills if you are prone to nausea on winding roads. Return tickets are not available, so buy tickets for the return journey on arrival in Petrópolis.

To **Angra dos Reis**, buses run at least hourly Mon-Sat from the *rodoviária* with **Costa Verde**, www.costaverdetransportes.com.br, some direct; several go through Copacabana, Ipanema and Barra then take the *via litoral*, sit on the left, US$15, 2½ hrs. You can flag down the bus in Flamengo, Copacabana, Ipanema, Barra da Tijuca,

but it may well be full on Sat and bank holidays. To link up with the ferry to Ilha Grande be sure to catch a bus before 1000.

Interstate and international

For full information on the latest routes and prices see www.buscaonibus.com.br.

Campo Grande, **Florianopolis**, **Curitiba** and **Foz do Iguaçu** are all reachable from Rio. Buses also run to **São Paulo**, **Camburiu** and **Porto Alegre**. To **Buenos Aires**, **Crucero Del Norte**, T021-2253 2960, www.crucerodelnorte.com.ar, and **Pluma**, www.pluma.com.br, run buses from the *rodoviária* via Porto Alegre and **Santa Fe** (Argentina), 48 hrs, US$105 (book 2 days in advance).

To **Santiago de Chile** (**Pluma** or **Gen Urquiza**), 70 hrs, US$167. There are no direct buses from Rio to **Asunción** (Paraguay).

Car

Service stations are closed in many places on Sat and Sun. Road signs are notoriously misleading in Rio and you can end up in a favela (take special care if driving along the Estr da Gávea to São Conrado as it is possible to unwittingly enter Rocinha, Rio's biggest slum).

Car hire

There are many agencies on Av Princesa Isabel, Copacabana. A credit card is essential for hiring a car. Recent reports suggest it is cheaper to hire outside Brazil; you may also obtain more comprehensive insurance this way. See also page 192. **Avis**, Antônio Carlos Jobim International Airport, T021-3398 5060; Santos Dumont Airport, T021-3814 7378; Av Princesa Isabel 150A and B, Copacabana, T021-2543 8481, www.avis.com.br. **Hertz**, international airport, T021-3398 4338; Av Princesa Isabel 500, Copacabana, T021-2275 7440. **Localiza**, international airport, T021-3398 3107; Santos Dumont Airport, T0800-992000; Av Princesa Isabel 150, Copacabana, T021-2275 3340. **Nobre**, Av Princesa Isabel 7, Copacabana, T021-2295 1799. **Telecar**, R Figueiredo Magalhães 701, Copacabana, T021-2548 6778.

Ferry

Every 10 mins ferries and launches cross Guanabara Bay for **Niterói** from the 'Barcas' terminal at Praça 15 de Novembro, www.barcas-sa.com.br. The journey takes 20-30 mins and costs US$1. Catamarans (*aerobarcas*) also leave every 10 mins but take just 12 mins and cost US$1 (the same price as a *barca* ferry). There are also more expensive catamarans and motor boats that take 9 mins. The slow, cheaper ferry gives the best views. From Niterói, ferries and catamarans return to Rio de Janeiro from the city centre terminal at Praça Araribóia and at Charitas district.

Metrô

The underground railway, the **metrô**, T0800-2595 1111, www.metrorio.com.br, currently has 2 lines. **Linha 1 (Orange)** operates between the inner suburb of Tijuca (station Saens Peña), to Ipanema (station General Osório) via the railway station (Central), Glória, Botafogo and Arcoverde. **Linha 2 (Green)** runs from the northern outskirt suburb of Pavuna to Botafogo, passing Engenho da Rainha, the Maracanã stadium, Central and then goes along the shore parallel to Line 1.

Trains run Mon-Sat 0500-2400 (though a few close as early as 1700; check the website for timetables); Sat 0500-2400 (with some stations closing at 1400); Sun and bank holidays 0700-2300 (with at least a quarter of stations not opening at all). Trains run 24 hrs during Carnaval.

Tickets cost R$3.70/US$1 for a single journey and for the connecting 'Metrô na Superfície' Gávea/Barra express bus which passes through Ipanema and Leblon. Multi-tickets and integrated bus/*metrô* tickets are available with connections as far as Barra and Jacarepaguá (on express buses). There is also a pre-paid card, **Cartão Pré-Pago**; the minimal initial payment is US$3, any minimal additional after that US$1.50. These can only be bought at the stations. Free *metrô* maps are available at the counter.

Tip...
Rio *metrô* has a women-only designated wagon Mon-Fri 0600-0900 and 1700-2000; it is the last wagon of each train, with a pink stripe across the top, but many women still prefer to travel with men, and often some distracted men pop into the pink wagon.

The *metrô* is currently undergoing expansion with sporadic station closures in Copacabana and Ipanema. By (or shortly after) the 2016 Olympics, the service will extend to Leblon, Rocinha, São Conrado and Jardim Oceânico in Barra da Tijuca where they will link with **BRT Express** buses (which have their own designated road) to Barra, Recreio and beyond. From 2016 a new BRT route called the Transolímpica will connect the Olympic parks in Barra and Deodoro with the TransOeste in Recreio. *Metrô* stations often have a number of different access points. Substantial changes in bus operations are taking place because of the extended *metrô* system; buses connecting with the *metrô* have a blue-and-white symbol in the windscreen.

Rio committed itself to building a new line (**Linha 4**) between the city centre and Barra da Tijuca in the south, in time for the Olympics in 2016. However it is extremely unlikely to be ready on time. As this book went to press in Jan 2016 the most optimistic expectations were that the *metrô* would reach Leblon, with stations in Gávea and Barra to open in 2017. There are also even grander plans to build **Linha 3** to Niterói via an underwater tunnel beneath Guanabara Bay; however, this is not scheduled for completion before 2020, if at all.

Taxi

The common taxis in Rio are yellow and blue, and use meters. There are 2 price bands, and there is a little flag on the meter that the driver tugs to choose the band. Bandeira 1 runs Mon-Sat 0600-2100, with the meter starting at R$4.30 (US$1.15) and then adding R$1.40 (US$0.37) per km. Bandeira 2 runs Mon-Sat 2100-0600, Sun and bank holidays, it starts at R$5.70 (US$1.52), adding R$2.46 (US$0.65) per km. The website www.tarifadetaxi.com/rio-de-janeiro has a Rio map and calculates the approximate taxi price for you. The fare between Copacabana and the centre is around US$20. Taxis from Glória metrô to Santa Teresa cost around US$3. It's a good idea to print out a copy of the map and keep it handy so you can monitor your journey; some taxis drivers sneakily choose the long way round in order to overcharge. Also, make sure meters are cleared and on the right price band.

Taxis have red number plates with white digits (yellow for private cars, with black digits). Smaller ones (mostly Volkswagen) are marked 'TAXI' on the windscreen or roof. It is safest to use taxis from *pontos* (taxi ranks), which are abundant throughout the city. *Ponto* taxis have the name of the *ponto* painted on the outside, indicating which *ponto* they belong to.

Radio taxis are safer but almost twice as expensive; each co-op has a different colour: **Central Táxi**, yellow and blue, T021-2195 1000, www.centraltaxi.com.br; **Coopacarioca**, yellow and blue, T021-2158 1818, www.cooparioca.com.br; **Coopertramo**, white, T021-2209 9292, www.radio-taxi.com.br; **Cootramo**, blue, T021-3976 9944, www.cootramo.com.br; **Transcoopass**, red, T021-2209 1555, www.transcoopass.com.br. If you get a radio/co-op taxi (*taxi especial*) at the airport you pay in advance,

buying the ticket at a special booth. In this case the meter will be off; but if you get into one outside the airport, the meter should be turned on. It will cost you US$40-45 to Copacabana or Ipanema. It is better to buy the ticket in advance – you will know for sure how much you are paying.

Taxis should always be booked through a hostel or hotel, or caught from a designated taxi *posto*; the name of the *posto* should be written in navy blue on the side of the taxi.

Train

Buses marked 'E Ferro' go to the train station. There are suburban trains to **Nova Iguaçu**, **Nilópolis**, **Campo Grande** and elsewhere. **Supervia** is the main company that sells tickets, www.supervia.com.br (in Portuguese only). None of the destinations are of tourist interest and they can be rough and dangerous, mainly at night. The station **Central do Brasil** (see page 53) is worth a visit and occasionally hosts cultural events and music concerts.

Tram

See also Santa Teresa, page 54. The famous yellow Santa Teresa tram service – the oldest in Latin America – was closed in 2011 following a serious accident involving one of the old tram cars. It reopened in 2015 with a single new car and thus a very limited service (1000-1600, US$2). More cars are expected to be completed by mid-2016, when VLT trams will also connect Santos Dumont airport, the Rodoviária and Av Rio Branco with the Porto Maravilha complex in the old city centre.

There are also infrequent trams from the Largo da Carioca (there is a museum open Fri 0830-1700) across the old aqueduct (Arcos) to Dois Irmãos or Paula Mattos in **Santa Teresa**; a beautiful journey, US$0.40.

East of
Rio de Janeiro

Rio de Janeiro state is one of Brazil's smallest, but it is packed with great things to see. East of Rio the country gets drier and looks more Mediterranean. The coast, which is lined with fabulous beaches for hundreds of kilometres, is backed by a long series of saltwater lakes and drifting sand dunes. Most visitors ignore Niterói, the city immediately opposite Rio across Guanabara Bay, despite the fact is has ocean beaches as good as or better than Rio's. Instead, they head straight for the surf towns around Cabo Frio or the fashionable little resort of Búzios, which has good beaches and lively summer nightlife.

Cariocas are rude about everywhere, but they are especially rude about their neighbour across Guanabara Bay. The only good thing about Niterói, they say, is the view it has of Rio de Janeiro. As a result few visitors make it here. However, its ocean beaches are less polluted and far less crowded than Rio's and the views from them across the bay, especially at sunset, are wonderful. Oscar Niemeyer's Museu de Arte Contemporânea, a flying-saucer-shaped building perched on a promontory, is one of his very best buildings. There is no reason to stay overnight in Niterói but the city is well worth visiting as a day trip or on the way to Búzios.

Sights

Surrounded by long curved walkways, the space-age building of the **Museu de Arte Contemporânea** ① *Mirante da Boa Viagem, T021-2620 2400, www.macniteroi.com.br, Tue-Sun 1100-1800, when this book went to press the museum was temporarily closed for repairs and due to reopen in time for the 2016 Olympics, US$2.65, free Wed,* is rapidly becoming the most famous work by Brazil's celebrated disciple of Le Corbusier, Oscar Niemeyer. It is in a fabulous location, sitting above a long beach with a sweeping view across Guanabara Bay to Rio as a backdrop. The building itself looks like a Gerry Anderson vision of the future; one can almost imagine *Thunderbird 1* taking off through its centre. The main gallery is a white circle of polished concrete perched on a low monopod and sitting in a reflection pool. It is reached by a coiling, serpentine ramp which meets the building on its second storey.

The exhibitions comprise seasonal shows and a permanent collection of Brazilian contemporary art of all disciplines. The top level is devoted to temporary displays and the intermediate to the permanent collection. Niemeyer overcomes the problem of the unsuitability of a curved space for the exhibition of art by using an inner hexagonal core enclosed by flat screen walls. More difficult to overcome is that the glimpses of the stunning panorama of Rio through the gaps in the hexagon are far more captivating than most of the art.

The building is worth seeing at dusk when it is lit; the sky above the streetlights of Rio is light peacock blue infused with lilac and the distant figure of the Corcovado Christ shines brilliant xenon-white over the dark mass of mountains.

Essential Niterói

Finding your feet

Boats from Rio arrive at the Praça Araribóia city centre terminal in Niterói and at Charitas district.

Bus Nos 761D Gávea–Charitas (via Jardim Botânico and Botafogo), 751D Galeão–Charitas, and 741D Leme–Charitas (via Copacabana, Botafogo, Lapa and Santos Dumont Airport), US$3, and Frescões Gávea–Charitas, Galeão–Charitas, all run between Rio and Niterói. If you are driving, the bridge across Guanabara Bay is well signposted; there is a toll of US$1 per car.

Getting around

To get to the ocean beaches from Niterói, take bus Nos 38 or 52 from Praça General Gomes Carneiro or a bus from the street directly ahead of the ferry entrance, at right angles to the coast road. For Jurujuba take bus No 33 from the boat dock; sit on the right-hand side, it's a beautiful ride.

Many buildings associated with the city's period as state capital are grouped around the **Praça da República**. None are open to the public. The city's main thoroughfare, Avenida Ernâni do Amaral Peixoto, runs from the *praça* and is lined with buildings similar to Avenida Presidente Vargas in Rio. At the end of the avenue is the dock for Rio, a statue of the indigenous chief, Araribóia, and the **Bay Market Shopping Centre**.

Perched on a rocky promontory at the mouth of Guanabara Bay, the 16th-century **Fortaleza Santa Cruz** ⓘ *Estrada General Eurico Gaspar Dutra, Jurujuba, T021-2711 0462, Tue-Sun 0900-1600, US$1.60, compulsory guided tour in Portuguese only,* is still used by the Brazilian military and is the most important historical monument in Niterói. As well as the usual range of cannon, dungeons and bulwarks the tour includes a visit to gruesome execution sites and a little chapel dedicated to Saint Barbara. The statue of the saint inside was originally destined for Santa Cruz dos Militares in Rio. However, unlike most Cariocas, the saint obviously prefers Niterói: any attempts to move her image from here have allegedly been accompanied by violent storms.

Beaches

The beaches closest to the city centre are unsuitable for bathing (Gragoatá, Vermelha, Boa Viagem, das Flechas). The next beaches along, also in the city and with polluted water, have more in the way of restaurants, bars and nightlife and some of the best views in the whole country, especially at sunset and sunrise. **Icaraí** is the smartest district, with the best hotels and good nightlife. There are superb views of Rio from here, especially at sunset, while neighbouring **São Francisco** and **Charitas** also have good views.

The road continues round the bay, past Preventório and Samanguaiá to **Jurujuba**, a fishing village at the end of the No 33 bus route. About 2 km from Jurujuba along a narrow road are the attractive twin beaches of **Adão** and **Eva** beneath the Fortaleza Santa Cruz with more lovely views of Rio across the bay. These beaches are often used for *candomblé* (Brazilian-African spirit religion) ceremonies.

About 40 minutes from Niterói, through picturesque countryside, are four fabulous stretches of sand, the best in the area: **Piratininga**, **Camboinhas**, **Itaipu** and **Itacoatiara**. Buses leave from the street directly ahead of the ferry entrance, at right angles to the coast road. The undertow at Itacoatiara is dangerous, but the waves are popular with surfers and the beach itself is safe. Itaipu is also used by surfers.

Tourist information

Neltur
Estrada Leopoldo Fróes 773, São Francisco,
T021-2710 2727, www.niteroiturismo.com.br.

Where to stay

$$$ Icaraí Praia
R Belizário Augusto 21, T021-2612 5030,
www.icaraipraiahotel.com.br.
Plain rooms in a faded 1980s beachfront tower.

$$$ Tower Hotel
Av Almte Ari Parreiras 12, Icaraí, T021-
2612 2121, www.towerhotel.com.br.
Niterói's smartest hotel (3-star) with ordinary,
rather faded rooms, an indoor pool, sauna
and reasonable business facilities.

Restaurants

$$$ Olimpo
Estação Hidroviária de Charitas, 2nd floor,
Av Quintino Bocaiúva, s/n, Charitas, T021-
2711 0554, www.restauranteolimpo.com.br.
Brazilian and European cooking in
a Niemeyer building surrounded by
windows overlooking Guanabara Bay.

$$ La Sagrada Familia
R Domingues de Sá 325, Icaraí, T021-
2610 1683, www.lasagradafamilia.
com.br/niteroi.htm.
The best restaurant in Niterói, housed in a
beautiful colonial building, with a varied
menu and reasonable wine list.

Festivals

Mar-May Festa do Divino, a festival
that traditionally begins on Easter Sun
and continues for the next 40 days, in
which the *bandeira* (banner) *do Divino*
is taken around the local municipalities.
The festival ends at Pentecost with
sacred and secular celebrations.

Transport

Boat Ferries and launches run between
the terminal at Praça Araribóia (for Niteroi
city centre) and Charitas beach and the
'Barcas' terminal at Praça 15 de Novembro in
Rio de Janeiro city centre, every 10 mins (20-
30 mins, US$1.70), www.barcas-sa.com.br.
There are also catamarans (*aerobarcas*)
every 10 mins (12 mins, US$1.70). The slow,
cheaper ferry gives the best views.

Bus Buses running between Niterói and
Rio de Janeiro include No 761D Gávea–
Charitas (via Jardim Botânico and Botafogo),
751D Aeroporto Galeão–Charitas 740-D
and 741D Leme–Charitas (via Copacabana,
Botafogo, Lapa and Santos Dumont Airport),
US$3. Also available are Frescões Gávea–
Charitas, Galeão–Charitas.

To the east of Niterói lies a series of saltwater lagoons, the Lagos Fluminenses. Two small lakes lie behind the beaches of Piratininga, Itaipu and Itacoatiara, but they are polluted and ringed by mud. The next lakes, Maricá and Saquarema, are much larger; although they are still muddy, the waters are relatively unpolluted and wildlife abounds in the scrub and bush around the lagoons. This is a prime example of the *restinga* (coastal swamp and forest) environment. The RJ-106 road runs behind the lakes en route to Cabo Frio and Búzios, but an unmade road goes along the coast between Itacoatiara and Cabo Frio, giving access to the many long, open beaches of Brazil's Costa do Sol. The whole area is perfect for camping.

Saquarema

Saquarema (population 44,000) is a fishing and holiday village, known as the centre for surfing in Brazil. Its cold, open seas provide consistent crashing waves of up to 3 m. Frequent national and international championships take place here, but beware of strong currents.

The lovely white church of **Nossa Senhora de Nazaré** (1675) is on a green promontory jutting into the ocean. Local legend has it that on 8 September 1630, fishermen, saved from a terrible storm, found an image of the Virgem de Nazaré in the rocks. A chapel was founded on the spot and subsequent attempts to relocate the Virgin (as when the chapel was falling into disrepair) resulted in her miraculously returning to the original site.

Araruama

At 220 sq km, **Lagoa Araruama** (population 66,500) is one of the largest lakes in Brazil and is famous for its medicinal mud. The salinity is high, the waters calm and almost the entire lake is surrounded by sandy beaches, making it popular with families looking for unpolluted bathing. The constant breeze makes the lake perfect for windsurfing and sailing.

At the eastern end of the lake, also inland, is **São Pedro de Aldeia**, which has a population of 55,500 and, despite intensive development, still retains much of its colonial charm. There is a lovely **Jesuit church** built in 1723.

Arraial do Cabo

The rather ugly little salt industry town of Arraial do Cabo (population 21,500) near Cabo Frio is considerably less busy than the resort at Cabo Frio a little to the north, and provides access to equally good beaches and dunes. The lake and the ocean here are divided by the Restinga de Massambaba, a long spit of sand mostly deserted except for the beaches of **Massambaba** and **Seca**, at the western end, and **Grande** in the east at Arraial do Cabo town itself. Arraial has lots of other small beaches on the bays and islands that form the cape, round which the line of the coast turns north, including the long, busy stretch at **Anjos**, **Praia do Forno** and **Prainha**. Trips can be made by boat around the islets and by jeep or buggy over the sand dunes.

While Arraial is not a dive destination of international quality in its own right, it is one of the best in Brazil and there are a number of sites of varying difficulty with caverns and swim-throughs that are well worth exploring. Cold and warm currents meet here just off the coast and the marine life is more abundant than almost anywhere else on mainland southern Brazil. Expect to see schools of tropical and subtropical reef fish such as batfish and various tangs and butterfly fish, the occasional turtle, colonies of gorgonians and beautiful (though invasive) soft corals probably brought here on oil tankers from the Indo-Pacific. Dolphins are frequent visitors. The best visibility is between November and May. Water temperature is always below 20°C.

The little town is also establishing itself as an adventure sports destination with activities including dune boarding, parachuting, kitesurfing and kayaking available. See also What to do, below.

Praia do Farol, on Ilha do Cabo Frio, is one of Brazil's best beaches, with sand dunes and crystal-clear water.

Listings Costa do Sol

Tourist information

Saquarema

Tourist office
R Coronel Madureira 77, Centro Saquarema, T022-9972 7251, www.saquarema.rj.gov.br.

Araruama

Tourist office
Av Brasil 655, Parque Hotel, T022-2665 4145, www.araruama.rj.gov.br.

Arraial do Cabo

Tourist office
Praça da Bandeira, T022-2622 1949, www. arraialdocabo-rj.com.br/zarony.html.

Where to stay

Saquarema

$$ Pousada do Holandês
Av Vilamar 377, Itaúna beach, www.pousadadoholandes.com.br.
Many languages spoken by Dutch owner and his Brazilian wife. Good meals – follow the signs, or take a taxi, from Saquarema. Recommended.

$$ Pousada Pedra d'Água Maasai
Trav de Itaúna 17, Praia de Itaúna, T022-2651 1092, www.maasai.com.br.
Good little beachfront hotel with 18 apartments, pool, sauna and a reasonable seafood restaurant.

Araruama

$$$ Enseada das Garças
R José Costa 1088, Ponta da Areia, about 5 km from São Pedro de Aldeia, T022-2621 1924, www.enseadadasgarcas.com.br.
Beautiful little hotel overlooking the sea with access to good walking trails.

Arraial do Cabo

$$$ Pousada Nautillu's
R Marcílio Dias 100, T022-2622 1611, www.pousadanautillus.com.br.
Medium-sized *pousada* with a pool, sauna, bar and restaurant. Recommended.

What to do

Arraial do Cabo
Barco Lindo Olhar, *T022-2647 4493*. For trips to Ilha do Cabo Frio; ask for Vadinho or Eraldo in the town's main marina.
Deep Trip, *Av Getulio Vargas 93, Praia Grande, Arraial do Cabo, T021-9942 3020 (mob), www. deeptrip.com.br.* The only PADI-affiliated dive operator in Arraial, with a range of courses and dive trips.
Gas, *Av Litoranea 80, Praia Grande, T022-9956 1222, www.arraialdocabo-rj.com.br/gas.* Various adventure sports including dune boarding, parachuting and kayak surfing. Runs dive trips but is not PADI accredited.
K-Kite School, *R da Alegria 15, T021-9351 7164, www.kkite.hpg.ig.com.br.* Windsurfing and kitesurfing, and lessons.

Zarony Tours, *Marina dos Pescadores, 2nd pier on Praia dos Anjos, T022-7836 7952 (mob), www.arraialdocabo-rj.com.br/zarony. html.* For trips to Ilha do Cabo Frio.

Transport

A very steep road connects the beaches of Itaipu and Itacoatiara with RJ-106 (and on to Bacaxá and Araruama) via the village of Itaipu-Açu. Most maps do not show a road beyond Itaipu-Açu; it is certainly too steep for buses. An alternative to the route from

Niterói to Araruama through the lagoons is further inland than the RJ-106, via Manilha, Itaboraí and Rio Bonito on the BR-101 and RJ-124; this is a fruit-growing region.

Saquarema
Bus To **Rio de Janeiro** (Mil e Um, 1001), www.autoviacao1001.com.br/en, every 2 hrs 0625-1950, about 2 hrs, US$10.

Arraial do Cabo
Bus To **Rio de Janeiro**, www. autoviacao1001.com.br/en, US$17.

Cabo Frio

popular middle-class Brazilian seaside resort

The busy tourist town of Cabo Frio (population 127,000), 168 km from Rio, overflows at the weekend with Cariocas. Although the town itself is very touristy, there are some attractive white-sand beaches, some with dunes and good surf and windsurfing, and accommodation nearby. Bring mosquito repellent.

Cabo Frio vies with Porto Seguro for the title of Brazil's first city. The navigator Amerigo Vespucci landed here in 1503 and returned to Portugal with a boatload of *pau brasil*. Since the wood in these parts was of better quality than that further north, the area subsequently became the target for loggers from France, the Netherlands and England. The Portuguese failed to capitalize on their colony here and it was the French who established the first defended settlement. Eventually the Portuguese took it by force but it was not until the second decade of the 17th century that they planned their own fortification, the **Forte São Mateus** ① *daily 0800-1800*, which was started in 1618 on the foundations of the French fort. It is now a ruin at the mouth of the Canal de Itajuru, with rusting cannons propped up against its whitewashed ramparts. The canal connects Lagoa Araruama with the ocean.

The town beach, **Praia do Forte**, is highly developed and stretches south for about 7.5 km to Arraial do Cabo, its name changing to **Praia das Dunas** (after the dunes) and **Praia do Foguete**. These waters are much more suited to surfing.

North of the canal entrance and town is the small under-developed beach of **Praia Brava** (popular with surfers and naturists) and the wine-glass bay of **Praia das Conchas**, which has a few shack restaurants. Next is **Praia do Peró**, 7 km of surf and sand on the open sea with a small town behind it and cheap accommodation. The best dunes are at Peró, Dama Branca (on road to Arraial) and the Pontal dunes at Praia do Forte.

Tourist information

Tourist office
Av do Contorno s/n, Algodoal, T022-2647 1689, www.cabofrio.tur.br or www.cabofrioturismo.rj.gov.br. Located in a big orange building.

Where to stay

$$$ La Plage
R das Badejos 40, Peró, T022-2647 1746, www.laplage.com.br. Cheaper in low season. Fully equipped suites; those upstairs have a sea view, excellent for families. Right on the beach, services include pool and bar, à la carte restaurant, hydro-massage, sauna, 24-hr cyber café, garage.

$$ Pousada São Lucas
R Goiás 266, Jardim Excelsior, T022-2645 3037, www.pousadasaolucas.com.br (formerly a youth hostel). 3 mins from the *rodoviária*. Price is for double room with TV. Also has dorms with hot shower, breakfast and fan (a little cheaper in low season).

Restaurants

The neat row of restaurants on Av dos Pescadores are worth a browse for good-value seafood and pasta. They have French-style seating on the pavement under awnings.

$$$-$$ Picolino
R Mcal F Peixoto 319, Blvd Canal, T022-2647 6222, www.restaurantepicolino.com.br. In a nice old building, very smart, with a mixed menu of seafood and a few international dishes.

Transport

Air The **airport**, Estrada Velha do Arraial do Cabo s/n, T022-2647 9500, www.aeroporto cabofrio.com.br, receives flights in high season from **Rio de Janeiro**, **Belo Horizonte**, **São Paulo**, **Ribeirão Preto**, and **Uberlândia** with **GOL**, www.voegol.com.br.

Local bus **Salineira** and **Montes Brancos** run the local services. US$1.35 to places such as **Búzios**, **São Pedro da Aldeia**, **Saquarema**, **Araruama**, **Arraial do Cabo**. The urban bus terminal is near Largo de Santo Antônio, opposite the BR petrol station.

Long distance bus The inter-city and interstate *rodoviária* is 2 km from the centre. Buses to **Rio de Janeiro** every 30 mins, 2½ hrs, from US$11.50. To **Búzios**, from the local bus terminal in the town centre, every hour, US$1. **Útil** to **Belo Horizonte**, from US$30. **Macaense** runs frequent services to **Macaé**. To **São Paulo**, at 1000 and 2100, US$30, with **Auto Viação 1001**.

For the route from Cabo Frio to **Vitória** either take **Macaense** bus to **Macaé** (5¼ hrs), or take **1001** to **Campos** (3½ hrs, US$5.60), and change. **1001** stops in Campos first at the **Shopping Estrada** *rodoviária*, which is the one where the bus connection is made, but it's outside town (US$3 taxi to the centre, or local bus US$0.35). The **1001** then goes on to the local *rodoviária*, closer to the centre, but there are no long-distance services from that terminal. Shopping Estrada *rodoviária* has a tourist office, but no cheap hotels nearby. **Aguia Branca** buses to **Vitória** at 0900 and 1900, US$8.10, 3 hrs 40 mins.

Búzios (population 18,000) is the principal resort of choice for Carioca and Mineira upper-middle classes searching for their idea of St Tropez sophistication. When it was discovered by Brigitte Bardot in 1964 it was little more than a collection of colonial fishermen's huts and a series of pristine beaches hidden beneath steep hills covered in maquis-like vegetation. Now traffic is so heavy there are one-way streets, as well as strings of hotels behind all of those beaches. The huts have become lost within a designated tourist village of bars, bikini boutiques and restaurants, most of which are strung along the main street, Rua das Pedras.

Bardot sits here too, cheesily immortalized in brass, and subsequently in tens of thousands of pictures taken by the troops of cruise line passengers who fill the streets of Búzios in high season. St Tropez this is not, but it can be fun for 20-somethings who are single and looking not to stay that way. The beaches are beautiful and there are a few romantic hotels with wonderful views.

Beaches
During the daytime, the best option is to head for the beaches, of which there are 25. The most visited are **Geribá** (many bars and restaurants; popular with surfers), **Ferradura** (deep-blue sea and calm waters), **Ossos** (the most famous and close to the centre), **Tartaruga** and **João Fernandes**. The better surf beaches, such as **Praia de Manguinhos** and **Praia de Tucuns**, are further from the town centre. To help you to decide which beach suits you best, you can join one of the local two- or three-hour schooner trips (contact **Buziana** ① *T022-2623 2922, www.buzianatour.com.br, US$30*, which pass many of the beaches, or hire a beach buggy (available from agencies on Rua das Pedras or through most hotels and hostels).

Essential Búzios

Finding your feet
The Búzios *rodoviária* is a few blocks' walk from the centre. Some *pousadas* are within 10 mins' walk, while for others you'll need to take a local bus (US$0.73) or taxi. The buses from Cabo Frio run the length of the peninsula and pass several *pousadas*.

Tip...
Avoid travelling back to Rio on Sun nights and during the peak holiday season because the traffic can be appalling.

Listings Búzios

Tourist information

For most of the hotels and services on the peninsula check www.buziosonline.com.br or www.buzios.rj.gov.br. Maps are available from hotels and tourist offices.

Main tourist office
Manguinos, Pórtico de Búzios s/n, T022-2633 6200, T0800-249999, www.buziosturismo.com. Open 24 hrs.

At the entrance to town on the western edge of the peninsula. It has helpful staff, some of whom speak English. There's another office at Praça Santos Dumont (T022-2623 2099), in the centre of Búzios town, which is more limited.

Where to stay

Rooms in Búzios are overpriced and during peak season, overbooked. Prior reservations are needed in summer, during holidays such as Carnaval and New Year's Eve, and at weekends. For cheaper options and better availability, try Cabo Frio.

Several private houses rent rooms, especially in summer and holidays. Look for the signs: 'Alugo quartos'.

$$$$ Casas Brancas
Alto do Humaitá 10, T022-2623 1458, www.casasbrancas.com.br.
Mock-Mykonos buildings with separate terraces for the pool and spa areas. Sweeping views over the bay. Wonderfully romantic at night when it is lit by candlelightIf you can't afford to stay, come for dinner. The **Abracadabra** (www.abracadabrapousada. com.br) next door is owned by **Casas Brancas** and is similar though cheaper and less stylish. The hotel runs a decent streetside pizza restaurant below the hotel.

$$$$ Pousada Byblos
Alto do Humaitá 14, T022-2623 1162, www.byblos.com.br.
Lovely views out over the bay and bright, light rooms with tiled floors and balconies.

$$$ Pousada Hibiscus Beach
R 1 No 22, quadra C, Praia de João Fernandes, T022-2623 6221, www.hibiscusbeach.com.
A peaceful spot, run by its British owners, overlooking Praia de João Fernandes,
15 pleasant bungalows, a/c, satellite TV, garden, pool, light meals available, help with car/buggy rentals and local excursions. One of the best beach hotels.

$$$ Pousada Pedra da Laguna
R 6, lote 6, Praia da Ferradura, T022-2623 1965, www.pedradalaguna.com.br.
Spacious rooms, the best with a view, 150 m from the beach. Part of the **Roteiros de Charme** group (see page 24).

$$$ Pousada Santorini
R 9, Lote 28, Quadra C, Praia João Fernandes, T022-2623 2802, www.pousadasantorini. com.br.
Good service, lovely beach views from a maquis-covered ridge, clean mock-Greek island design and spacious rooms and public areas.

$$ Ville Blanche
R Manoel T de Farias, 222, T022-2623 1201, http://villeblanchebuzios.blogspot.co.uk.
A hostel and hotel right in the centre in the street parallel to R da Pedras with a/c dorms for up to 10, and light-blue tiled doubles with fridges, en suites and a balcony. Can be noisy.

Restaurants

See also Casas Brancas, page 114, for fine views and romantic dining.

$$$ Bar do Ze
Orla Bardot 282, www.bardozebuzios.com.br.
Lovely spot for candlelit dinner. Come at sunset for a caipirinha and then follow with

starlit alfresco dining and delicious seafood dishes like prawn (*camarão*) risotto or octopus (*polvo oriental*).

$$$ Satyricon
Av José Bento Ribeiro Dantas 500, Orla Bardot Praia da Armação (in front of Morro da Humaitá), T022-2623 2691.
The most illustrious restaurant in Búzios, specializing in Italian seafood. Decent wine list.

$$$ Sawasdee Bistrô
Av José Bento Ribeiro Dantas 422, Orla Bardot, T022-2623 4644, www.sawasdee. com.br.
Marcos Sodré's Brazilian take on Thai (and Indonesian) food is strong on flavour but very light on spice (for those used to genuine article). Try the *tom yam* prawn and coconut milk soup made with crustaceans brought in straight from the sea. Vegetarian options.

$$$-$$ O Barco
Av José Bento Ribeiro Dantas 1054, Orla Bardot, T022-2629 8307.
Very simple restaurant overlooking the water, run and owned by a fishmonger, and offering the freshest seafood. Come early to ensure a table. Very popular.

Bars and clubs

In season, nightlife in Búzios is young, beautiful and buzzing. Out of season it is non-existent.

Most of the bars and the handful of clubs are on Orla Bardot. These include **Zapata**, a bizarrely shaped Mexican theme-bar and restaurant with dancing and electronica; and **Privilege** (Av José Bento Ribeiro Dantas 550, Orla Bardot). **Pacha** (R das Pedras 151, T021-2292 9606, www.pachabuzios.com), is Búzios's main club and the sister of its namesake in Ibiza, with pumping techno, house and hip-hop and a cavernous dance floor. There are plenty of others on and around Av José Bento Ribeiro Dantas.

Shopping

Many of Brazil's fashionable and beautiful come here for their holidays and Búzios is therefore a good place to pick up the kind of beach clothes and tropical cuts that they would wear. Although seemingly expensive these clothes are a fraction of what you would pay for labels of this quality in Europe, the US or Australia. Shopping is best on R das Pedras. Aside from the boutiques, there is little else of interest beyond the expected range of tourist tack shops. Of the boutiques the best are as follows: Osklen, Salinas, Farm, Reserva and Lenny Niemeyer.

What to do

Tour operators
Malizia, *Av José Bento Ribeiro Dantas, Orla Bardot, T022-2623 2022, www.malizia tour.com.br.* Money exchange, car hire and other services.
Mister Tours, *R Germiniano J Luís 3, Centro, T022-2623 2100, www.mistertours.com.br.*

Transport

Beach buggies A popular way to get around the cobbled streets of Búzios. Buggy rental is available through most *pousadas* and travel agencies on R das Pedras, or through **Malízia**, T022-2623 2022.

Bus The Búzios *rodoviária* is a few blocks' walk from the centre. **1001**, T021-4004 5001, www.autoviacao1001.com.br, to **Rio de Janeiro**, US$12-16, 2 hrs 40 mins (be at the bus terminal 20 mins before departure), 7 departures daily. Buses running between the *rodoviária* Novo Rio in **Rio de Janeiro** and **Cabo Frio** stop at Búzios and are more frequent. Cabo Frio is a 30-min journey from Búzios. Buying the ticket in advance is only recommended on high season and major holidays.

Car By car via the BR-106 takes about 2½ hrs to **Rio de Janeiro** and can take far longer on Sun nights and on Brazilian public holidays.

Inland resorts
& coffee towns

The mountain resorts of Petrópolis, Teresópolis and Nova Friburgo are set high in the scenic Serra do Mar behind Rio. All three are lovely mountain retreats with accommodation in charming *fazendas* (coffee estates). The imperial city of Petrópolis retains many of its original buildings and boasts what is perhaps Brazil's finest museum. This is a beautiful area and is becoming increasingly popular for walking, as well as horse riding and other activities. The resorts were originally established because the cool mountain air offered a respite from the heat of Rio and from yellow fever and other diseases that festered in the unhealthy port in the 19th century. They also provided the routes that brought first gold, then coffee from the interior to the coast.

Emperor Pedro I, who tired of the sticky summer heat in Rio, longed for a summer palace in the cool of the Atlantic coastal mountains but abdicated before he could realize his dream. When the new emperor, Pedro II, took the throne, he soon approved plans presented by the German architect Julius Friedrich Köler for a palace and a new city, to be settled by immigrants. The result was Petrópolis (population 290,000).

The city was founded in 1843 and in little over a decade had become a bustling Germanic town and an important imperial summer retreat. The emperor and his family would spend as much as six months of each year here and, as he had his court in tow, Köler was able to construct numerous grand houses and administrative buildings. Many of these still stand – bizarre Rhineland anomalies in a neotropical landscape.

Sights

Three rivers dominate the layout of Petrópolis: the **Piabanha**, **Quitandinha** and the **Palatino**. In the historic centre, where most of the sites of tourist interest are to be found, the rivers have been channelled to run down the middle of the main avenues. Their banks are planted with flowering trees and the overall aspect is unusual in Brazil; you quickly get a sense that this was a city built with a specific purpose and at a specific time in Brazil's history.

Petrópolis's main attraction is its imperial palace. The **Museu Imperial** ① *R da Imperatriz 220, T024-2237 8000, www.museuimperial.gov.br, Tue-Sun 1100-1730, last entry 1700, US$2.70, under 6s free, expect long queues on Sun during Easter and high season*, is so

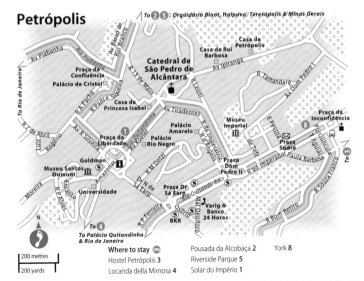

Petrópolis

Where to stay
Hostel Petrópolis **3**
Locanda della Mimosa **4**

Pousada da Alcobaça **2**
Riverside Parque **5**
Solar do Império **1**

York **8**

well kept you might think the imperial family had left the day before, rather than in 1889. It's modest for an emperor, neoclassical in style and fully furnished, and is worth a visit if just to see the crown jewels of both Pedro I and Pedro II. The palace gardens in front are filled with little fountains, statues and shady benches. Descendants of the original family live in a house behind the palace. Horse-drawn carriages wait to be hired outside the gate; not all the horses are in good shape.

Opposite the Museu Imperial is the handsome **Palácio Amarelo** ① *Praça Visconde de Mauá 89, T024-2291 9200, Tue-Sun 0900-1800, free*, built in 1850 as the palace of another Brazilian baron and now the Câmara Municipal (town hall). The twin shady *praças* **dos Expedicionários** and **Dom Pedro II** (which has a pigeon-covered statue of the emperor) lie opposite each other at the junction of Rua do Imperador and Rua da Imperatriz, 100 m south of the Museu Imperial (left as you leave the museum). A small **market** is held here on Sundays and there are a handful of cafés and restaurants.

At the northern end of Rua da Imperatriz (turn right out of the museum and follow the river as it curves left along Avenida Tiradentes) is the Gothic revival **Catedral de São Pedro de Alcântara** ① *R São Pedro de Alcântara 60, T024-2242 4300, Tue-Sun 0800-1200 and 1400-1800, free*, where Emperor Pedro II, his wife Princesa Teresa, Princesa Isabel and Count D'Eu are entombed in mock-European regal marble.

This lies at the end of the city's most impressive avenue, **Avenida Koeler**, which is lined with mansions built by the imperial and republican aristocracy. Among them are the neoclassical **Palácio Rio Negro** ① *Av Koeler 255, T024-2246 9380, Mon 1200-1700, Wed-Sun 0930-1700, free, multilingual guides*, built in 1889 by the Barão do Rio Negro as the summer retreat of Brazilian presidents, and the **Casa da Princesa Isabel** ① *Av Koeler 42, outside visits only*, the former residence of Dom Pedro II's daughter and her husband the Count D'Eu.

Avenida Koeler ends at the **Praça da Liberdade** (formerly known as Praça Rui Barbosa) where there are cafés, goat-drawn carts for children and very photogenic views of the cathedral. A further 100 m west of the *praça* (away from Avenida Koeler) is the **Museu Santos Dumont** ① *R do Encanto 22, T024-2247 3158, Tue-Sun 0930-1700, US$2, free for under 6s*. The summer home of Alberto Santos Dumont, who Brazilians claim was the first man to fly an aeroplane, was designed in 1918 as a mock-Alpine chalet. Santos Dumont called it 'the enchanted one', and it is a delightful example of an inventor's house. Steps to the roof lead to an observation point and are carefully designed to allow visitors only to ascend right foot first. His desk doubled up to become his bed. The alcohol-heated shower is said to be the first in Brazil.

The city has a handful of other interesting buildings. The **Casa de Rui Barbosa** ① *Av Ipiranga 405, private residence*, was the home of the Bahian media mogul and writer who was instrumental in abolishing slavery in Brazil. The **Casa de Petrópolis** ① *Av Ipiranga 716, outside visits only*, is a magnificent Gothic folly set in formal French gardens and was built in 1884 by José Tavares Guerra, the grandson of the founder of industrialization in Brazil, the Barão de Maúa. Taking centre stage in the Praça da Confluência is the **Palácio de Cristal**, which was commissioned and built in France following London's great exhibition, when such palaces were all the rage in Europe. It opened to great aplomb, fell into disrepair in the 20th century and is now the home of weekend concerts and shows.

Some 10 km from the centre, on the way to the BR-040 to Rio, is the **Palácio Quitandinha** ① *Av Joaquim Rolla 2, T024-2237 1012, Tue-Sat 1000-1700, Sun 1000-1600, free, guided tour US$2.70*, a vast mock-Bavarian edifice that was built in 1944 to be the largest casino in South America. The lake in front of the building is in the shape of Brazil. Further out of town still is the **Orquidário Binot** ⓘ *R Fernandes Vieira 390, T024-2248 5665, Mon-Fri 0800-1100 and 1300-1600, Sat 0700-1100.* This nursery has one of the best collections of Brazilian orchids in the state and is well worth visiting even if you don't intend to buy.

Tourist information

Tourist office
Praça da Liberdade, at the far southwestern end of Avenida Koeler. Mon-Sat 0900-1800, Sun 0900-1700.
It has a list of tourist sights and hotels, a good, free, colour map of the city, and a useful pamphlet in various languages. Some staff are multilingual and very helpful.

Where to stay

Good budget accommodation is hard to find, but bargaining is possible Mon-Fri.

$$$$ Locanda della Mimosa
Alameda das Mimosas, Vale Florido, T024-2233 5405, www.locanda.com.br.
A 6-room *pousada* in a terracotta Palladian villa in the mountains near town, overlooking a little pool. The owner is one of the finest chefs in Brazil, see Restaurants, below.

$$$$ Pousada da Alcobaça
R Agostinho Goulão 298, Correas, T024-2221 1240, www.pousadadaalcobaca.com.br.
In the **Roteiros de Charme** group (see page 24). Delightful, family-run large country house set in flower-filled gardens leading down to a river, with pool and sauna.

$$$$ Solar do Império
Av Koeler 376, T024-2103 3000, www.solardoimperio.com.br.
A luxury boutique hotel with period furniture in a converted mansion opposite the Palácio Rio Negro. Excellent spa and restaurant.

$$$ Riverside Parque
R Hermogéneo Silva 522, Retiro, 5 mins from the centre, T024-2246 9850, www.hoteis-riverside.com.br.

Mock-colonial hotel with a nice outdoor pool set in attractive gardens with views of the surrounding countryside. The helpful owner can arrange tours.

$$ Hostel Petrópolis
R Santos Dumont 345, Centro, T024-2237 3811, www.hostel petropolisoficial.com.br.
Well-kept and well-run hostel situated in a brightly painted red townhouse conveniently located in the city centre.

$$ York
R do Imperador 78, near the rodoviária, T024-2243 2662, www.hotelyork.com.br.
Convenient package-tour hotel with faded 1980s rooms, decent breakfast.

Restaurants

Bakeries and cheap eateries are located by the *rodoviária*.

$$$ Locanda della Mimosa
Alameda das Mimosas, Vale Florido, T024-2233 5405, www.locanda.com.br.
One of the best restaurants in Brazil, offering fusion cooking with a focus on game. Danio Braga was 4 times *Quatro Rodas* chef of the year. The 3000-bottle wine cellar includes heavyweights like 1990 Château Haut-Brion.

What to do

Rio Serra, *T024-2235 7607, www.rioserra.com.br/trekking.* Horse riding, trekking, whitewater rafting and a range of trips into the scenic mountain area, multilingual guides.
Roz Brazil, *T024-9257 0236, www.rozbrazil.com.* Some of the best drive and light walk tours around Petrópolis, Teresópolis and the Serra dos Órgãos with British Brazilian Rosa Thompson, who has been living in the area for decades. Pick-ups from Rio.

Transport

Bus Buses run to **Rio de Janeiro** every 30 mins throughout the day (US$6.50), Sun every hour, 1-1¼ hrs, sit on the right-hand side for best views, www.unica-facil.com.br. Ordinary buses arrive in Rio at the *rodoviária*; a/c buses run hourly and arrive at Av Nilo Peçanha, US$4. Book your return journey as soon as you arrive in Petrópolis. Bus to **Niterói**, US$7.20; to **Cabo Frio**, US$16. To **Teresópolis**, 8 a day, US$3. To **São Paulo** daily at 2330.

Teresópolis

a useful base for visiting the nearby Serra dos Órgãos

At 910 m Teresópolis (population 140,000) is the highest city in the state of Rio de Janeiro. It was the favourite summer retreat of Empress Teresa Cristina and is named after her. However, development in recent years has destroyed some of the city's character. It's a good base for visiting Serra dos Órgãos (see opposite).

Listings Teresópolis

Tourist information

Secretaria de Turismo
Praça Olímpica, T021-2742 3352, ext 2082.
Information is also available from the **Terminal Turístico Tancredo Neves** (Av Rotariana, T021-2642 2094, www.teresopolis.rj.gov.br), which is at the entrance to town from Rio. There are very good views of the serra from here.

Where to stay

Many cheap hotels are on R Delfim Moreira.

$$$$ Fazenda Rosa dos Ventos
Km 22 on the road to Nova Friburgo, T021-2644 9900, www.hotelrosadosventos.com.br.
Part of the **Roteiros de Charme** chain. One of the best hotels in inland Rio with a range of chalets in 1 million sq m of private forest and with wonderful views. Excellent restaurant.

$ Recanto do Lord Hostel
R Luiza Pereira Soares 109, Centro-Artistas, T021-2742 5586, www.teresopolishostel.com.br.
Family-oriented hostel with rooms and dorms, kitchen, cable TV and barbecue area. Camping is permitted beside the hostel.

Transport

Bus The *rodoviária* is at R 1 de Maio 100. Buses to **Rio de Janeiro** Novo Rio *rodoviária* every 30 mins. Book your return journey as soon as you arrive in Teresópolis. Fare US$3.60. From Teresópolis to **Petrópolis**, 8 a day, US$3.

These mountains near Teresópolis, named after their strange rock formations, which are said to look like organ pipes, preserve some of the most diverse stretches of Atlantic coast forest in the state of Rio de Janeiro. The flora and fauna (especially birdwatching) here are excellent, as are the walking and rock climbing.

The best way to see the park is on foot. A number of trails cut through the forest and head up into the alpine slopes, including the ascent of the **Dedo de Deus** (God's Finger); a precipitous peak that requires some climbing skills. Other trails lead to the highest point in the park, the **Pedra do Sino** (Bell Rock), 2263 m, a three- to four-hour climb up a 14-km path. The west face of this mountain is one of the hardest climbing pitches in Brazil.

Other popular walks include the **Pedra do Açu trail** and paths to a variety of anatomically named peaks and outcrops: O Escalavrado (The Scarred One), O Dedo de Nossa Senhora (Our Lady's Finger), A Cabeça de Peixe (Fish Head), A Agulha do Diabo (The Devil's Needle) and A Verruga do Frade (The Friar's Wart).

Flora and fauna

The park belongs to the threatened Mata Atlântica coastal rainforest, designated by **Conservation International** as a global biodiversity hot spot and the preserve of what are probably the richest habitats in South America outside the Amazonian cloudforests. There are 20- to 30-m-high trees, such as *paineiras* (floss-silk tree), *ipês* and *cedros*, rising above palms, bamboos and other smaller trees. Flowers include begonias, bromeliads, orchids and *quaresmeiras* (glorybushes).

The park is home to numerous rare and endemic birds including cotingas, the rarest of which is the grey-winged cotinga, as well as guans, tanagers, berryeaters and trogons. Mammals include titi and capuchin monkeys, all of the neotropical rainforest cats including jaguar and ocelot, tapir and white collared peccary. Reptiles include the *sapo-pulga* (flea-toad), which at 10 mm long vies with the Cuban pygmy frog as the smallest amphibian in the world.

Essential Serra dos Órgãos

Getting around

If you have a car, a good way to see the park is to do the Rio–Teresópolis–Petrópolis–Rio road circuit, stopping off for walks in the forest. This can be done in a day. The park has two ranger stations, both accessible from the BR-116: the **Sede** (headquarters, T021-2642 1070), is closer to Teresópolis (from town take Avenida Rotariana), while the **Sub-Sede** is just outside the park proper, off the BR-116. By the Sede entrance is the Mirante do Soberbo, with views to the Baía de Guanabara. Both the Sede station and the Mirante can be reached on the bus marked 'Mirante do Soberbo', which leaves every half an hour from the Teresópolis *rodoviária* and city centre.

Entry information

Anyone can enter the park and hike the trails from the Teresópolis gate, but if you intend to climb the Pedra do Sino, you must sign a register (those under 18 must be accompanied by an adult and have permission from the park authorities). Entrance to the park is US$2, with an extra charge for the path to the top of the Pedra do Sino. For information, contact the Rio de Janeiro branch of **Ibama** (T021-2231 1772).

Reserva Ecológica de Guapi Assu (REGUA)

www.regua.org, Feb-Dec (closed Jan) dawn to dusk daily, overnight full board and guiding from US$150.

This reserve is a 9100-ha private reserve run by the Anglo-Brazilian Locke family protecting one of the few truly pristine stretches of Atlantic coastal wild country close to Rio, in the Serra dos Órgãos. Not only are there large stretches of Mata Atlântica rainforest but Regua is one of the few locations in southeast Brazil with large stretches coastal restinga alongside wetlands. The biodiversity is very high and thanks to constant vigilance by park guards rare species exist in burgeoning numbers. They include America's biggest primate, the Muriqui, which looks like a small yeti, as well as marmoset monkeys small enough to sit in your palm and 470 species of bird.

Listings Serra dos Órgãos

Where to stay

Ibama has some hostels but they are a bit rough.

$$$$ Reserva Ecológica de Guapi Assu (REGUA)
Cachoeiras de Macacu-RJ, T021-2745 3998, www.regua.co.uk.
A British-run conservation NGO and ecotourism project focused on a large main house with several rooms, set in primary rainforest. Expert guided walks into the reserve, in one of the richest areas in the state for birds, mammals and orchids.

$$$$ Serra dos Tucanos
Caixa Postal 98125, Cachoeiras do Macacu, T021-2649 1557, www.serradostucanos.com.br.
One of the best wildlife and birdwatching lodges in Brazil with excellent guiding, equipment and accommodation in a comfortable lodge set in the Atlantic coastal rainforest.

What to do

Tours are available through the tourist office or the HI **Recanto do Lord** (www.recantodolord.com.br) in Teresópolis.
See also **Roz Brazil**, page 97.
Lazer Tours, *T024-2742 7616*. Tours of the park are offered by Francisco (find him at the grocery shop on R Sloper 1). Recommended.

West of
Rio de Janeiro

Towns to the west of Rio are mostly spread along the ugly Rio–São Paulo motorway known as the Via Dutra. None are appealing. But the mountains that watch over them preserve important tracts of Atlantic coast rainforest, particularly around Itatiaia. This is one of the best places close to Rio for seeing wild animals and virgin rainforest and is the country's oldest protected area. The little mock-Alpine resort of Visconde de Mauá sits in the same mountain chain a little further towards São Paulo, although the forest here is less well preserved.

Itatiaia is a must for those who wish to see Brazilian forest and animals and have a restricted itinerary or limited time. Itatiaia's virgin rainforest hides rocky clear-water rivers and icy waterfalls. Little winding trails pass through a whole swathe of different ecosystems, watched over by some of world's rarest birds and mammals. There are hotels and guesthouses to suit all budgets from which to explore them. And all are within easy reach of Rio or São Paulo.

This 30,000-ha mountainous park is Brazil's oldest. It was founded in 1937 to protect Atlantic coast rainforest in the Serra de Mantiqueira mountains, and important species still find a haven here, including jaguars and pumas, brown capuchin and black-faced titi monkeys.

This is good hiking country with walks through subtropical and temperate forests, grasslands and *paramo* to a few peaks just under 3000 m. The best trails head for Pedra de Taruga, Pedra de Maçã and the Poranga and Véu de Noiva waterfalls. The Pico das Agulhas Negras and Serra das Prateleiras (up to 2540 m) offer good rock climbing. There is a **Museu de História Natural** ① *Tue-Sun 1000-1600*, near the park headquarters with a depressing display of stuffed animals from the 1940s.

Flora and fauna

The park is particularly good for birds. It has a list of more than 350 species with scores of spectacular tanagers, hummingbirds (including the ultra-rare Brazilian ruby, with emerald wings and a dazzling red chest), cotingas (included the black and gold cotinga, which as far as we are aware has never been photographed) and manakins. Guans squawk and flap right next to the park roads.

The vegetation is stratified by altitude so that the plateau at 800-1100 m is covered by forest, ferns and flowering plants (such as orchids, bromeliads, begonias), giving way on the higher escarpments to pines and bushes. Higher still, over 1900 m, the distinctive rocky landscape has low bushes and grasses, isolated trees and unique plants adapted to high winds and strong sun. There is also a great variety of lichens.

Hiking trails

The park also offers excellent trail walking, one of the best ways of seeing a good cross section of the habitats and their flora and fauna. There are peaks with magnificent views out over the Atlantic coastal forest and the Rio de Janeiro coastline and a series of beautiful waterfalls; many of which are easily accessible from the park road. The trails, most of which begin just behind the Hotel Simon or around the visitor centre, cut through the forest, bushland and up into the alpine paramo, dotted with giant granite boulders. The views from here are breathtaking.

Be sure to take plenty of water, repellent and a fleece for the higher areas. Temperatures can drop well below 0°C in the winter. Information on the trails is available from the visitor centre (see under Tourist information, below), which holds maps and gives directions to all the trail heads (though English is poor). The adjacent museum has a collection of stuffed animals, all of which exist in fully animated form in the park itself.

Maciço das Prateleiras peak, one of the highest in the park (2548 m) is a full day's walk for experienced hikers. When there is no mist the views are magnificent. To get there, take the trail from Abrigo Rebouças mountain lodge, reached from the BR354 road that

Essential Parque Nacional de Itatiaia

Finding your feet

Itatiaia lies just off the main São Paulo–Rio highway, the Dutra. A bus marked '504 Circular' runs from Itatiaia town four times a day (variable hours) to the park, calling at the hotels in town. The bus can also be caught at Resende, at the crossroads before Itatiaia. Tickets are sold at a booth in the large bar in the middle of Itatiaia main street.

The alternative option involves adding another 10- to 15-km on to your journey depending on where you are staying in town. There is one bus that goes to the park used mostly by the park employees. The bus leaves at 0700 from the road that leads to the park's gate. It takes about 30 minutes and costs about US$1; stay in the bus until the last stop. Check out the return time in advance. There are also guides that provide their own transport. A local guide for this trek costs US$10 per person.

Getting around

The best way to see the park is to hire a car or with a tour operator (see What to do, below). There is only one way into the park from Itatiaia town and one main road within it – which forks off to the various hotels, all of which are signposted.

Entry information

Entry per day is US$8.

> **Tip...**
> Avoid weekends and Brazilian holidays if wildlife watching is a priority.

heads north out of Engenheiro Passos – the next town beyond Itatiaia on BR116 (The Dutra). From here it is around 1½ hours. **Pico das Agulhas Negras** is the highest point in the park (2787 m) and is reached via the same route as Maçico das Prateleiras, but with a turn to the east at the Abrigo Rebouças (instead of west). The upper reaches are only accessible with a rope and moderate climbing experience. This is another full day's walk. **Tres Picos** is a six-hour walk, leaving from a trail signposted off to the right, about 3 km beyond the visitor centre. It is one of the best for a glimpse of the park's various habitats. The first half of the trail is fairly gentle, but after about an hour the path gets progressively steep. An hour or so beyond the steep trail is the **Rio Bonito** – a great place for a break, where there is a beautiful waterfall for swimming and refreshment. There are wonderful views from the top, which is another 45 minutes further on. The **Piscina do Maromba** is a natural pool formed by the Rio Campo Belo and situated at 1100 m. It's one of the most refreshing places to swim in the park – although most Brazilians find it far too cold. Trails leave for here from behind Hotel Simon.

There are a number of **waterfalls** in the park; most of which have pools where you can swim. The most accessible is **Cachoeira Poranga** – left off the park road about 3.5 km beyond the visitor centre. **Itaporani** and **Véu da Noiva** are reached by a path just beyond the Poranga trail; which leaves from next to the road bridge and divides after about 1 km – left for Véu da Noiva, right for Itaporani.

Engenheiro Passos

Further along the Dutra highway (186 km from Rio) is the small town of Engenheiro Passos (population 3500), from which a road (BR-354) leads to São Lourenço and Caxambu in Minas Gerais. By turning off this road at the Registro Pass (1670 m) on the Rio–Minas border, you can reach the **Pico das Agulhas Negras**.

The mountain can be climbed from this side from the **Abrigo Rebouças** refuge at 2350 m, which is manned all year round; US$2.70 per night, take your own food.

Listings Parque Nacional de Itatiaia

Tourist information

See www.icmbio.gov.br/parnaitatiaia/en for lots of useful information (in English) on the park.

Administração do Parque Nacional de Itatiaia
Estrada Parque Km 8.5, www.ibama.gov.br/ parna_itatiaia.
The park office has information and maps. Information can also be obtained from Ibama (T024-33521461 for the local headquarters, or T021-3224 6463 for the Rio de Janeiro state department).

Clube Excursionista Brasileiro
Av Almirante Barroso 2, 8th floor, Rio de Janeiro, T021-2252 9844, www.ceb.org.br.
Information on trekking.

Where to stay

Basic accommodation in cabins and dormitories is available in the village strung along the road leading to the park. There are some delightful options inside the park but they are more expensive. The Administração do Parque Nacional de Itatiaia (see Tourist information, above) operates several refuges in the park, including Abrigo Rebouças (see under Engenheiro Passos, above).

$$$ Hotel Donati
T024-3352 1110, www.hoteldonati.com.br.
One of the most delightful hotels in the country – mock-Swiss chalets and rooms, set in tropical gardens visited by animals every night and early morning. A series of trails leads off from the main building and the hotel can organize professional birding

guides. Decent restaurant and 2 pools. Highly recommended.

$$ Hotel do Ypê
T024-3352 7453, www.hoteldoype.com.br.
Inside the park with sauna and heated pool.

$$ Pousada Aldeia dos Passaros
T024-3352 1152, pousadaaldeiadospassaros. com.br.
10 chalets with fireplaces and balconies in secondary forest overlooking a stream in the lower reaches of the park. Great breakfasts, good off-season rates and a riverside sauna.

$$ Pousada Country
Estrada do Parque Nacional 848, T024-3352 1433, www.pousadacountry.com.br.
A bit cheaper but outside the park on the paved access road. There are a couple of other smaller hotels and a restaurant close by.

$$ Pousada Esmeralda
Estrada do Parque, T024-3352 1643, www.pousadaesmeralda.com.br.
Very comfortable chalets set around a lake in a lawned garden and furnished with chunky wooden beds, tables and chests of drawers and warmed by log fires. Be sure to book a table for a candlelit dinner.

$ Ypê Amarelo
R João Maurício Macedo Costa 352, Campo Alegre, T024-3352 1232, www.pousadaypeamarelo.com.br.
Set in an attractive garden visited by hummingbirds.

Engenheiro Passos
Around Engenheiro Passos there are many *fazenda* hotels.

$$$$ Hotel Fazenda 3 Pinheiros *Caxambu, Km 23, T024-2108 1000, www.3pinheiros.com.br.* Large resort charging all inclusive rates with 3 meals provided. Special rates for trekkers that only sleep over are negotiable.

What to do

Edson Endrigo, *T024-3742 8374, www. avesfoto.com.br.* One of Brazil's foremost birding guides, offering birdwatching trips in Itatiaia and throughout Brazil. English spoken.
Ralph Salgueiro, *T024-3351 1823, www.ecoralph.com.* Offers general tours.

Engenheiro Passos
Levy, *T024-3352 6097, T024-8812 0006 (mob), www.levyecologico.com.br.* Experienced guide that takes trekking groups to the high region of Itatiaia Park. Portuguese only.
Miguel, *T024-3360 5224, T024-7834 2128 (mob).* Local guide who knows the region really well. Portuguese only.

Transport

Bus Bus '504 Circular' to/from **Itatiaia town** 4 times daily, picks up from **Hotel Simon** in the park and stops at **Resende** (at the crossroads before Itatiaia) and hotels in town.

Itatiaia town has bus connections with **São Paulo** and **Rio de Janeiro** and it's possible to buy through tickets from the middle of the main street.

Costa
Verde

The Rio de Janeiro–Santos section of the BR-101 is one of the world's most spectacular highways, hugging the forested and hilly Costa Verde southwest of Rio. The Serra do Mar mountains plunge down to the sea in a series of spurs that disappear into the Atlantic to reappear as a cluster of islands offshore. The most beautiful of these is Ilha Grande: an 80,000-ha mountain ridge covered in rainforest and fringed with wonderful beaches. Beyond Ilha Grande, further down the coast towards São Paulo, is one of Brazil's prettiest colonial towns, Paraty, which sits surrounded by long white beaches in front of a glorious bay of islands. Seen from the harbour in the morning light, this is one of Brazil's most photographed sights.

The islands in the bay of Angra dos Reis (population 120,000) are the private playgrounds of Carioca playboys or media islands, owned by magazines devoted to the cult of the Brazilian celebrity, and permanently twinkling with camera flashes. A few islands are thronged with bikinis and board shorts in high season and pulsate to *forró* and samba beats. And many islands are as wild and unspoilt as they were when the Portuguese arrived 500 years ago. Yachts and speedboats flit across the bay, ferrying their bronzed and smiling cargo between the islands and beaches. In between, they dock at floating bars and restaurants for an icy caipirinha or catch of the day, and at night to dance or be lulled by the gentle sound of bossa nova.

Angra town itself is down at heel and a little more than a jumping-off point to the private islands and to Ilha Grande, but it's an increasingly popular destination for international travellers. This is a result of the migration of the wealthy out of Rio and their acquisition of beaches and property from the local fishermen, whose families now live in the favelas that encrust the surrounding hills.

Angra was once a pretty colonial town like Paraty further along the coast, and several buildings remain from its heyday. Of particular note are the church and convent of **Nossa Senhora do Carmo**, built in 1593 on Praça General Osório, the **Igreja Matriz de Nossa Senhora da Conceição** (1626) in the centre of town and the church and convent of **São Bernardino de Sena** (1758-1763) on the Morro do Santo Antônio. On the Largo da Lapa is the church of **Nossa Senhora da Lapa da Boa Morte** (1752) and a **Museum of Sacred Art** ① *Thu-Sun 1000-1200, 1400-1800*.

Essential Costa Verde

Finding your feet

The BR-101 is paved all the way to Santos, which has good links with São Paulo. Buses from Rio run to Angra dos Reis, Paraty, Ubatuba, Caraguatatuba and São Sebastião, where it may be necessary to change for Santos or São Paulo. Hotels and *pousadas* have sprung up all along the road, as have expensive housing developments, though these have not spoiled the views. The drive from Rio to Paraty should take four hours, but it would be better to break the journey and enjoy some of the attractions. The coast road has lots of twists and turns so, if prone to motion sickness, get a seat at the front of the bus to make the most of the views.

On the Península de Angra, west of the town, is the **Praia do Bonfim**, a popular beach; offshore is the island of the same name, on which the **hermitage of Senhor do Bonfim** (1780) is located. Some 15 km east are the ruins of the **Jacuecanga seminary** (1797).

Angra is connected to Rio and Paraty by regular buses, to Ilha Grande by ferry and fishing boat, and to Ilha do Gipóia by fishing boat.

ON THE ROAD

The caiçaras

Brazilians of mixed Indian, African and Portuguese race living on the coast and leading traditional lives fishing and hunting are known as *caiçaras*. Until the 1970s almost all the beaches and islands between Rio de Janeiro and Santos were home to *caiçara* communities. But then the Rio to Santos main highway was constructed and floods of visitors began to pour in. With them came developments – for luxury private houses, hotels and condominiums like Laranjeiras – which is home to members of Brazil's wealthy and allegedly highly corrupt elite. *Caiçara* communities were bought off for pittance or forced from their land with threats of violence or even death. And an entire way of life and knowledge of the Atlantic coast forest, strongly rooted in indigenous traditions is in danger of being entirely lost.

Many of the favelas in Angra dos Reis bear the name of a different beach on Ilha Grande or the beaches and islands around the bay. Nowadays there are *caiçara* communities only on a few isolated stretches between Rio and Santos – like the Ponta da Joatinga peninsula south of Paraty and Aventureiros beach in Ilha Grande. Many think that carefully managed, sensitive ecotourism will help protect them and spread the story of their plight, which is little known even within Brazil.

Listings Angra dos Reis and around

Tourist information

Tourist office
Av Julio Maria, behind the Cais de Santa Luiza quay, T024-3365 2041, www.angra-dos-reis. com, www.angra.rj.gov.br.
The websites have more information than the office.

Where to stay

Only stay in Angra town if you miss your bus or boat. There are a few cheap hotels near the port and main *praça*.

$$$$ Pestana
Estr do Contorno 3700, Km 13, T024-3367 2754, www.pestanahotels.com.br.
A range of bungalows on a forested hillside overlooking an emerald green sea. Very pretty, peaceful and secluded.

$$ Caribe
R de Conceição 255, T024-3365 0033, www.angra2reis.com.br/caribe.

Central and well kept with rather cheesy 1970s rooms in a tower near the centre.

What to do

See **Angatu**, under Paraty, page 141.

Transport

Bus Costa Verde buses (T021-3622 3123, www.costaverdetransportes.com.br) run at least hourly to the *rodoviária* in **Rio de Janeiro**, some are direct, others take the *via litoral* and go through Barra, Ipanema and Copacabana, US$11, 3-3½ hrs. Sit on the right for the best views. Busy at weekends. There are also regular buses to and from **São Paulo**, **Paraty**, **Ubatuba** and the São Paulo coast.

Ferry Ferries run to Ilha Grande, see below. Fishing boats will also take passengers for around US$3.50 per person before 1300 or when full. Boat charters cost around US$40-70.

a relatively undeveloped forest-clad island with stunning beaches

Ilha Grande is a mountain ridge covered in tropical forest protruding from the emerald sea and fringed by some of the world's most beautiful beaches. There are no cars and no roads, just trails through the forest. With luck it will remain undeveloped, as much of Ilha Grande forms part of a state park and biological reserve, and cannot even be visited.

That the island has so much forest is largely a fluke of history. The island was a notorious pirate lair in the 16th and 17th centuries and then a landing port for slaves. By the 20th century it was the site of an infamous prison for the country's most notorious criminals, including the writer Graciliano Ramos, whose *Memórias do Cárcere* relate his experiences. The prison closed in 1994 and is now overgrown. Since then Ilha Grande has been a well-kept Brazilian secret, and is gradually becoming part of the international backpacker circuit.

The weather is best from March to June and the island is overrun during the Christmas, New Year and Carnaval periods. Be wary of undercover police searching for backpackers smoking cannabis on Ilha Grande's beaches. Banks are only open at weekends.

Beaches and walks

The beach at **Abraão** may look beautiful to new arrivals but those further afield are far more spectacular. The two most famous are: **Lopes Mendes**, a long stretch of sand on the eastern (ocean side) backed by flatlands and patchy forest; and **Aventureiro**, fringed by coconut palms and tropical forest, its powder-fine sand pocked with boulders and washed by a transparent aquamarine sea. Lopes Mendes is two hours' walk from Abraão. Aventureiro is over six hours, but it can be reached by boat. A few fishermen's huts and *barracas* provide food and accommodation here but there is no camping.

Good beaches closer to Abraão include the half-moon bay at **Abraãoozinho** (15 minutes' walk) and **Grande das Palmas**, which has a delightful tiny whitewashed

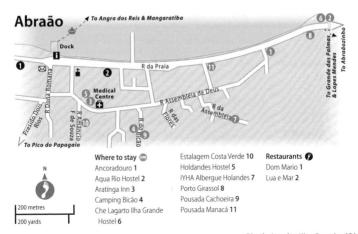

Abraão

Where to stay
Ancoradouro 1
Aqua Rio Hostel 2
Aratinga Inn 3
Camping Bicão 4
Che Lagarto Ilha Grande
  Hostel 6

Estalagem Costa Verde 10
Holdandes Hostel 5
IYHA Albergue Holandes 7
Porto Girassol 8
Pousada Cachoeira 9
Pousada Manacá 11

Restaurants
Dom Mario 1
Lua e Mar 2

chapel (one hour 20 minutes' walk). Both lie east of the town past **Hotel Sagu**. There are boat trips to **Lagoa Azul**, with crystal-clear water and reasonable snorkelling, **Freguesia de Santana** and **Saco do Céu**.

There are a couple of good treks over the mountains to **Dois Rios**, where the old jail was situated. There is still a settlement of former prison guards here who have nowhere to go. The walk is about 13 km each way, takes about three hours and affords beautiful scenery and superb views. Another three-hour hike is to **Pico do Papagaio** (980 m) through forest; it's a steep climb for which a guide is essential, however, the view from the top is breathtaking. **Pico da Pedra d'Água** (1031 m) can also be climbed.

Listings Ilha Grande *map p131*

Tourist information

There is a helpful **tourist office** on the jetty at Abraão. Further information and pictures can be found at www.ilhagrande.com.

Where to stay

Accommodation on the island is in *pousadas* at Vila do Abraão or camping elsewhere. It is possible to hire a fisherman's cottage on Aventureiro Beach, which can be reached on the *Maria Isabel* or *Mestre Ernani* boats (T021-3361 9895 or T021-9269 5877) that leave from the quay in front of the BR petrol station in Angra dos Reis. Alternatively boats can be chartered direct from Angra dos Reis (2-3 hrs). There's a handful of upmarket options in isolated locations reachable only by boat. **Hidden Pousadas Brazil** (www. hiddenpousadasbrazil.com) offers some of the best accommodation on Ilha Grande, both in Abraão and on the quieter beaches.

Abraão

Reservations are only necessary in peak season or on holiday weekends.

$$$ Aratinga Inn
Vila do Abraão, www.aratingailhagrande. com.br, or through Hidden Pousadas.
The simple furnishing in the rooms (there's little more than a bed and a table) are more than made up for by the lovely location, nestled in a lush tropical garden dotted with

boulders right under the brow of Papagaio peak, and the excellent service which includes Anglo-Australian afternoon tea.

$$$ Estrela da Ilha
Praia Pequena da Freguesia de Santana, www.estreladailha.com, or through Hidden Pousadas.
Isolated location northwest of Abraão with magnificent ocean views from airy, rustic but romantic chunky wood rooms and easy access to snorkelling sites and broad sandy beaches. On-site yoga and healthy food; full board.

$$$-$$ Pousada Manacá
Praia do Abraão, T024-3361 5404, www.ilhagrandemanaca.com.br.
Friendly French-Brazilian *pousada* right on the beach with homey light blue rooms decked out with colourful floor tiles, raw brick and with baclonies overlooking the little garden and the beach. Public areas are decorated with art from the Amazon. Wi-Fi throughout.

$$ Ancoradouro
R da Praia 121, T024-3361 5153, www.pousadancoradouro.com.br.
Clean, simple rooms with en suite in a beach-front building, 10 mins' walk east of the jetty.

$$ Aqua Rio Hostel
Town Beach, Abraão, T024-3361 5405, www.aquariohostel.com.
Party hostel on a peninsula overlooking the beach. Dorms, scruffy rooms, a large,

relaxing bar area, seawater pool and great ocean views.

$$ Che Lagarto Ilha Grande Hostel
Town Beach, Abraão, T024-3361 9669, www.chelagarto.com.
Large beachside party hostel with well-kept dorms, doubles, bar and tours including trail walking and kayaking.

$$ Holdandes Hostel
R Assembleia de Deus, T024-3361 5034, www.holandeshostel.com.br.
HI hostel with dorms, doubles and 4 little chalets in the forest on the edge of town. Breakfast included, laundry and advice on boats and tours. Good atmosphere. Book ahead.

$$ Porto Girassol
R do Praia 65, T011-3085 0289/021-99918 7255, http://ilhagrande.org/portogirassol.
Simple whitewash a/c rooms with pine beds and bedside tables in a mock-colonial beach house set in a small garden, 5 mins east of the jetty. The best have balconies with ocean views.

$$ Pousada Cachoeira
12-min walk from centre, T024-3361 9521, www.cachoeira.com. Price per person.
Great little *pousada* full of character, with small rooms in chalets in a forest garden. Run by a German-Brazilian couple; English spoken. Good breakfast.

$$ Pousada Sanhaço
R Santana 120, T024-3361 5102, www.pousadasanhaco.com.
A range of a/c rooms, the best of which have balconies with sea views and cosy en suites. The *pousada* is decorated with paintings by local artists. Wi-Fi throughout, generous breakfast.

$ Estalagem Costa Verde
R Amâncio Felicio de Souza 239a, half a block behind the church, T024-3361 5808, www.estalagemcostaverde.com.br.
Bright hostel with light, well-maintained rooms decorated with a little thought. Great value.

Camping

Camping Bicao
R do Bicão s/n, T024-3361 5061, www.ilhagrande.org/campingdobicao.
Hot showers, lockers, electricity a campsite with lots of shade. There are plenty of other campsites; see www.ilhagrande.com for details in English.

Restaurants

Food on the island is fairly basic: fish, chicken or meat with beans, rice and chips. There are plenty of restaurants serving these exciting combinations in Abraão. We list the very few better options.

$$$ Lua e Mar
Abraão, on the waterfront, T024-3361 5113.
The best seafood restaurant in Abraão with a menu including *bobó do camarão*, fish fillets and various *moquecas*.

$$ Dom Mario
R da Praia, T024-3361 5349.
Good Franco-Brazilian dishes and seafood from a chef who honed his art at the **Meridien** in Rio. Try the fillet of fish in passion fruit sauce.

What to do

Boat trips
These are easy to organize on the quay in Abraão on Ilha Grande.

Scuba diving
Ilha Grande Dive, *R da Praia s/n, Vila do Abraão, T021-3361 5512, igdive@bol.com.br (next to the* farmacia *on the seafront).* Offers trips around the entire bay.

Transport

Bus All the towns are served by Costa Verde buses leaving from the *rodoviária* in Rio.

Ferry For the most up-to-date boat and ferry timetables see www.ilhagrande.org. Fishing boats and ferries (**Barcas SA**, T0800

721 10 12, www.grupoccr.com.br/barcas in Portuguese only) leave from Angra dos Reis, Conceição de Jacareí and Mangaratiba, taking 2 hrs or so to reach **Vila do Abraão**, the island's only real village. From Angra there are 4 daily yachts and catamarans and one ferry (at 1530) leaving 0730-1600, and an extra ferry at 1330 on weekends and public holidays. Note the Angra catamaran leaves from Santa Luiza pier (not the ferry pier). From Conceição de Jacareí there are 7 yacht sailings daily 0900-1815, with an occasional late boat at 2100 on busy Fri. From Mangaratiba there is a ferry at 0800 and a yacht at 1400. Schedules change frequently and it's well worth checking www. ilhagrande.org, which details the names and phone numbers of all boats currently sailing.

Ferries cost US$1.70 on weekdays and double that on weekends, yachts US$6 and catamarans US$20. Buy at least 1 hr in advance to ensure this price, and a place.

From Abraão to Angra there's a boat at 1000, and to Mangaratiba at 1730.

Easy Transfer, T021-99994 3266, www. easytransferbrazil.com, offers a van and boat service from Rio to Ilha Grande; door to door from the city (US$22.60) and from the airport (price depends on flight times and numbers); and from Ilha Grande to Paraty (US$20). There are discounts on multi-trips (eg Rio–Ilha Grande–Paraty–Rio).

Paraty (population 30,000) is one of Rio de Janeiro state's most popular tourist destinations. It is at its most captivating at dawn, when all but the dogs and chickens are sleeping. As the sun peeps over the horizon the little rectilinear streets are infused with a rich golden light, which warms the whitewash and brilliant blue-and-yellow window frames of the colonial townhouses and the façades of the Manueline churches. Brightly coloured fishing boats bob up and down in the water in the foreground and behind the town the deep green of the rainforest-covered mountains of the Serra da Bocaina sit shrouded in their self-generated wispy cloud.

At the weekend Paraty buzzes with tourists who browse in the little boutiques and art galleries or buy souvenirs from the Guarani who proffer their wares on the cobbles. At night they fill the little bars and restaurants, many of which, like the *pousadas*, are owned by the bevy of expat Europeans who have found their haven in Paraty and who are determined to preserve its charm. During the week, especially off season, the town is quiet and intimate, its atmosphere as yet unspoilt by the increasing numbers of independent travellers.

The town's environs are as beautiful as Paraty itself. Just a few kilometres away lie the forests of the **Ponta do Juatinga Peninsula**, fringed by wonderful beaches, washed by little waterfalls and still home to communities of Caiçara fishermen who live much as they have done for centuries. Islands pepper the bay, some of them home to ultra-rare animals such as the tiny golden lion tamarin monkey, which is found nowhere else. The best way to visit these destinations is on a boat trip with one of the town's fishermen from the quay.

Sights

The town was founded in the 17th century as a gold port and most of its historic buildings date from this period. In keeping with all Brazilian colonial towns, Paraty's churches were built according to social status and race. There are four churches in the town, one for the 'freed coloured men', one for the blacks and two for the whites. The recently renovated **Santa Rita** (1722), built by the 'freed coloured men' in elegant Brazilian baroque, faces the bay and the port. It is probably the most famous picture postcard image of Paraty and houses a small **Museum of Sacred Art** ① *Wed-Sun 0800-1200, 1400-1700, US$0.50.* **Nossa Senhora do Rosário e São Benedito** ① *R do Comércio, Tue 0900-1200,* (1725, rebuilt 1757) built by black slaves, is small and simple; the slaves were unable to raise the funds to construct an elaborate building.

Nossa Senhora dos Remédios ① *Mon, Wed, Fri, Sat 0900-1200, Sun 0900-1500,* is the town's parish church, the biggest in Paraty. It was started in 1787 but construction continued until 1873. The church was never completely finished as it was built on unstable ground; the architects decided not to add weight to the structure by putting up

Essential Paraty

Finding your feet

The *rodoviária* is at the corner of Rua Jango Padua and Rua da Floresta. Taxis charge a set rate of US$3 from the bus station to the historic centre, which is pedestrianized and easily negotiable on foot.

When to go

The wettest months are January, February, June and July. In spring, the streets in the colonial centre may flood, but the houses remain above the waterline.

the towers. The façade is leaning to the left, which is clear from the three doors (only the one on the right has a step). Built with donations from the whites, it is rumoured that Dona Geralda Maria da Silva contributed gold from a pirate's hoard found buried on the beach.

Capela de Nossa Senhora das Dores ⓘ *Thu 0900-1200*, (1800), is a chapel facing the sea. It was used mainly by wealthy 19th-century whites.

There is a great deal of distinguished Portuguese colonial architecture in delightful settings. **Rua do Comércio** is the main street in the historic centre. It was here that the prominent traders lived, the two-storey houses having the commercial establishments on the ground floor and the residences above. Today the houses are occupied by restaurants, *pousadas* and tourist shops.

The **Casa da Cadeia**, close to Santa Rita Church, is the former jail, complete with iron grilles in the windows and doors. It is now a public library and art gallery.

On the northern headland is a small fort, **Forte do Defensor Perpétuo**, built in 1822, whose cannon and thick ruined walls can be seen. From the fort there are good views of the sea and the roofs of the town. It's about 15 minutes' walk from the centre. To get there, cross the Rio Perequê Açu by the bridge at the end of the Rua do Comércio; climb the small hill, which has some attractive *pousadas* and a cemetery, and follow the signs.

Also here is the **Museum of Arts and Popular Traditions** ⓘ *Wed-Sun*, in a colonial-style building. It contains carved wooden canoes, musical instruments, fishing gear and other

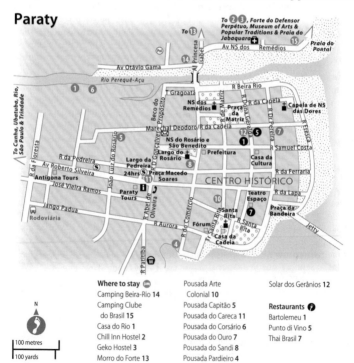

Paraty

items from local communities. On the headland is the gunpowder store and enormous hemispherical iron pans that were used for extracting whale oil, which was used for lamps and to mix with sand and cement for building.

Boat trips and beaches

The most popular trip from Paraty, and highly recommended, is a four-hour **schooner tour** around the bay for swimming (US$21, US$18 online, lunch is an optional extra, book via www.infoparaty.com/en). Smaller boats are available for US$10 an hour or US$20 for three hours. Many beautiful beaches are visited.

Praia do Pontal is the town beach, five minutes' walk from the historic centre: cross the bridge and turn right along the river. The water and sand are not very clean but the handful of *barracas* under the trees are a nice place to hang out. **Praia do Jabaquara** is about 20 minutes away on foot: cross the bridge and continue straight up the hill. There are a few *barracas* here and the sand is cleaner, but the water tends to be muddy.

There are other beaches further from town, many of which make worthwhile excursions. Scruffy **Boa Vista** is just south of town and beyond this (reachable only by boat) are, in order, the long, broad and clean stretches of **Praia da Conçeicao, Praia Vermelha** and **Praia da Lula**, all of which have simple restaurants and are backed by forest and washed by gentle waves. The **Saco da Velha**, further south still, is small and intimate, protected by an island and surrounded by rainforested slopes.

The small town of **Paraty Mirím**, is 17 km away and has a vast sweeping beach with a Manueline church built on the sand and some ruined colonial buildings. It is reached by boat or by four buses a day (three on Sunday) and has simple restaurants and places to camp. Fishing boats leave from here for other islands and beaches including the **Praia do Pouso da Cajaíba**, which has lodgings of the same name, and the spectacular sweep at **Martim do Sá**. The **Saco do Mamanguá** is a long sleeve of water that separates the Ponta da Juatinga and Paraty Mirím, which has good snorkelling.

Caminho do Ouro (Gold Trail)

This partly cobbled trail through the mountains was built by slaves in the 18th century to bring gold down from Ouro Preto before transporting it to Portugal. Now restored, it can be visited, along with the ruins of a toll house, on foot or horseback as a day trip. Tours leave at 1130 Thursday to Sunday from the **Caminho do Ouro information centre** (T024-3371 1897, http://www.paraty.com.br/caminhodoouro/passeio.htm in Portuguese only) in Penha, 8.5 km from Paraty, and cost US$5.30 per person.

There are several *cachoeiras* (waterfalls) in the area, such as the **Cachoeira da Penha**, near the church of the same name. It is 10 km from town on the road to Cunha; take a local bus from the *rodoviária*, US$1, there are good mountain views on the way. The tourist office and travel agencies have details on the waterfalls and hikes.

A recommended excursion is to **Fazenda Murycana** ⓘ *T024-3371 3930 for tours and information*, an old sugar estate and 17th-century *cachaça* distillery with original house and waterwheel. You can taste and buy the different types of *cachaça*; some are aged in oak barrels for 12 years. Try the *cachaça com cravo e canela* (with clove and cinnamon). There is an excellent restaurant and horse riding is available but English is not spoken by the employees. Mosquitoes can be a problem at the *fazenda*, take repellent and don't wear shorts. To get there, take a 'Penha/Ponte Branca' bus from the *rodoviária*, four a day; alight where it crosses a small white bridge and then walk 10 minutes along a signed, unpaved road. There is a good chance of hitching a lift back to Paraty.

Tourist information

There is a good town map in the *Welcome to Paraty* brochure, www.eco-paraty.com. More information is available at www.paraty.com.br.

Centro de Informações Turísticas
Av Roberto Silveira, near the entrance to the historic centre, T024-3371 1266. Staff at this tourist office are friendly and helpful and some speak English.

Where to stay

There are many options in Paraty and 2 beautiful places in the hills nearby. **Hidden Pousadas Brazil** (www.hiddenpousadasbrazil.com) has some attractive options in the old town and around. Ponta do Corumbe (T024-9981 2610, www.pontadocorumbe.com.br) has the best of the *pousadas*, private houses and homestays in and around Paraty, including on the myriad beautiful beaches, islands and peninsulas in the bay. The most exclusive have private beaches, and the properties include the stunning Bernardes Jacobsen house used for the honeymoon scene in *Twilight Breaking Dawn*. Also browse www.paraty.com.br/frame.htm.

$$$$ Bromelias Pousada and Spa
Rodovia Rio–Santos, Km 562, Graúna, T024-3371 2791, www.pousadabromelias.com.br. An Asian-inspired spa *pousada* with its own aromatherapy products and a range of massage treatments. Accommodation is in tastefully decorated chalets perched on a hillside forest garden overlooking the sea and islands.

POUSADA DO **ouro** PARATY

Nested in the heart of Paraty's historical centre.
Tel. +55 24 3371 4300 / +55 24 3371 2033
w w w . p o u s a d a o u r o . c o m . b r

$$$$ Pousada do Ouro
R Dr Pereira (or da Praia) 145, T024-3371 4300,
www.pousadaouro.com.br.
Near Paraty's eastern waterfront and built
as a private home with a fortune made on
the gold route. Plain rooms in an annexe
and suites in the main building. The tropical
garden houses an open-air poolside pavilion.
Pictures of previous guests such as Mick
Jagger, Tom Cruise and Linda Evangelista
adorn the lobby.

$$$$ Pousada do Sandi
Largo do Rosário 1, T024-3371 2100,
www.pousadadosandi.com.br.
The most comfortable in town set in an
18th-century building with a grand lobby,
comfortable mock-colonial rooms and a very
good adjoining restaurant and pool area.
Superior breakfast, parking and excellent
tours organized through www.angatu.com.

$$$$ Pousada Pardieiro
R do Comércio 74, T024-3371 1370,
www.pousadapardieiro.com.br.
Tucked away in a quiet corner, with a calm,
sophisticated atmosphere. Attractive colonial
building with lovely gardens, delightful
rooms facing internal patios and a little
swimming pool. No children under 15.

$$$ Le Gite d'Indaitiba
Rodovia Rio–Santos (BR-101)
Km 562, Graúna, T024-3371 7174,
www.legitedindaiatiba.com.br.
French-owned *pousada* with one of the best
restaurants in southeastern Brazil. Sweeping
views of the sea and bay of islands and a
2-m-wide spring-water swimming pool.

$$$ Morro do Forte
R Orlando Carpinelli, T024-3371 1211,
www.pousadamorrodo forte.com.br.
Lovely garden, good breakfast, pool, German
owner Peter Kallert offers trips on his yacht.
Out of the centre. Recommended.

$$$ Pousada Bartholomeu
R Dr Samuel Costa 176, T024-3371 5032,
www.bartholomeuparaty.com.br.

A handsome Portuguese townhouse, with
a handful of simple rooms situated above
Alexandre Righetti's gourmet restaurant.

$$$ Vivenda and Maris
R Beija Flor 9 and Flor 11, Caboré,
www.vivendaparaty.com and
www.marisparaty.com.br.
These identical-twin *pousadas*, with lovely
garden chalet rooms in bright white and
marble clustered around a jewel-like pool,
offer friendly, personal service and quiet,
intimate and discreet accommodation
10 mins' walk from the city centre.

$$ Chill Inn Hostel and Pousada
R Orlando Carpinelli 3, Praia do Pontal,
T024-3371 2545, www.chillinnhostel.com.
Beachfront accommodation from dorms
($ pp) to private rooms, all with bathrooms
and a/c. Breakfast at beach bar, free taxi
and internet.

$$ Geko Hostel
R Orlando Carpinelli 5, Praia do Pontal,
T024-3371 7504, www.gekohostel.com.
Doubles and dorms ($ pp), breakfast
included, free pickup from bus station,
Wi-Fi, tours arranged.

$$ Pousada Arte Colonial
R da Matriz 292, T024-3371 7231,
www.pousadaartecolonial.com.br.
One of the best deals in Paraty. A beautiful
colonial building in the centre decorated
with style and a personal touch by its French
owner, with artefacts and antiques from all
over the world.

$$ Pousada Capitão
R Luiz do Rosário 18, T024-3371 1815,
www.paraty.com.br/capitao.
Converted colonial building, close to the
historic centre, swimming pool, English
and Japanese spoken.

$$ Pousada do Corsário
Beco do Lapeiro 26, T024-3371 1866,
www.pousadacorsario.com.br.
With a pool and its own gardens, next to the
river and 2 blocks from the centre. Simple,

stylish rooms, most with hammocks outside. With a branch in Búzios (see website).

$$ Solar dos Gerânios
Praça da Matriz, T024-3371 1550, www.paraty.com.br/geranio.
Beautiful colonial family house on the main square in traditional rustic style that is a welcome antidote to the more polished *pousadas*.

$ Casa do Rio
R Antônio Vidal 120, T024-3371 2223, www.paratyhostel.com.
Youth hostel in a little house with riverside courtyard and hammocks. There's a kitchen and price includes breakfast. Trips by jeep or on horseback to waterfalls, mountains and beaches. Dorms a little crowded.

$ Pousada do Careca
Praça Macedo Soares, T024-3371 1291, ww.pousadadocareca.com.
Simple rooms. Those without street windows are musty.

Camping

Camping Beira-Rio
Just across the bridge, before the road to the fort.

Camping Clube do Brasil
Av Orlando Carpinelli, Praia do Pontal, T024-3371 1877.
Small, good, very crowded in Jan and Feb, US$8 per person.

Restaurants

The best restaurants in Paraty are in the historic part of town and are among the best in the southeast outside Rio or São Paulo. Watch out for surreptitious cover charges for live music, which are often very discreetly displayed. The less expensive restaurants, those offering *comida por kilo* (pay by weight) and the fast-food outlets are outside the historic centre, mainly on Av Roberto Silveira.

Paraty's regional specialities include *peixe à Parati* (local fish cooked with herbs and green bananas), served with *pirão* (a mixture of manioc flour and the sauce that the fish was cooked in). Also popular is the *filé de peixe ao molho de camarão* (fried fish fillet with a shrimp and tomato sauce). There is plenty of choice in Paraty so have a browse. Also see **Le Gite d'Indaitiba**, page 139.

$$$ Bartolomeu
R Samuel Costa 179, T024-3371 5032, www.bartholomeuparaty.com.br.
A sumptuous menu of European-Brazilian fusion dishes (including a delicious, tangy bass (*robalo*) fillet with plantain purée (*puree de banana da terra*) and pumpkin sauce (*emoção de abóbora*). Be sure to try the guava petit gateau with cheese and walnut sorbet, which melts on the tongue, and kick off a meal with one of the tangerine and passion fruit caipirinhas.

$$$ Caminho do Ouro
R Samuel Costa 236, T024-3371 1689.
Mineira Ronara Toledo cooks *caiçara* food with a gourmet twist using locally produced ingredients. Try her filet mignon in *jabuticaba* sauce or her bass in passion fruit and *pupunha* berry sauce.

$$$ Punto Di Vino
R Mcal Deodoro 129, historical centre, T024-3371 1348.
The best for seafood in town; owned and run by a Neapolitan who catches his own 'catch of the day'. Great wood-fired pizza, live music and an excellent selection of wine.

$$$ Thai Brasil
R Dona Geralda 345, historic centre, T024-3371 0127, www.thaibrasil.com.br.
Well-executed Thai standards without spices (Brazilians yelp in pain at the sight of a chilli).

$$ Vila Verde
Estr Paraty–Cunha, Km 7, T024-3371 7808, www.villaverdeparaty.com.br.
It's worth a stop off here on the way to or from the waterfalls, the Caminho Douro or

Cunha. The restaurant serves light Italian and its open sides overlook a tropical garden that attracts numerous morpho butterflies, hummingbirds and tanagers.

$ Kontiki
Ilha Duas Irmãs, T024-9999 9599, www.ilha kontiki.com.br. Daily 1000-1500 and Fri and Sat for dinner. Reservations recommended.
A tiny island, 5 mins from the pier where a small speed boat runs a (free) shuttle service. Wonderful island setting; ordinary food.

Entertainment

Theatre
Teatro Espaço, *R Dona Geralda 327, T024-3371 1575, www.ecparaty.org.br. Wed, Sat 2100, US$10.* This world-famous puppet show should not be missed. The puppets tell stories (in mime) with incredible realism. The short pieces (lasting 1 hr) are works of pure imagination and emotion and a moving commentary on the human condition.

Festivals

Feb/Mar Carnaval, hundreds of people cover their bodies in black mud and run through the streets yelling like prehistoric creatures (anyone can join in).
Mar/Apr Semana Santa (Easter Week) with religious processions and folk songs.
Jun-Jul FLIP (Festa Literária Internacional de Paraty).
Mid-Jul Semana de Santa Rita, traditional foods, shows, exhibitions and dances.
Aug Festival da Pinga, the *cachaça* fair at which local distilleries display their products and there are plenty of opportunities to overindulge.
Sep (around the 8th) **Semana da Nossa Senhora dos Remédios**, processions and religious events.
Sep/Oct Spring Festival of Music, concerts in front of Santa Rita Church.
31 Dec New Year's Eve, a huge party with open-air concerts and fireworks (reserve accommodation in advance).

What to do

Angatu, *T011-3872 0945, www.angatu.com.* The best private tours and diving around the bay in luxurious yachts and motor cruisers, with private entries to the exclusive island parties. Also offers private villa rental in and around Paraty (see Where to stay, page 139). Book well ahead. Highly recommended.
Paraty Tours, *Av Roberto Silveira 11, T024-3371 1327, www.paratytours.com.br.* Good range of trips. English and Spanish spoken.
Rei Cigano, *contact through Bartolomeu restaurant (see Restaurants, page 140), or ring Tuca T024-7835 3190, thiparaty@hotmail.com.* Day overnight trips or even expeditions along the Brazilian coast in a beautiful 60-ft sailing schooner with cabins.
Soberana da Costa, *R Dona Geraldo 43, in Pousada Mercado do Pouso, T024-3371 1114, www.facebook.com/soberanodacostaparaty.* Schooner trips. Recommended.

Transport

There are direct bus connections with Rio and São Paulo several times daily, and with a number of destinations along the coast.

Bus On public holidays and in high season, the frequency of bus services usually increases. **Costa Verde** (www.costaverde transportes.com.br) runs 13 buses a day to **Rio de Janeiro** (241 km, 4½ hrs, US$18.60).
To **Angra dos Reis** (98 km, 1½ hrs, every 40-60 mins, US$4); 3 a day to **Ubatuba** (75 km, just over 1 hr, **São José** company, US$4), **Taubaté** (170 km) and **Guaratinguetá** (210 km); 2 a day to **São Paulo**, 1100 and 2335 (304 km via **São José dos Campos**, 5½ hrs, US$10 (**Reunidas** book up quickly and are very busy at weekends), and **São Sebastião. Easy Transfer** (see page 134) offers transfers along the Costa Verde to and from Paraty.

Taxi Set rate of US$4 for trips within the historic centre.

spectacular setting between rainforested slopes and emerald sea

Ramshackle little Trindade (pronounced *Tringdajee*) may not be as attractive in its own right as Paraty, 30 km away, but it's in beautiful surroundings and, unlike Paraty, it has a long, broad beach. The town has long been a favourite hang-out for young middle-class surf hippies from São Paulo and Rio, who come here in droves during the holiday period. It is now also finding its place on the international backpacker circuit and it's easy to see why. The beach is stunning, the *pousadas* and restaurants cheap and cheerful, and there are a number of campsites.

Sadly, there is no sewage treatment and when the town is full, foul black water flows onto the sand. There are plenty of unprepossessing restaurants along the town's main drag, **Avenida Principal**. All serve the usual 'beans and rice and chips' combinations. Avoid coming here during Christmas, New Year, Carnaval and Easter.

Tip...
Bring cash with you because Trindade has no banks.

Around Trindade

Beyond Trindade and the upmarket condominium at **Laranjeiras** there is a series of beaches. **Sono** is a long, sweeping stretch of sand backed by *barracas*, some of which have accommodation to rent. Sanitation is a problem, however.

Ponta Negra is a little *caiçara* village, beautifully situated in a cove between rocky headlands. It has its own beach, simple but elegant homestay accommodation, fishing-boat trips and organized treks into the surrounding forest, which is rich in birdlife and full of waterfalls. It is possible to climb to the highest peak on the peninsula for views out over the Paraty area. The community is traditional and conservative; visits should be arranged in advance through village leaders. See Where to stay, below. Sono and Ponta Negra are reached from the Sono trailhead, which lies at the end of the bus route to Trindade/Laranjeiras. The path is easy to find and follow. Allow 1½ hours for Sono and three hours for Ponta Negra. There are several buses a day to Trindade and the trailhead from Paraty. See Transport, below.

Tourist information

Information is available at the booth at the entrance to town (no English spoken) or through the Paraty website, www.paraty.com.br, and tourist office.

Where to stay

Places to stay are basic in Trindade.

$ Chalé e Pousada Magia do Mar
T024-3371 5130.
Thatched hut with space for 4. Views out over the beach.

$ Ponta da Trindade Pousada and Camping
T024-3371 5113.
Simple fan-cooled rooms and a sand-floored campsite with cold showers and no electricity.

$ Pousada Marimbá
R Principal, T024-3371 5147.
Simple colourful rooms and a breakfast area.

Around Trindade

$ Ponta Negra homestays
Ponta Negra, contact Teteco, T024-3371 2673, teteco@paratyweb.com.br, or Cauê, francocvc@hotmail.com.

Transport

Trindade is reached by a steep, winding 7-km road branching off the Rio–Santos road (BR-101). **Paraty–Ubatuba** buses all pass the turning to Trindade and will pick you up or drop you off from here. Ask for 'Patrimonio' or 'Estrada para Trindade'. In high season there are vans from Trindade to the turning (US$2). In low season you'll have to hitch or walk; cars pass regularly. Be wary of carrying any drugs – the police at the turn-off post are very vigilant and searches are frequent. There are 14 direct **Colitur** (T024-3371 1224, www.paratytrindade.com.br) buses a day running between Paraty and Trindade which also call in on **Laranjeiras** for the trailhead to **Sono** and **Ponta Negra**.

Minas
Gerais

Belo
Horizonte

The capital of Minas Gerais, Belo Horizonte (population 2.38 million), is the sixth largest city in Brazil and the third largest metropolitan area. It was one of the country's first planned cities, built at the advent of the republic. It remains an attractive capital, pocked with hills that rise and fall in waves of red-tiled houses, tall apartment blocks and jacaranda- and ipê-lined streets. The city has rapidly grown since its foundation and the extensive metropolitan area stretches to all sides of the natural bowl-shaped valley in which it sits, encircled by dramatic mountains, ideal conditions to trap pollution. Like much of urban Brazil, Belo Horizonte suffers from streets clogged with cars during the morning and evening rush hours, a situation that has led the municipal government to introduce an efficient integrated public transport system linking the bus and *metrô* networks, in imitation of Curitiba.

Essential Belo Horizonte

Finding your feet

International and many national flights land at **Tancredo Neves International Airport**, more commonly referred to as **Confins**, 39 km north of Belo Horizonte. A bus takes an hour to the city centre, or there are taxis. The domestic airport at **Pampulha** (a name by which it is also known) is officially called **O Aeroporto Carlos Drummond de Andrade** and is 9 km north of the centre. The bus to the centre takes 25 minutes. Interstate buses arrive at the *rodoviária* next to Praça Rio Branco at the northwest end of Avenida Afonso Pena. See also Transport, page 154.

Getting around

The city has a good public transport system (www.bhtrans.pbh.gov.br). A **BRT** (**Bus Rapid Transit**) links the city centre to the Mineirao stadium in Pampulha. Some city buses link up with the regional overground *metrô*. At present, the *metrô* is limited to one line and connects a limited portion of the north and west of the city to the centre. However, there are plans to extend the service to Pampulha and Praça de Estação centre by 2020.

Orientation

Belo Horizonte centres on the large Parque Municipal in the heart of downtown Belo Horizonte and on the broad main avenue of Afonso Pena. This is constantly full of pedestrians and traffic, except on Sunday morning when cars are banned and part of it becomes a huge open-air market. Daytime activity is concentrated on and around the main commercial district on Avenida Afonso Pena, which is the best area for lunch. At night, activity shifts to Savassi, southwest of the centre, which has a wealth of restaurants, bars and clubs.

Safety

As in any large city, be vigilant in the centre and at the bus station. The Parque Municipal and the streets around the *rodoviária* are not safe after dark.

When to go

Central Minas enjoys an excellent climate (16-30°C) except for the rainy season (December to March). The average temperature in Belo Horizonte is 21°C.

Central Belo Horizonte is a pleasant place to spend an afternoon. The city began here as a circular grid of streets ringed by Avenida Contorno planned and executed by Pará engineer Aarão Reis, who razed the original (tiny village) of Belo Horizonte to the ground. It was intended to be a bold statement in stone of the power and promise of the new Republic.

1 Belo Horizonte orientation & Pampulha

➡ **Belo Horizonte maps**
1 Belo Horizonte orientation
   & Pampulha, page 148
2 Belo Horizonte centre, page 150

The centre focuses around the stately Praça da Liberdade, a piece of architectural propaganda whose neoclassical buildings of state (which would have looked modern and progressive at the time) occupy the highest ground. This is in contrast to the old state capital, Ouro Preto, where baroque churches occupy this role. The name of the praça and the Avenida da Liberdade which runs to it emphasize the liberty brought to the people by the republican coup d'état.

Also in the centre is the appealing **Parque Municipal** ① *Tue-Sun 0600-1800*, and the elegant **Palácio das Artes** ① *Afonso Pena 1537, T031-3236 7400, 1000-2200, Sun 1400-2200*, which contains the **Centro de Artesanato Mineiro** (with a craft shop), exhibitions, cinema and theatres.

There are numerous small museums spread around the praça. The **Memorial Minas Gerais** ① *Praça da Liberdade s/n at R Gonçalves Dias, T031-3343 7317, www.memorialvale. com.br, Tue-Wed 1000-1730, Thu 1000-2130, Fri-Sat 1000-1730, Sun 1000-1330, free*, is devoted to the history of Minas Gerais through the lives of famous Mineiros such as Tiradentes and JK, and the work of famous Mineiros including writers Carlos Drummond de Andrade, Guimarães Rosa, painter Lygia Clark, photographer Sebastião Salgado and musician Milton Nascimento.

The **Museu de Artes e Ofícios** ① *Praça Rui Barbosa s/n, T031-3248 8600, Tue 1200-1900, Wed-Thu 1200-2100, Fri 1200-1900, Sat and Sun 1100-1700*, in a converted late 19th-century railway station, houses some 2000 18th- and 19th-century objects telling the story of various public and private professions in Minas.

The **Museu Mineiro** ① *Av João Pinheiro 342, T031-3269 1103, Tue-Wed and Fri 1000-2100, Thu 1200-1900, Sat and Sun 1000-1600*, houses religious and other art in the old senate building, close to the centre. There is a section dedicated specifically to religious art, with six pictures attributed to Mestre Athayde, exhibitions of modern art, photographs and works by naïf painters. Also of interest are the woodcarvings by Geraldo Teles de Oliveira (GTO). Away from the centre, the **Museu Histórico Abílio Barreto** ① *Av Prudente de Morais 202, Cidade Jardim, T031-3277 8573, www.amigosdomhab.com.br, Tue, Wed, Sat-Sun 1000-1700, Thu-Fri 1000-2100*, is in an old *fazenda* which has existed since 1883, when Belo Horizonte was a village called Arraial do Curral d'el Rey. The *fazenda* now houses antique furniture and historical exhibits. To get there, take bus No 2902 from Avenida Afonso Pena.

The new **Museu Clube da Esquina** ① *Rua Paraisópolis 738, Santa Teresa district, T031-2512 5050, www.museuclubedaesquina.org.br, Mon-Sat 0900-0100*, is devoted to the group of artists and musicians (including Milton Nascimento, Lo Borges and Beto Guedes) and has exhibition spaces and live music in the museum's bar (for agenda see www.bardomuseuclubedaesquina.com).

The **Museu das Minas e do Metal** ① *Praça da Liberdade s/n, T031-3516 7200, www.mmm.org.br, Tue-Sun 1200-1800, Fri open until 2200, free*, housed in a handsome turn-of-the-20th-century building is devoted to the story of mining in Minas, with interactive displays and a replica mine.

Pampulha
To reach Pampulha take the BRT from the centre. Linha S51 or 52 (Circular Pampulha) run around the neighbourhood (US$0.90).

The city's most interesting attraction by far is the suburb of Pampulha: a complex of Oscar Niemeyer buildings set around a lake in formal gardens landscaped by Roberto Burle Marx.

The project was commissioned by Juscelino Kubitschek in the 1940s, when he was governor of Minas Gerais and a decade before he became president. Some see it as a prototype for Brasília, for this was the first time that Niemeyer had designed a series of buildings that work together in geometric harmony. It was in Pampulha that he first experimented with the plasticity of concrete; the highlight of the complex is the **Igreja São Francisco de Assis** ① *Av Otacílio Negrão de Lima, Km 12, T031-3427 1644, Tue-Sat 0900-1700, Sun 1200-1700 US$1.50.* This was one of Niemeyer's first departures from the orthodox rectilinear forms of modernism and one of the first buildings in the world to mould concrete, with its series of parabolic waves running together to form arches. Light

② Belo Horizonte centre

➡ **Belo Horizonte maps**
1 Belo Horizonte orientation & Pampulha, page 148
2 Belo Horizonte centre, page 150

Where to stay 🛏
Chalé Mineiro 1
Dayrell Minas 2
O Sorriso do Lagarto Hostel 3
Quality Hotel Afonso Pena 4

Restaurants 🍴
Café com Letras 1
Dona Derna 2
Dona Lucinha 3
Eddie Fine Burger 4
Kauhana 5
Taste Vin 7
Vecchio Sogno 8

Xapuri 9

Bars & clubs 🍸
A Obra 10
Jack Rock Bar 11
Stonehenge 12
Vinnil 13

500 metres
500 yards

pierces the interior through a series of louvres and the curves are offset by a simple free-standing bell tower. The outside walls are covered in azulejo tiles by Candido Portinari, Brazil's most respected modernist artist. These were painted in a different style from his previous social realism, as exemplified by pictures such as O Mestiço. The building provoked a great deal of outrage because of its modernist design. One mayor proposed its demolition and replacement by a copy of the church of Saint Francis in Ouro Preto.

There are a number of other interesting Niemeyer buildings on the other side of the lake from the church. With its snaking canopy leading up to the main dance hall, the **Casa do Baile** ① *Av Octacílio Negrão de Lima 751, Tue-Sun 0900-1900, free*, is another example of his fascination with the curved line. There are wonderful views out over the lake. People would dance here and then take a boat to the glass and marble **Museu de Arte de Pampulha** (**MAP**) ① *Av Octacílio Negrão de Lima 16585, T031-3443 4533, www.comartevirtual.com.br, Tue-Sun 0900-1900, free*, which was then a casino set up by Kubitschek. Today it houses a fine collection of Mineira modern art and more than 900 works by national artists.

Just 700 m south of the lake are the twin stadia of **Mineirão** and **Mineirinho**, clear precursors to the Centro de Convenções Ulysses Guimarães in Brasília, which was designed by Niemeyer's office though not the architect himself. Mineirão is the second largest stadium in Brazil after the Maracanã in Rio, seating 92,000 people. It was completely refurbished and largely rebuilt for the 2014 FIFA World Cup™. See also box, page 16.

Listings Belo Horizonte *maps p148 and p150*

Tourist information

The free monthly Guía Turística lists events and opening times. The websites www.visiteminasgerais.com.br and www.belohorizonteturismo.com.br are also useful.

Belotur
R Pernambuco 284, Funcionários, T031-3220 1310, www.turismo.mg.gov.br, www. belohorizonte.mg.gov.br.
The municipal tourist office lies in a big purpose-built office on the outskirts of the city, but operates booths at Mercado Municipal, Praça da Liberdade, Veveco (Av Otacílio Negrão de Lima 855, Pampulha), the airports and *rodoviária*, offering hotel, sightseeing and cultural information and maps.

Instituto Chico Mendes de Conservação da Biodiversidade (ICMBio)
Av do Contorno 8121, Cidade Jardim, T031-3337 2624.
Has information on national parks.

SETUR
Rodovia Prefeito Américo Gianetti s/n, Prédio Gerais, 11th floor, Bairro Serra Verde, T031-3915 9454, www.minasgerais.com.br. Mon-Fri 0800-1800.
The tourism authority for Minas Gerais is very helpful.

Where to stay

There are cheap options near the *rodoviária* and on R Curitiba, but many of these hotels rent by the hour and the area is tawdry; you'll have a more comfortable stay in one of the youth hostels. You can spend the night in the *rodoviária* if you have an onward ticket (police check at 2400). Many chain hotels have opened in the city since the football in 2014. Some are mentioned below; others include **Holiday Inn**, **Ramada**, **Royal** (www.royalhoteis.com.br) and **Promenade**, of which a good example is **Promenade Toscanini** (R Arturo Toscanini 61, Santo Antônio, T031-3064 2200, www.promenade.com.br/toscanini), with 5 others in Savassi.

$$$$ Dayrell Minas
R Espírito Santo 901, T031-3248 1000,
www.dayrell.com.br.
One of the best and most central business
hotels, with a very large convention centre
and full business facilities, fax and email
modems in the rooms. Rooftop pool.
Not much English spoken.

$$$$-$$$ Quality Hotel Afonso Pena
Av Afonso Pena 3761, Savassi, T031-2111 8900,
www.atlanticahotels.com.br.
Spacious practical modern rooms with work
desks and on the upper floor city views,
decent business facilities, helpful staff,
generous breakfast, a pool and a pocket-
sized gym.

$$-$ O Sorriso do Lagarto Hostel
R Cristina 791, São Pedro, T031-3283 9325,
www.osorrisodolagarto.com.br.
Simple little hostel in a converted townhouse
with kitchen, internet and fax service,
breakfast, lockers, washing machines and a
living area with DVD player. Also has a branch
in Ouro Preto.

$ Chalé Mineiro
*R Santa Luzia 288, Santa Efigênia, T031-3467
1576, www.chalemineirohostel.com.br.*
Attractive and well maintained, with
dorms and doubles, a small pool and
shared kitchen, TV lounge and telephones.
Bus No 9801 stops right in front of
the hostel and it's 300 m away from
the nearest metro station.

Restaurants

Mineiros love their food and drink and Belo
Horizonte has a lively café dining and bar
scene. Savassi and nearby Lourdes make
up the gastronomic heart of the city, and
are overflowing with bohemian streetside
cafés, bars and restaurants. Savassi takes
its name from an Italian bakery founded
here in the 1940s whose cakes became so
popular that the square became known as
'Praça Savassi', which in turn lent its name
to the neighbourhood. There is a lively,
cheap street food market in Savassi on
R Tomé de Souza, between Pernambuco
and Alagoas, every Thu 1900-2300.

There are plenty of cheap per kilo restaurants
and *padarias* near the budget hotels in the
centre. The **Mercado Central** is a great spot
for lunch or a snack, with many restaurants,
stalls and cafés.

   Pampulha, on the outskirts, has the best
of the fine-dining restaurants, which are well
worth the taxi ride.

$$$ Taste Vin
R Curitiba 2105, Lourdes, T031-3292 5423,
www.tastevin-bh.com.br.
Decent, if a little salty mock-French food.
Celebrated for its soufflés and Provençale
seafood. The respectable wine list includes
some Brazilian options.

$$$ Vecchio Sogno
*R Martim de Carvalho 75 and R Dias Adorno,
Santo Agostinho, under the Assembléia
Legislativo, T031-3292 5251, www.vecchio
sogno.com.br. Lunch only on Sun.*
The best Italian in the city with an inventive
menu fusing Italian and French cuisine with
Brazilian ingredients. Excellent fish. Good
wine list.

$$$ Xapuri
R Mandacaru 260, Pampulha, T031-3496 6198,
www.restaurantexapuri.com.br. Closed Mon.
Comida mineira, great atmosphere, live
music, very good food, expensive and a bit
out of the way but recommended.

$$$-$$ Dona Derna
R Tomé de Souza, Savassi, T031-3223 6954.
Several restaurants in one. There is Italian
fine dining with excellent dishes and a
respectable wine list, as well as traditional
Italian home cooking.

$$$-$$ Dona Lucinha
R Sergipe 811, T031-3261 5930,
www.donalucinha.com.br.
A Gula award-winning eatery founded by
an old lady from Serro who devoted her
life to preserving and recreating 18th- and
19th-century Mineiro cuisine. The modern
restaurant serves a buffet of steaming
Mineiro plates (like *frango com quiabo* and
feijao tropeiro). Traditional decor and staff
in uniform.

$$ Eddie Fine Burger
R da Bahia 2652, T031-3282 4606,
www.eddieburger.com.br.
US-style diner serving North American
and Brazilian burgers, including *bauru*
and cheeseburgers, all made with prime
Brazilian beef.

$$-$ Café com Letras
R Antônio de Albuquerque, 781, Savassi,
T031-3225 9973, www.cafecomletras.com.br.
Arty little a/c café-bar and bookshop with
live music on Mon and Sun, with a varied
menu of healthy, well-prepared *petiscos*,
sandwiches, salads and light lunches like
risottos and pasta.

$$-$ Kauhana
R Tomé de Souza, Savassi, T031-3284 8714.
Tasty wood-fired pizzas. Pleasant open-air
dining area.

Bars and clubs

There's a cluster of bars around Tomé
de Souza in Savassi, where a young and
arty crowd spills out onto the street, and
the beer and caipirinhas are cheap and
plentiful. Come after 1030 0n Thu-Sat for
the liveliest crowds both here and in Santa
Teresa – the neighbourhood where Clube
da Esquina first met. The Edifício Maleta is
a big blocky office building with a string
of well-known bars and restaurants; it was
one of the city's pioneering nightlife spots
in the 1960s and 1970s. Check out www.
guiadasemana.com.br/belo-horizonte to
find out what's on.

A Obra
R Rio Grande do Norte 1168, Savassi,
T031-3215 8077, www.aobra.com.br.
The leading alternative music venue in
the city. Great for DJs and new Minas acts.

Jack Rock Bar
Av do Contorno, 5623, T031-227 4510,
www.jackrockbar.com.br.
Low-lit rock bar with live tribute bands
and local rock and metal acts.

Stonehenge
R Tupis 1448, T031-3271 3476,
www.stonehengerockbar.com.br.
Live rock music and metal.

Vinnil
R dos Incofidentes 1068, Savassi,
T031-3261 7057, www.vinnil.com.br.
Funky retro club-bar housed in a 1940s
building decorated with art and hosting
great live acts at weekends.

Shopping

Fashion and jewellery
Íris Clemência, *Sta Catarina 1587, Lourdes.*
Gorgeous figure-hugging dresses, evening
gowns and smart casual wear. Also stocks
clothing by bag and accessory designer of
the moment Rogerio Lima.
Manoel Bernardes, *BH Shopping and*
Shopping Patio Savassi, T031-3505 5170,

www.manoelbernardes.com.br. Beautifully crafted jewellery, made with Brazilian gold and precious stones.

Ronaldo Fraga, *R Fernandes Tourinho 81, Savassi, T031-3282 5379, www.ronaldofraga. com.br*. One of Brazil's leading new designers famous for his bright stamps and elegant cuts.

Markets

Spend at least a few hours wandering through the **Mercado Central**, Av Augusto de Lima 744. A temple to Minas produce, there's everything from cheeses, *cachaças*, arts and crafts, herbs and spices and bric-a-brac, as well as many cafés and restaurants. There is a Sun handicraft fair on **Av Afonso Pena**. Hippies still sell their wares on **R Rio de Janeiro**, 600 block, each evening. A **flower market** is held at Av Bernardo Monteiro, near Av Brasil, every Fri 1200-2000. Also here on Sat is a **food and drinks market**.

What to do

Tour operators

Minas Golden Tours, *R da Bahia 1345, T031-3023 1451, www.minasgoldentours.com.br*. The best tour operator in Minas with a broad range of tours throughout the state (and connections with Rio, São Paulo, Brasília and Bahia) and around Belo Horizonte, including to Inhotim, Caraça and the colonial towns.

Transport

Air

From **Tancredo Neves International Airport**, more commonly referred to as **Confins** (39 km north of Belo Horizonte, T031-3689 2415, www.aeroportoconfins.net) a taxi to the centre costs US$45. **Unir** (www. conexaoaeroporto.com.br), kiosk next to baggage reclaim, runs executive buses from Confins to the *rodoviária* and the city centre from the *pista interna* road outside the terminal, US$4.80, 50 mins. There are also comfortable 'normal' buses 5250 or 5270

(from the *pista externa* road at the far end of the pedestrian walkway running through the car park, hourly, US$2.20, 60 mins to the centre). Some buses run via Pampulha, stopping outside the **Plaza** hotel.

There are international flights to **Lisbon (TAP)**, **Buenos Aires (TAM)**, **Miami (American Airlines)** and **Panama City (COPA)**, with connections throughout the Americas. Domestic flights include those to **São Paulo**, **Brasília**, **Salvador**, **Rio de Janeiro** and most state capitals with **Avianca**, **Azul**, **GOL**, **Pantanal** and **TAM**.

The domestic airport at **Pampulha** (a name by which it is also known) is officially called **O Aeroporto Carlos Drummond de Andrade** (9 km north of the centre, T031-3490 2001). Blue bus No 1202 runs to the centre from across the street (25 mins, US$1.80), passing the *rodoviária* and the cheaper hotel district.

From Pampulha Airport there are ever fewer flights, but shuttle services remain to several cities including **Campinas**, **São Paulo** and destinations within Minas. Airlines serving the airport are limited to **Passaredo** and **TRIP**.

Bus

Local The city has a good public transport system (www.bhtrans.pbh.gov.br). Red buses run on express routes and charge US$0.90; yellow buses have circular routes around the Contorno, US$0.90; blue buses run on diagonal routes charging US$0.90.

A **BRT (Bus Rapid Transit)** links the city centre to the Mineirao stadium in Pampulha running along Pedro I/Antônio Carlos, Cristiano Machado and Região Central. By 2017 it will also run along *avenidas* Pedro II, Carlos Luz, Nossa Senhora do Carmo, Afonso Pena, Anel Rodoviário and the Anel Intermediário. It will not run to the airport.

Long distance The *rodoviário* (bus station) is clean and well organized with toilets, a post office, telephones, left-luggage lockers (open 0700-2200, US$1.50) and shops. For bus routes, companies, prices and times see www.rodoviariabelohorizonte.com.br.

Within Minas To **Ouro Preto** at least once an hour 0600-2300 (2 hrs, US$.7.50); change here for Mariana. To **São João del Rei**, 7 daily, more on Fri (4 hrs, US$ 17, US$21 via Barabacena). To **Congonhas**, twice daily direct, once on Sun all before 1030 and numerous passing the turn-off from where you can get a 10-min taxi-ride into town (1½ hrs, US$8.50). To **Diamantina**, 8 daily (5 hrs, US$22). To **Serra da Canastra** catch one of the 6 daily buses bus to Piumhi (3¾ hrs, US$18.30) and change there for São Roque de Minas (3 daily, 1½ hrs, US$6). To **Inhotim**, 1 **Saritur** *colectivo* Tue-Sun at 0815 (90 mins, US$7.50) leaving from Belo Horizonte bus station. To **Caraça** catch one of the 9 daily buses to Santa Barbara (3 hrs, US$6-10) and take a taxi from there (US$25).

Interstate buses To **Rio** at least 6 a day (6-7 hrs, from US$22.60). To **Vitória**, numerous (8-9 hrs, US$23). To **Brasília**, 5 daily, all at night (10 hrs, US$36). To **São Paulo**, numerous (8½ hrs, US$29). To **Salvador** 4 daily, all at night (24 hrs, US$75). To **Porto Seguro** twice daily at night (17 hrs direct, via Nanuque and Eunápolis, US$50).

Car hire
All the major companies have offices at Confins airport and in the city.

Metro
Some buses link up with the regional overground *metrô*. At present, the *metrô* is limited to 1 line and connects a limited portion of the north and west of the city to the centre. However, there are plans to extend the service to Pampulha and Praça de Estação centre by 2020. Tickets cost US$0.95.

captivating contemporary art complex and a wolf reserve

Inhotim

Rua B 20, Inhotim, Brumadinho, T031-3571 9700, www.inhotim.org.br, Tue-Fri 0930-1630, Sat and Sun 0930-1730, Tue and Thu US$6.30, US$10 (Fri-Sun), free (Wed), reduced price 'passport' for 2-day visits. Bring your own food, restaurants are very overpriced; there are 2 expensive but good restaurants and several cheaper snack bars dotted about the site. There are lots of drinking fountains and toilets on site. Electric buggies take visitors to far-flung galleries, US$5 for unlimited use (free for disabled visitors), but you must pay at the entrance, otherwise you can walk everywhere. You are given a map on arrival. It can get very crowded on Sat and at long weekends. Visits should be organized through a tour operator like Minas Golden Tours, see page 154, or hire a car.

After the colonial towns and cities, the most visited attraction near Belo Horizonte is this art complex, one of the most unusual contemporary art galleries in the world. The complex as a whole covers some 1255 ha, with dozens of purpose-built galleries and interactive spaces nestled in tropical forest surrounds and showcasing the work of myriad Brazilian and international artists. These include Tunga, Olafur Eliasson, Hélio Oiticica, Dan Graham, Chris Burden, Cildo Meireles, Zhang Huan and Miguel Rio Branco. The galleries are stunning; Branco's looks like a vast rusting ship hull, its gloomy interior perfectly offsetting his religiously iconographic photographs, some of which are projected onto flowing cotton sheets, allowing visitors literally to walk through them.

Tip...
Set aside at least a day for a full leisurely visit.

Santuário e Parque Natural de Caraça

www.santuariodocaraca.com.br. Daily 0800-1700; if staying overnight you cannot leave after 2100. Entrance fee US$2.50.

This remarkable reserve sits in the heart of the Serra do Espinhaço mountains about 120 km east of Belo Horizonte and is perhaps the best place in South America for seeing maned wolf. The park ranges in altitude from 720 m to 2070 m. The lower areas are rich in Atlantic forest while the higher areas support Cerrado, grassland and other mountain habitats. There are lakes, waterfalls and rivers.

Essential Santuário e Parque Natural de Caraça

Access

There are frequent buses to Santa Bárbara from Belo Horizonte. There is also a bus service to Mariana, a beautiful route, via Catas Altas, which has an interesting church and a *pousada* belonging to the municipality of Santa Bárbara. To get to the park, turn off the BR-262 (towards Vitória) at Km 73 and go via Barão de Cocais to

Caraça (120 km). There is no public transport to the seminary. Buses go as far as Santa Bárbara, from where a taxi is US$35. Book the taxi to return for you, or hitch (which may not be easy). The park entrance is 10 km before the seminary. The alternative is to book at tour from Belo Horizonte (see **Minas Golden Tours**, page 154) which will work out cheaper than going under your own steam if you can join a group.

Since the early 1980s, the monks have been leaving food for maned wolves on the seminary steps, and at least four can usually be seen in the every evening. Other endangered mammals in the park include southern masked titi monkeys, which can often be spotted in family groups, tufted-eared marmosets and brown capuchin monkeys. Birdlife includes various toucans, guans and hummingbirds (such as the Brazilian ruby and the white-throated hummingbird), various tanagers, cotingas, antbirds, woodpeckers and the long-trained and scissor-tailed nightjars. Some of the bird species are endemic, others are rare and endangered.

The trails for viewing the different landscapes and the wildlife are marked at the beginning and are quite easy to follow, although a guide (available through the seminary) is recommended.

The **seminary buildings** and the church are beautifully set in a shallow valley 1220 m above sea level and surrounded on three sides by rugged mountains that rise to 2070 m at the Pico do Sol. The name Caraça means 'big face', so called because of a hill that is said to resemble the face of a giant who is looking at the sky. This can be best appreciated by climbing up to the cross just above the church. The church itself has a painting of the Last Supper attributed to Mestre Athayde with a trompe l'oeil effect. The eyes of Judas Iscariot (the figure holding the purse) seem to follow you as you move.

Part of the seminary has been converted into a hotel, which is the only place to stay in the park (see Where to stay, below). It is also possible to stay in Santa Bárbara, 25 km away on the road to Mariana, which has a few cheap hotels, and hitchhike to Caraça.

Listings Around Belo Horizonte

Where to stay

Parque Natural de Caraça

$$$ Santuário do Caraça
Reservations: Caixa Postal 12, Santa Bárbara, T031-3837 2698, www.santuariodocaraca.com.br.

This onsite hotel has reasonable rooms and the restaurant serves good food (lunch 1200-1330). No camping is permitted.

Colonial
towns

The colonial gold-mining towns of Minas are the highlights of any visit to the state and some of the prettiest towns in South America. Streets of whitewashed 18th-century Portuguese houses with deep blue or yellow window frames line steep and winding streets leading to lavishly decorated churches with Manueline façades and rich gilt interiors. Behind lies a backdrop of grey granite hills swathed with green forests, still filled with tiny marmoset monkeys and flocks of canary-winged parakeets. The most spectacular is Ouro Preto, which preserves some of the finest baroque architecture in the country. The town is easily visited from Belo Horizonte or on the way to or from Rio or São Paulo.

Essential colonial towns

Orientation

The towns fall into two groups: south of Belo Horizonte (Ouro Preto, Mariana, Congonhas do Campo, São João del Rei and Tiradentes); and north (Diamantina). The southern towns are on the main Rio highway (Ouro Preto being the closest to the state capital and São João del Rei the furthest from it). To the north, Diamantina is a longer journey from Belo Horizonte, off the inland route to Bahia.

Time required

The most famous of the towns, Ouro Preto, is often visited on a day trip from Belo Horizonte. However, one day is not enough. Allow at least two or three and use Ouro Preto

as a base for visiting nearby Mariana – either by bus or on the *Maria Fumaça* diesel train – and Congonhas. At the centre of Congonhas is a spectacular church reached by a walkway lined with Aleijadinho's famous statues of the prophets; the town is easily visited in a morning or afternoon. Tiradentes, further south, is perhaps the prettiest of all the cities, though it lacks the spectacular sights of Ouro Preto and feels somewhat touristy and twee. Nearby, São João del Rei is more decrepit but very much a real city. They are linked at weekends by a 30-minute steam train ride and daily by frequent buses. Diamantina is far to the north and can be visited en route to Bahia or as a trip from Belo Horizonte.

BACKGROUND
Colonial towns

Like the Spanish, the Portuguese looked to their colonies for easy money. Outside the Jesuit reduction cities, there were never plans to invest in empire, only to exploit the land and the local people as ruthlessly as possible. At first it was wood that attracted the Portuguese, and then indigenous slaves for the cane plantations that stretched along the northern coast. But it was the ultimate in rich pickings that led to colonial Brazil becoming more than a coastline empire.

In 1693, whilst out on a marauding expedition, a Paulista *bandeirante* found *ouro preto* (gold made black by a coat of iron oxide) in a stream south of modern Belo Horizonte. When news reached home, an influx of adventurers trekked their way from São Paulo through the forests to set up makeshift camps along the gold streams. These camps developed into wealthy towns such as Ouro Preto and Mariana. Later, with the discovery of diamonds and other gemstones, a captaincy was established and named, prosaically, 'General Mines'.

The wealth of Minas was reflected in its streets and in the baroque churches, whose interiors were covered in gold plate and decorated with sculptures by the best artisans in Brazil. And with the wealth came growing self-importance. The Inconfidência Mineira, the most important rebellion in colonial Brazil, began in Ouro Preto in the late 18th century under a group of intellectuals educated in Portugal who were in contact with Thomas Jefferson and English industrialists. The Inconfidência never got beyond discussion but it was decided that the only non-aristocratic member of the group, José Joaquim da Silva, would be in charge of taking the governor's palace, occupied by the hated Visconde of Barbacena, who was responsible for levying the imperial taxes. Da Silva was derisively known as Tiradentes (the tooth puller) by his compatriots. Today he is the only Inconfidênte rebel that most Brazilians can name, and he is celebrated as a folk hero – one of the common people who dared to challenge the powerful elite, and who was cruelly martyred as a result.

After Brazil changed from an empire into a republic, Minas Gerais vied for power with the coffee barons of São Paulo and, in the 20th century, produced two Brazilian presidents. Juscelino Kubitschek, an establishment figure chosen by the electorate as the best alternative to the military, opened up Brazil to foreign investment in the 1960s, and founded Brasília. Tancredo Neves, who also opposed the Brazilian military, was elected to power in 1985. A few days before his inauguration, he died in mysterious circumstances. His last words were reportedly "I did not deserve this". He was replaced by José Sarney, a leading figure in the Brazilian landowning oligarchy.

Ouro Preto (population 67,000, altitude 1000 m), named after the black iron oxide-coated gold that was discovered here by the adventurer Antônio Dias, was one of the first of the Minas gold towns to be founded. It became the wealthiest and most important town in the region and, until the establishment of the republic, was the state capital of Minas Gerais. Although it now has a hinterland of ugly blocks of flats and crumbling favelas, the town preserves some of the most significant colonial architecture in Brazil. In homage to its historical importance Ouro Preto becomes the capital of Minas Gerais once again every year for one day only, on 24 June.

The modern city bustles with young Brazilians studying and partying at the various local universities and has a thriving café and nightlife scene. Sadly the historic centre, once closed to traffic, is now overrun with buses and cars, which is taking its toll on some of the beautiful buildings.

Praça Tiradentes and around

The city has a number of churches and chapels as well as some beautiful *chafariz* (public fountains), *passos* (oratories) and stone bridges. The best place to start exploring the city is the central **Praça Tiradentes**, where you'll see a statue of Tiradentes, one of the leaders of the Inconfidêntes, a group who conspired to rid Brazil of Portuguese colonizers. Another Inconfidênte, the poet Tomás Antônio Gonzaga, lived at Rua Cláudio Manoel 61 near the São Francisco de Assis church, and was exiled to Africa. Most Brazilians know his poem based on his forbidden love affair with the girl he called Marília de Dirceu. Guides will show you the romantic bridge and decorative fountain where the lovers held their trysts. The house where she lived, on the Largo Marília de Dirceu, is now a school.

On the north side of Praça Tiradentes is a famous **Escola de Minas** (School of Mining). It was founded in 1876, is housed in the fortress-like Palácio dos Governadores (1741-1748) and includes the **Museu de Ciencia e Tecnica** ① *No 20, Tue-Sun 1200-1700, US$1, astronomical observatory (on a different site, Sat 2000-2200)*, which has one of the finest displays of rocks, minerals, semi-precious and precious stones in South America, including Minas black gold and rare locally sourced crystals. Just north of the *praça*, towards the *rodoviária*, is the church of Nossa Senhora das Mercês e Misericórdia (1773-1793).

On the south side of the *praça*, next to Carmo church, is the **Museu da Inconfidência** ① *No 139, T031-3551 1121, www.museudaincondencia.gov.br, Tue-Sun 1000-1800, US$2.50*, a fine historical and art museum in the former Casa de Câmara e Cadeia, containing drawings by Aleijadinho and the Studio of Manoel da Costa (Mestre) Athayde.

West of Praça Tiradentes

The church of **Nossa Senhora do Carmo** ① *R Brigadeiro Mosqueira, Tue-Sun 1300-1700, entry is shared with Nossa Senhora do Pilar*, built 1766-1772, was planned by Manoel Francisco Lisboa, and both his son and Mestre Athayde worked on the project. It was a favourite church of the aristocracy. Housed in an annexe of the church, the modern and well-appointed **Museu do Oratório** ① *T031-3551 5369, http://museudooratorio. org.br, Wed-Mon 0930-1730, US$1.25*, is the city's best museum. Inside is a selection of exquisitely crafted 18th- and 19th-century prayer icons and oratories, many of them with strong indigenous design and some disguised as bullet cases. On the opposite side of

ON THE ROAD

O Aleijadinho

Brazil's greatest sculptor, Antônio Francisco Lisboa (1738-1814), son of a Portuguese architect and a black slave woman, was known as O Aleijadinho (the little cripple). A debilitating disease – probably leprosy – left him so badly maimed that he was forced to work on his knees and later on his back with his chisels strapped to his useless hands. Like Mestre Athayde and many other Mineira baroque artists his art was political. He was strongly sympathetic with the Inconfidêntes movement and was probably a friend of Tiradentes. Many of his sculptures contain subtle references to Tiradentes's martyrdom and veiled criticisms of the Portuguese. His most remarkable works are the haunting, vivid statues of the prophets in Congonhas (which are so lifelike that they almost seem to move), and the church decoration in Ouro Preto. Aleijadinho was also responsible for the design of the expanded Igreja Matriz de Santo Antônio in Tiradentes.

the road, the **Teatro Municipal** ⓘ *R Brigadeiro Musqueiro, Mon-Fri 1200-1800*, is the oldest functioning theatre in Latin America, built in 1769.

A block north of the theatre, **Casa Guignard** ⓘ *R Conde de Bobadela 110, T031-3551 5155, Tue-Fri 0900-1200 and 1300-1800, free*, displays the paintings of Alberto da Veiga Guignard.

Further west, just before the river, the **Casa das Contas** ⓘ *R São José 12, T031-355 1444, Tue-Sat 1230-1730, Sun and holidays 0900-1500, free*, built 1782-1784, houses a museum of money and finance on its upper storeys. Far more interesting is the damp, dark basement where slaves were formerly housed. In colonial Ouro Preto a slave's life was literally worth less than a chicken: swapping an African Brazilian for poultry was considered a good deal.

Following Rua Teixeira Amaral across the river, the church of **São José** was begun in 1752, but not completed until 1811; some of the carving is by Aleijadinho (see box, above). Up on the hill, **São Francisco de Paula** ⓘ *0900-1700*, was started in 1804, making it the last colonial church in Ouro Preto.

Further west, on the Largo do Rosário, the church of **Nossa Senhora do Rosário** dates from 1785, when the present church replaced a chapel on the site. It has a curved façade, which is rare in Brazilian baroque. The interior is more simple than the exterior, but there are interesting side altars.

One of the city's grandest churches, **Nossa Senhora do Pilar** ⓘ *just north of R do Pilar, Tue-Sun 0900-1045 and 1200-1645, US$2.50*, was attended by the Portuguese upper classes. The ceiling painting by João de Carvalhães features a trompe l'oeil effect – as you walk to the front of the church the lamb appears to move from one side of the crucifix to the other – a symbol of the resurrection. Manoel Lisboa, Aleijadinho's father, was responsible for all the carving except the heavily gilded work around the altar, which is by Francisco Xavier de Brito who was almost certainly Aleijadinho's master and who was largely responsible for the magnificent interior in the church of **Ordem Terceira de São Francisco da Penitência** in Rio (see page 45). The museum in the church vaults is one of the best in Minas, preserving some stunning gold and silver monstrances and some of Xavier de Brito's finest sculptures, including a wonderful image of Christ.

East of Praça Tiradentes

A block southeast of Praça Tiradentes, on the Largo São Francisco, is one of the masterpieces of Brazilian baroque, the church of **São Francisco de Assis** ⓘ *Largo de Coimbra, T031-3551 3282, Tue-Sun 0830-1200, 1330-1700, US$2.50; keep your ticket for the museum, which houses the collection from Nossa Senhora da Conceição until that it re-opens in 2016.* Built 1766-1796, Aleijadinho (see box, page 161) worked on the general design and the sculpture of the façade, the pulpits and many other features. The harmonious lines of the exterior and the gentle beauty of the interior are exceptional – far less ornate than the opulent gold-covered churches of Salvador, and with artwork altogether more subtle and refined. The relatively modest appearance and quiet atmosphere of the church

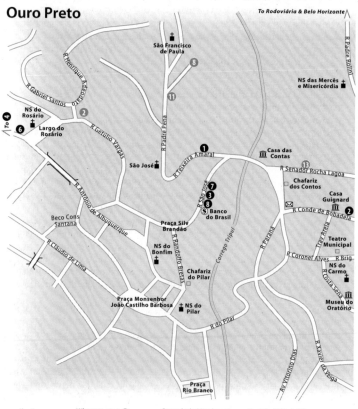

Ouro Preto

N		

Where to stay 🛏	Pousada do Mondego **5**	Pousada Solar de NS
Brumas **11**	Pousada dos	do Rosário **2**
Colonial **1**	Bandeirantes **4**	Pousada Tiradentes **9**
Grande **13**	Pousada Nello Nuno **15**	Pouso Chico Rei **10**
Luxor Pousada **3**	Pousada São Francisco	Solar das Lajes **12**
Pousada Casa Grande **6**	de Paula **8**	

suggest that it is a model of tolerance and piety. But it's far from it. When it was built the church was a bastion of Portuguese social propriety. Aleijadinho was a *mulatto* – as were Mestre Athayde's wife and children – and as such they were prohibited from entering white churches like São Francisco, from eating any meat other than offal, ears and trotters and they had no rights in civil society. *Mulatto* sculptors were not even considered to be artists; they were referred to as artisans or *artistas de sangue sujo* (artists of dirty blood).

The church is full of subtle criticisms of the Portuguese encoded in the art by Athayde and Aleijadinho. The model for the Virgin (depicted in the highest heaven, surrounded by cherubs and musicians and saints Augustine, Hieronymous, Gregory and Ambrosius), is said to have been Mestre Athayde's *mulatto* wife. She has her breasts showing, open legs

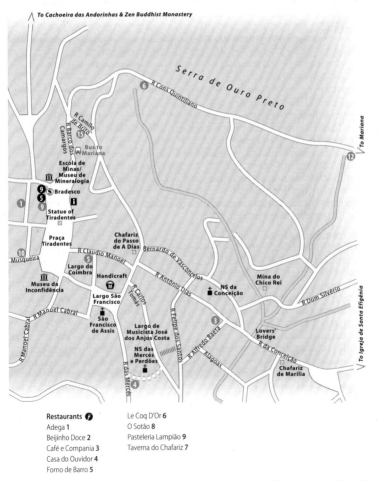

Restaurants 📍
Adega **1**
Beijinho Doce **2**
Café e Compania **3**
Casa do Ouvidor **4**
Forno de Barro **5**

Le Coq D'Or **6**
O Sotão **8**
Pasteleria Lampião **9**
Taverna do Chafariz **7**

and her face shows African traces; all of which can only be noticed with careful attention and all of which would have been anathema to the Portuguese. The *Last Supper* painting in the sanctuary replaces the apostles with Portuguese feeding on meat and being attended to by Brazilian servants. And Aleijadinho's *Sacred Heart of Jesus* near the altar has its hands and feet cut into quarters in a reference to the fate that befell Tiradentes at the hands of the Portuguese. A museum at the back of the church has a small selection of paintings of serious-looking saints and a fountain by Aleijadinho depicting *Blind Faith* holding up a banner saying "such is the path to heaven".

In the largo outside São Francisco is a handicraft market. South of here, the church of **Nossa Senhora das Mercês e Perdões** ① *R das Mercês, Tue-Sun 1000-1400,* (1740-1772), was rebuilt in the 19th century. Some sculptures by Aleijadinho can be seen in the main chapel.

Further east, **Nossa Senhora da Conceição** ① *Tue-Sat 0830-1130, 1330-1700, Sun 1200-1700,* was built in 1722 and is the parish church of Antônio Dias (one of the original settlements that became Vila Rica de Albuquerque). It is heavily gilded and contains Aleijadinho's tomb. The adjacent museum devoted to him is closed for renovation until 2016, and the works it preserves are currently on display in the Igreja São Francisco de Assis museum.

Across the river, the 18-km-long **Mina do Chico Rei** ① *R Dom Silvério, 0800-1700, US$2.50,* is not as impressive as some other mines in the area, but is fun to descend on the pulley, crawl through the narrow tunnels and learn how the gold was mined. The Chico Rei who gave his name to the mines was supposedly an African king called Francisco, who was enslaved but bought his freedom working in the mine.

On the eastern edge of town, **Santa Efigênia** ① *Ladeira Santa Efigênia and Padre Faria, Tue-Sun 0800-1630, US$1,* built 1720-1785, has wonderful panoramic views of the city. This was a church used by black Brazilians only and the gilt that lines the interior is said to have been made from gold dust washed out of slaves' hair. Manuel Francisco Lisboa (Aleijadinho's father) oversaw the construction and much of the carving is by Francisco Xavier de Brito (Aleijadinho's mentor).

Trips from Ouro Preto

Minas da Passagem ① *T031-3557 5000, www.minasdapassagem.com.br, Mon-Tue 0900-1700 and Wed to Sun 0900-1730, US$6.50,* is the world's largest gold mine open to the public, located 8 km from Ouro Preto on the way to Mariana. It's an exciting place to visit, with a thrilling Indiana Jones descent on an old mining cart followed by a guided wander through gloomy passages and large artificial caverns to a dark crystal-clear lake. Much of the clunking machinery dates from the early 18th century. There is also the opportunity to pan for gold on the tour. Note that some signs for the mine say 'Mina de Ouro', omitting 'da Passagem'.

There is a waterfall nearby, the **Cachoeira Serrinha**, where swimming is possible; walk 100 m towards Mariana then ask for directions. The nearest town to the mine is **Passagem de Mariana**. The bus stops at the edge of town by the **Pousada Solar dos Dois Sinos**, which has a church behind it.

Tourist information

Avoid the unaccredited guides who hang around at the *rodoviária*.

Posto de Informações Turísticas
At the rodoviária, *T031-3551 5552. Mon-Fri 0700-1300.*

Tourist office
Praça Tiradentes 41, T031-3559 3269; and R Claudio Manoel 61, T031-3559 3287, www.ouropreto.org.br. Open 0800-1800.
Within the **Centro Cultural e Turistico** mini-mall (with the town's best exhibition space, as well as shops and cafés), the tourist office has details of accommodation in *casas de família*, *repúblicas* (see below under Student hostels) and other places. It also has leaflets showing the opening times of sights, which change frequently, and can organize a local accredited guide from the **Associação de Guias de Turismo** (**AGTOP**) (R Padre Rolim s/n, T031-3551 2655, Mon-Sun 0800-1800, Sat and Sun 0800-1700, little English spoken), which has its own office opposite the bus station.

Where to stay

Many hotels will negotiate lower prices off season. Ask at the tourist office for reasonably priced accommodation in *casas de família*. Avoid touts who greet you off buses and charge higher prices than those advertised in hotels; it is difficult to get hotel rooms at weekends and holiday periods. Rooms can be booked through www.ouro pretotour.com or www.ouropreto.com.

$$$$ Grande Hotel
R das Flores 164, Centro, T031-3551 1488, www.grandehotelouropreto.com.br.
One of a handful of gorgeous Niemeyer hotels dotted throughout Minas, with views over the city.

$$$ Luxor Pousada
R Dr Alfredo Baeta 16, Praça Antônio Dias, T031-3551 2244, http://hotelluxor.com.br.
Converted colonial mansion, no twin beds, comfortable and clean but spartan, great views, restaurant good but service slow.

$$$ Pousada Casa Grande
R Conselheiro Quintiliano 96, T031-3551 4314, www.hotelpousadacasagrande.com.br.
A large colonial townhouse with 21 smart, but simply appointed rooms with polished wooden floors, en suites and some with views out over the city.

$$$ Pousada do Mondego
Largo de Coimbra 38, T031-3551 2040, www.mondego.com.br.
Beautifully kept colonial house in a fine location by São Francisco church. Room rates vary according to view.

$$$ Pousada Solar de NS do Rosário
Av Getúlio Vargas 270, T031-3551 5200, www.hotelsolardorosario.com.br.
Fully restored historic building with a highly recommended restaurant, as well as a bar, sauna, pool; all facilities in rooms.

$$ Colonial
Trav Padre Camilo Veloso 26, close to Praça Tiradentes, T031-3551 3133, www.hotelcolonial.com.br.
A little colonial house with 14 rooms. All are well maintained. Some are distinctly smaller than others so it is worth looking at a few. Decor is modest, with furniture sitting on a polished wooden floor.

$$ Pousada Nello Nuno
R Camilo de Brito 59, T031-3551 3375, www.pousadanellonuno.com.br.
The friendly owner, Annamélia, speaks some French. Cheaper rooms have no bath. Highly recommended.

$$ Pousada São Francisco de Paula
R Pe José Marcos Pena 202, next to the São Francisco de Paula church, T031-3551 3156, www.pousadasaofranciscodepaula.com.br.
One of the best views of any in the city; from the rooms or from a hammock in the garden. The hostel has 8 rustic rooms including a dormitory, and is only 100 m from the *rodoviária*. Services and facilities include the free use of a kitchen. There are multilingual staff and trips are available.

$$ Pousada Tiradentes
Praça Tiradentes 70, T031-3551 2619, www.pousadatiradentesop.com.br.
The rooms are spartan but well kept and moderately comfortable. Each has a TV and a fridge. Conveniently located.

$$ Pouso Chico Rei
R Brig Musqueira 90, T031-3551 1274, www.pousodochicorei.com.br.
A fascinating old house with Portuguese colonial furnishings, very small and utterly delightful (room No 6 has been described as a 'dream'). Book in advance.

$$ Solar das Lajes
R Conselheiro Quintiliano 604, T031-3551 1116, www.hotelsolardaslajes.com.br.
A little way from the centre but with an excellent view and a pool, and well run.

$$-$ Brumas Hostel
R Antônio Pereira, 43 (next to the Museu da Inconfidência), T031-3551 2944, www.brumashostel.com.br.
Small well-kept rooms and dorms with parquet floors, chunky wooden bunks and in the double rooms, flatscreen TVs. Those on the upper corridor have views of the surrounding misty mountains. Excellent location in the heart of the colonial town overlooking the São Francisco church.

$ Pousada dos Bandeirantes
R das Mercês 167, T031-3551 1996.
Behind the São Francisco de Assis church and offering beautiful views.

Student hostels
During holidays and weekends students may be able to stay at the self-governing hostels, known as *repúblicas* (described as very welcoming, "best if you like heavy metal music" and "are prepared to enter into the spirit of the place"). The *prefeitura* has a list of over 50 *repúblicas* with phone numbers, available at the **Secretaria de Turismo**. Many are closed between Christmas and Carnaval.

Restaurants

Try the local firewater, *licor de jaboticaba*, made from a sweet Brazilian tropical fruit.

$$$ Le Coq D'Or
Solar do Rosário (see Where to stay), R Getúlio Vargas 270 (next to the Rosário church), T031-3551 5200.
Brazilian-French fusion cooking in a smart dining room with live music. One of the city's best.

$$ Adega
R Teixeira Amaral 24, T031-3551 4171. Open 1130-1530.
Vegetarian smorgasbord, US$5, all you can eat. Highly recommended.

$$ Beijinho Doce
R Conde de Bobadela 134.
Decent *bacalhau* and steak, delicious pastries, lousy coffee. Try the truffles.

$$ Café e Compania
R São José 187, T031-3551 0711. Closes 2300.
Very popular, *comida por kilo* at lunchtime, good salads and juices.

$$ Casa do Ouvidor
R Conde de Bobadela 42, T031-3551 2141.
The best in the city for traditional Minas fare, served in a lovely old mansion house 2 mins' walk from Praça Tiradentes.

$$ O Sotão
R São José 201, T031-8725 9434.
Great-value pancake and crêpe restaurant with some 40 different flavours ranging from *abobora com carne seca e catupiry* (pumpkin

with jerk meat and cream cheese) to *Da Casa* with mozzarella, sun-dried tomatoes, basil and mushrooms. Cocktails all have film names.

$$ Pasteleria Lampião
Praça Tiradentes.
Good views at the back (better at lunchtime than in the evening).

$$ Taverna do Chafariz
R São José 167, T031-3551 2828.
Good local food. Recommended.

$ Forno de Barro
Praça Tiradentes 54.
Decent Mineira buffet with varied plates and sweet puddings. Generous portions.

Festivals

Many shops close during Holy Week and on winter weekends.

Feb **Carnaval** attracts many people.
Mar/Apr Ouro Preto is famous for its **Holy Week** processions, which actually begin on the Thu before Palm Sun and continue (but not every day) until Easter Sun. The most famous is that commemorating Christ's removal from the Cross, late on Good Fri.
Jun **Corpus Christi** and **Festas Juninas**.
Jul The city holds the **Festival do Inverno da Universidade Federal de Minas Gerais** (**UFMG**), the 'Winter Festival', about 3 weeks of arts, courses, concerts and exhibitions.
8 Jul **Anniversary of the city**.
15 Aug **Nossa Senhora do Pilar**, patron saint of Ouro Preto.
12-18 Nov **Semana de Aleijadinho**, a week-long arts festival.

Shopping

Gems and jewellery
Gems are not much cheaper from freelance sellers in Praça Tiradentes than from the shops. If buying gems on the street, ask for the seller's credentials.
Gemas de Minas, *Conde de Bobadela 63.* One of the city's better jewellers.

Videmaju, *R Conselheiro Santana 175.* Vincente Júlio de Paula, a professor at the School of Mines, sells stones at very good prices.

Handicrafts
Buy soapstone carvings at roadside stalls rather than in the cities; they are much cheaper. Many artisans sell carvings, jewellery and semi-precious stones in the **Largo de Coimbra** in front of São Francisco de Assis church. Also worth buying is traditional cookware in stone, copper or enamelled metal.

What to do

Yoga centre, *down an alley between Nos 31 and 47 (Cine Teatro Vila Rica), Praça Alves de Brito, T031-3551 3337.* Offers shiatsu and Kerala massage.

Transport

Bus Ouro Preto's *rodoviária* (R Padre Rolim 661, T031-3559 3252), is 1 km north of Praça Tiradentes, and has a **Posto de Informações Turísticas** (see under Tourist information, above). A circular bus runs from the *rodoviária* to Praça Tiradentes, US$1.50. Taxis charge exorbitant rates.

Buses run to **Belo Horizonte** at least once an hour 0600-2300 (2 hrs, US$7.70). Day trips are possible; book your return journey to Belo Horizonte early if returning in the evening; buses get crowded. To **Mariana**, buses run from the Escola de Minas near Praça Tiradentes every 30 mins, US$1.95, 30 mins, all passing **Minas da Passagem** (buses also leave from Ouro Preto *rodoviária*). To **Congonhas** you will need to change bus in Ouro Branco: 3 daily to **Ouro Branco** from Ouro Preto, first at 0715 (US$1.50, 50 mins); 7 daily from Ouro Branco to **Congonhas** (US$1.40, 90 mins). Take the 1615 bus from Congonhas to Ouro Branco for the last bus back to Ouro Preto.

To **Rio** there are 4 daily buses including 2 night buses (from US$24, 7 hrs 40 mins). To **São Paulo**, 1 night bus daily (10½ hrs, US$36).

Train The **Maria Fumaça Trem da Vale** (Praça Cesário Alvim s/n, T031-3551 7310, www.tremdavale.org) is now a diesel train and not a steam locomotive. It leaves Fri-Sun at 1000, returning from **Mariana** at 1400, with an extra train leaving Ouro Preto at 1530 and from Mariana at 0800 on public holidays. Tickets start at US$14.40 for a return. For the best views during the 18-km 40-min journey, sit on the right side and in the back carriages.

Mariana

the oldest of the colonial mining towns in Minas Gerais

Mariana (population 47,000, altitude 697 m) has many fine colonial buildings, most of them constructed in the second half of the 18th century, but on the outskirts these are overshadowed by some ramshackle and ugly concrete edifices and an unsightly road. The artist Mestre Athayde was born here, as was the Inconfidênte Cláudio Manuel da Costa. The town was declared a National Monument in 1945.

Unlike its more famous neighbour, Ouro Preto, in whose shadow the town tends to sit, Mariana has remained a working mining centre. For many years the **Companhia do Vale do Rio Doce (CVRD)** had major operations here and provided a great deal of assistance for the restoration of the colonial heritage.

Mariana was founded by *bandeirantes* a few years before Ouro Preto, on 16 July 1696. At first, when it was little more than a collection of huts, it was called Arraial de Nossa Senhora do Carmo but by 1711 it had become the town of Vila de Nossa Senhora do Carmo, and by the mid-18th century it had grown to be the most important administrative centre in the newly created Capitania de São Paulo e Minas do Ouro. Its name was changed to Mariana in honour of the wife of Dom João V, Dona Maria Ana of Austria.

Sights

The historic centre of the town slopes gently uphill from the river and the **Praça Tancredo Neves**, where buses from Ouro Preto stop. The first street parallel with the Praça Tancredo Neves is Rua Direita, which is lined with beautiful, two-storey 18th-century houses with tall colonial windows and balconies. The **Casa do Barão de Pontal** ① *R Direita 54, not officially open to the public*, is unique in Minas Gerais, with its balconies carved from soapstone.

Rua Direita leads to the **Praça da Sé**, on which stands the cathedral, **Basílica de Nossa Senhora da Assunção**. Before Vila de Nossa Senhora do Carmo became a town, a chapel dating from 1703 stood on this spot. In various stages it was expanded and remodelled until its completion in 1760. The portal and the lavabo in the sacristy are by Aleijadinho (see box, page 161) and the painting in the beautiful interior and side altars is by Manoel Rabello de Sousa. Also in the cathedral is a wooden German organ (1701), made by Arp Schnitger, which was a gift to the first diocese of the Capitania de Minas do Ouro in 1747. It was restored in 1984 after some 50 years of silence. Concerts are held in the cathedral including regular organ concerts (Friday at 1100, Sunday at 1215, US$7.60; see the local press for details).

Turning up Rua Frei Durão, on the right is the **Museu Arquidiocesano** ① *R Frei Durão 49, Tue-Fri 0830-1200, 1330-1700, Sat-Sun and holidays 0900-1500, US$1.25*, which has fine church furniture, a gold and silver collection, Aleijadinho statues and an ivory cross. On the opposite side of the street is the **Casa da Intendência/Casa de Cultura** ① *R Frei Durão 84, 0800-1130, 1330-1700*, which holds exhibitions and has a museum of music. The ceilings in the exhibition rooms are very fine; in other rooms there are *esteiro* (flattened bamboo) ceilings.

ON THE ROAD
Sweet river, bitter spill

On 5 November 2015 Brazil experienced its worst ever single environmental disaster when two dams sealing off contaminated mining waste mud burst at a site near Mariana. The volume of waste mud was sufficient to overwhelm the Rio Doce. Some 50 million tons (enough to fill 20,000 Olympic swimming pools) of sticky brown effluent swamped 850 sq km of land, turning the entire river basin red, flooding into the water table, silting up the estuary and swathing the turtle-nesting beaches and mangrove forests of the coast. At least 17 people died (all the missing have yet to be accounted for), 500 were displaced and Bento Rodrigues, a satellite town of Mariana, was wiped off the map. In addition, 250,000 people lost access to drinking water and millions of fish died, depriving coastal and riverine fishing communities of their source of food and livelihood.

The dams were built and maintained by Samarco, the world's biggest mining company and a joint venture of huge multinational mining companies, including Anglo-Australian BHP Billiton and Brazilian Vale. Joint statements issued by the mining conglomerate and the Brazilian government after the disaster concluded that the chemicals released in the mud was harmless to human health, and that the long-term environmental impact would be minimal.

The UN concluded otherwise. On 25 November 2015 UN Special Rapporteurs found high levels of toxic heavy metals, including arsenic and mercury, and other toxic chemicals such as amines in the river Doce. They noted that the Doce "is now considered by scientists to be dead and the toxic sludge is slowly working its way downstream towards the Abrolhos National Marine Park where it threatens protected forest and habitat. Sadly, the mud has already entered the sea at Regência beach, a sanctuary for endangered turtles and a rich source of nutrients that the local fishing community relies upon." And they were scathing about the government and corporate response, calling it "unacceptable."

Samarco responded by stating that according to its data, the tailings were chemically stable. Government ministers also denied negligence, seizing the company's assets and announcing plans to sue for US$5.2 billion.

The large **Praça Gomes Freire** was where horses would be tied up (there is an old drinking trough on one side) and where festivals were held. Now it has pleasant gardens. On the south side is the **Palácio Arquiepiscopal**, while on the north side is the **Casa do Conde de Assumar**, home of the governor of the *capitania* from 1717 to 1720; it later became the bishop's palace.

Praça Minas Gerais has one of the finest groups of colonial buildings in Brazil. In the middle is the *Pelourinho*, the stone monument to justice at which slaves used to be beaten. The fine **São Francisco church** ① *daily 0800-1700*, built 1762-1794, has pulpits, a fine sacristy and an altar designed by Aleijadinho, and paintings by Mestre Athayde, who is buried in tomb No 94. The statue of São Roque is most important as he is the patron saint of the city (his day is 16 August). Among Athayde's paintings are the panels showing the life of St Francis, on the ceiling of the right-hand chapel. The church is one of the most simple in Mariana but, in terms of art, one of the richest. There is a small exhibition of the restoration work funded by CVRD.

At right angles to São Francisco is **Nossa Senhora do Carmo** ⓘ *daily 1400-1700*, built 1784, with steatite carvings, Athayde paintings, and chinoiserie panelling. Some consider its exterior to be the most beautiful in Mariana. Unfortunately this church was damaged by fire in 1999. Across Rua Dom Silvério is the **Casa da Cámara e Cadéia** (1768), once the Prefeitura Municipal. It is a superb example of civic colonial construction.

On Rua Dom Silvério, the **Colégio Providência**, at No 61, was the first college for boarding students in Minas Gerais. Also on this street is the Igreja da Arquiconfraria and, near the top of the hill, the Chafariz de São Pedro. On Largo de São Pedro is the church of **São Pedro dos Clérigos**, founded by Manuel da Cruz, first bishop of the town (1764), one of the few elliptical churches in Minas Gerais. It is unadorned, although there is a painting by Athayde, *A Entrega do Menino Jesus a Santo Antônio*. The cedar altar was made by José Pedro Aroca. Look for the cockerel, carved in memory of the biblical verses about St Peter betraying Christ before the cock has crowed three times. Ask to see the view from the bell tower.

Beyond the centre

The **Capela de Santo Antônio**, wonderfully simple and the oldest in town, is some distance from the centre on Rua Rosário Velho. Overlooking the city from the north, with a good viewpoint, is the church of **Nossa Senhora do Rosário** ⓘ *R do Rosário*, dating back to 1752, with work by Athayde and showing Moorish influence.

Outside the centre to the west, but within easy walking distance, is the **Seminário Menor**, now the Instituto de Ciencias Históricas e Sociais of the federal university.

South of the river, Avenida Getúlio Vargas leads to the new Prefeitura Municipal. It passes the Ginásio Poliesportivo and, across the avenue, the railway station. This is a romantic building with a clock tower, but it is rapidly falling into disrepair.

Listings Mariana

Tourist information

Mariana Turismo
R Direita 31.
Helpful staff.

Tourist office
Praça Tancredo Neves, T031-3557 9044, www.mariana.mg.gov.br.
Can organize guides and has a map and free monthly booklet, *Mariana Agenda Cultural*, full of information.

Where to stay

Most of these hotels are housed in colonial buildings. Further details can be found on www.mariana.mg.gov.br. Prices are often cheaper at weekends as most visitors to Mariana come on business.

$$$ Faísca
R Antônio Olinto 48, T031-3557 1206, www.hotelfaisca.com.br.
Up the street from the tourist office. Suites and rooms, breakfast included.

$$$ Pousada Solar dos Corrêa
R Josefá Macedo 70 and R Direita, T031-3557 2080.
A restored 18th-century townhouse with spacious a/c rooms.

$$$ Pouso da Typographia
Praça Gomes Freire 220, T031-3557 1577.
The best in town with fan-cooled rooms in an attractive colonial town house which once housed a printing works, overlooking the central *praça*. All are large with wooden floors, whitewashed walls, modest work desks and chunky beds.

$$ Pousada do Chafariz
R Cônego Rego 149, T031-3557 1492,
www.pousadadochafariz.com.br.
A converted colonial building with parking,
breakfast and a family atmosphere.
Recommended.

Restaurants

There are many restaurants dotted around
Praça Gomes Freire. Most are lunch only.

$$ Bistrô
R Salomão Ibrahim da Silva 61,
T031-3557 4138. Open at night.
Comida mineira, decent steaks, pasta,
pizza and *petiscos*. A menu of German-
Brazilian beers.

$$ Lua Cheia
R Dom Viçoso.58, T031-3557 3232.
Good-value lunchtime buffet with
Minas food, pasta, salads and juices.

Transport

Bus Buses from Ouro Preto and Belo
Horizonte stop at the *rodoviária*, out of town
on the main road, then at the Posto Mariana,
before heading back to the centre at Praça
Tancredo Neves. Many buses seem to go
only to the *posto* (petrol station) above the
town, but it's a long walk from the centre. A
bus from the *rodoviária* to the centre via the
posto and Minas da Passagem costs US$1.15.

Buses to **Ouro Preto** can be caught by
the bridge at the end of R do Catete, every
30 mins, US$1.95, 30 mins, all passing **Minas
da Passagem**. Frequent daily buses to **Belo
Horizonte** (2 hrs, US$8.15). Buses for **Santa
Bárbara** (near Caraça) leave from the *rodoviária*.

Train Maria Fumaça trains run between **Ouro
Preto** and Mariana; see Transport, page 168.

Around Mariana
Bus There are 3 buses a day from Mariana
to **Antônio Pereira**, Mon-Fri, 0800, 1200,
1445, plus 1100, 1750 and 2100 on Sat.

Congonhas do Campo
known for its handsome church designed by Aleijadinho, and its handicrafts

In the 18th century, Congonhas (population 42,000, altitude 866 m) was a mining
town. Today, in addition to the business brought by the tourists and pilgrims who
come to the sanctuary, it is known for its handicrafts. There is little need to stay in
Congonhas as the town's main sight, Aleijadinho's beautiful church and chapel-
lined stairway, can be seen in a few hours between bus changes. Leave your bags
at the information desk in the bus station.

O Santuário de Bom Jesus de Matosinhos
*Tue-Sun 0700-1900. Buses leave you at the rodoviária in Congonhas de Campo, 2 km from the
sanctuary. It's an easy walk or you can take a taxi for US$2. Alternatively, a bus marked 'Basílica'
runs every 30 mins from the rodoviária in Conselheiro Lafaiete to the sanctuary itself, 8 km, US$1,
or take a taxi, US$6 one-way, US$12.50 return including the wait while you visit the sanctuary.*

The great pilgrimage church and its Via Sacra dominate the town. The idea of building
a sanctuary belonged to a prospector, Feliciano Mendes, who promised to erect a cross
and chapel in thanks to Bom Jesus after he had been cured of a serious illness. The
inspiration for his devotion came from two sources in Portugal, the cult of Bom Jesus at
Braga (near where Mendes was born) and the church of Bom Jesus de Matosinhos, near
Porto. Work began in 1757, funded by Mendes' own money and alms he raised. The church

was finished in 1771, six years after Mendes' death, and the fame that the sanctuary had acquired led to its development by the most famous architects, artists and sculptors of the time as a Sacro Monte. This involved the construction of six linked chapels, or *pasos* (1802-1818), which lead up to a terrace and courtyard before the church.

There is a wide view of the country from the church terrace, below which are six small chapels set in an attractive sloping area with grass, cobblestones and palms. Each chapel shows scenes with life-size Passion figures carved by Aleijadinho (see box, page 161) and his pupils in cedar wood. In order of ascent they are: the chapel of the Last Supper; the chapel of the Mount of Olives; the chapel of the betrayal of Christ; the chapel of the flagellation and the crowning with thorns; the chapel of Jesus carrying the Cross; and the chapel of Christ being nailed to the Cross.

On the terrace stand the 12 prophets sculpted by Aleijadinho 1800-1805; these are thought of as his masterpieces. Carved in soapstone with a dramatic sense of movement, they constitute one of the finest works of art of their period in the world. Note how Aleijadinho adapted the biblical characters to his own cultural references. The prophets are sculpted wearing leather boots, as all important men in his time would have done. Daniel, who entered the lion's den, is represented with the artist's own conception of a lion, never having seen one himself: a large, maned cat with a face rather like a Brazilian monkey. Similarly, the whale that accompanies Jonah is an idiosyncratic interpretation. Each statue has a prophetic text carved with it. The statues "combine in a kind of sacred ballet whose movements only seem uncoordinated; once these sculptures cease to be considered as isolated units, they take on full significance as part of a huge composition brought to life by an inspired genius." (*Iberian-American Baroque*, edited by Henri Stierlin) The beauty of the whole is enhanced by the combination of church, Via Sacra and landscape over which the prophets preside.

Inside the church, there are paintings by Athayde and the heads of four sainted popes (Gregory, Jerome, Ambrose and Augustine) sculpted by Aleijadinho for the reliquaries on the high altar. Other artists involved were João Nepomuceno Correia e Castro, who painted the scenes of the life and passion of Christ in the nave and around the high altar, João Antunes de Carvalho, who carved the high altar, and Jerônimo Félix and Manuel Coelho, who carved the crossing altars of Santo Antônio and São Francisco de Paula. Despite the ornate carving, the overall effect of the paintwork is almost muted and naturalistic, with much use of blues, greys and pinks. Lamps are suspended on chains from the mouths of black dragons. To the left of the church, through the third door in the building alongside the church, is the Room of Miracles, which contains photographs and thanks for miracles performed.

Up on the hill, the Alameda das Palmeiras sweeps from the Hotel Colonial round to the **Romarias**, a large, almost oval area surrounded by buildings. This was the lodging where the pilgrims stayed. It now contains the **Espaço Cultural** and tourist office, as well as workshops, the museums of mineralogy and religious art, and the Memória da Cidade.

Other churches

Of the other churches in Congonhas do Campo, the oldest is **Nossa Senhora do Rosário**, Praça do Rosário, built by slaves at the end of the 17th century. The **Igreja Matriz de Nossa Senhora da Conceição**, in Praça 7 de Setembro, dates from 1749; the portal is attributed to Aleijadinho, while parts of the interior are by Manuel Francisco Lisboa. There are also two 18th-century chapels, Nossa Senhora da Ajuda, in the district of Alto Maranhão, and the church at Lobo Leite, 10 km away.

Tourist information

On the hill are a tourist kiosk, souvenir shops, the **Colonial Hotel** and **Cova do Daniel** restaurant (see below). There are public toilets on the Alameda das Palmeiras.

Fumcult
In the Romarias, T031-3731 1300 ext 114.
This place acts as the tourist office and is very helpful.

Where to stay

$$ Colonial
Praça da Basílica 76, opposite Bom Jesus, T031-3731 1834, www. hotelcolonialcongonhas.com.br.
This converted colonial townhouse is in a superb location right next to the *sanctuário* at the top of the hill. Rooms are spacious but can be noisy. Breakfast extra, cheaper without bath. The fascinating restaurant, **Cova do Daniel**, downstairs is full of colonial handicrafts and good local food.

Transport

Bus The *rodoviária* is 1.5 km outside town; a bus to the centre costs US$0.65. In town, the bus stops in Praça JK from where you can walk up Praça Dr Mário Rodrigues Pereira, cross the little bridge, then go up R Bom Jesus and R Aleijadinho to the Praça da Basílica.

5 daily buses to **Ouro Branco** (US$3, 90 mins, change in Ouro Branco for **Ouro Preto**). The last bus which enables you to make this connection leaves at 1615.

There are frequent daily direct buses to **Belo Horizonte** (US$8, 2 hrs) and Ouro Preto (US$6, 1 hr 45 mins). To **São João del Rei** (for **Tiradentes**) buses run twice a week on Sat and Sun afternoon (2½ hrs, US$9). At other times flag down the São João del Rei bus on the main BR-040 highway (7 daily). Alternatively, go via **Conselheiro Lafaiete**, frequent buses (20 mins) from where there are 7 daily buses to **São João del Rei**.

There are no direct buses to **Rio** or the other southern Minas towns. To reach Congonhas from these, change at Conselheiro Lafaiete, from where there is 1 direct bus daily to Rio, 9 hrs, US$21, and numerous buses for the rest of southern Minas.

cobbled streets and handsome baroque churches against a hilly backdrop

After Ouro Preto, Tiradentes (population 7000) is the most visited of the Minas colonial towns. Its winding, hilly streets lined with carefully restored baroque Portuguese churches and neat whitewashed cottages huddle around the Santo Antonio River, beneath the rugged hills of the Serra de São José. Inside are art galleries, restaurants, souvenir shops and some 200 *pousadas*, all busy with tourists, especially at weekends, while horse-drawn carriages regularly clatter along the cobbles.

At weekends a steam train towing Pullmans full of delighted children puffs its way slowly below the mountains to the pretty colonial town of São João del Rei (see page 179), 30 minutes away and served by frequent buses. With better bus connections with Rio, São Paulo, Belo Horizonte, Mariana and Ouro Preto than Tiradentes, São João is the access point to Tiradentes if you're travelling on public transport. Tiradentes is the more twee of the two and has a far greater choice of accommodation; São João is less pretty but is more of a real town.

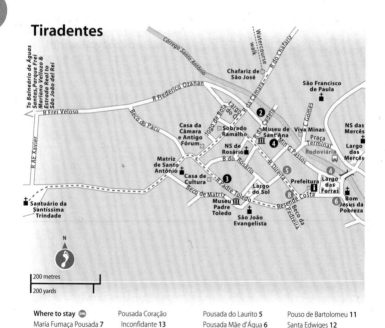

Tiradentes

Where to stay 🛏	Pousada Coração	Pousada do Laurito 5	Pouso de Bartolomeu 11
Maria Fumaça Pousada 7	Inconfidante 13	Pousada Mãe d'Água 6	Santa Edwiges 12
Pequena Tiradentes 1	Pousada da Sirlei 3	Pousada Três Portas 8	Solar da Ponte 9
Pousada Araújo Bazilio 2	Pousada do Largo 4	Pouso das Gerais 10	

Sights

A suggested walking tour is as follows. From the main *praça*, **Largo das Forras**, take Rua Resende Costa up to the Largo do Sol, a lovely open space where you'll find the simple church of **São João Evangelista** ⓘ *Wed-Mon 0900-1700*. Built by the Irmandade dos Homens Pardos (*mulattos*), it has paintings of the four Evangelists and a cornice painted in an elaborate pattern in pink, blue and beige. Beside the church is the **Museu Padre Toledo**, the house of this leader of the Inconfidência Mineira, which is now a museum protecting some handsome colonial furniture and a painted roof depicting the Five Senses. The **Casa de Cultura** ⓘ *not open to the public*, in the row of 18th-century houses on Rua Padre Toledo, which leads from Largo do Sol to the Igreja Matriz de Santo Antônio, is protected by the same organization.

The **Igreja Matriz de Santo Antônio** ⓘ *daily 0900-1700, US$1, no photography*, first built in 1710 and enlarged between 1733 and 1752, contains some of the finest gilded woodcarvings in the country. The main church is predominantly white and gold. Lamps hang from the beaks of golden eagles. The symbols on the panels painted on the ceiling of the nave are a mixture of Old Testament and medieval Christian symbolism (for instance, the phoenix and the pelican). A carved wooden balustrade separates the seating in the nave from richly carved side chapels and altars. The principal altar is also ornately decorated, as are the walls and ceiling around it. The church has a small but fine organ brought from Porto in the 1790s. The upper part of the reconstructed façade dating from between 1810 and 1816 is said to follow a design by Aleijadinho, executed by Cláudio Pereira Viana. In front of the church, on the balustrade which overlooks the main street and the town, are also a cross and a sundial said to be designed by him.

From Santo Antônio, it is well worth taking a detour up to the **Santuário da Santíssima Trindade**. The chapel itself is 18th century while the Room of Miracles associated with the annual Trinity Sunday pilgrimage is modern.

Heading back down past Santo Antônio along Rua da Câmara, you come to the **Câmara Municipal e Antigo Fórum**. Here the road divides, the left-hand street, Jogo de Bola, leads to the Largo do Ó (which rejoins the main street), while Rua da Câmara goes to the crossroads with Rua Direita. At this junction is the **Sobrado Ramalho**, said to be the oldest building in Tiradentes. It is believed to be where the gold was melted down, and contains many soapstone carvings. It has been beautifully restored as a cultural centre.

Before taking Rua Direita back to Largo das Forras, carry straight on towards the river and cross the bridge to the magnificent **Chafariz de São José** (public

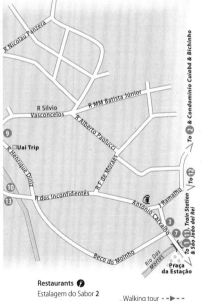

Restaurants 🍴
Estalagem do Sabor **2**
Quinto de Ouro **4**
Theatro da Villa **3**

Walking tour - - ▶ - -

fountain), installed in 1749 and undergoing renovation as this book went to press in 2016. The water is brought by a stone aqueduct from springs in the forest at the foot of Serra São José. It is still used for drinking, washing and watering animals.

Rua Direita has some interesting old buildings. The charming **Nossa Senhora do Rosário** ① *Praça Padre Lourival, Wed-Mon 1200-1600, US$0.50*, has fine statuary and ornate gilded altars. On its painted ceiling colonnades rise to heaven; two monks stand on a hill and the Virgin and Child are in the sky. Other ceiling panels depicting the life of Christ are in poor shape. The church contains statues of black saints, including São Benedito, patron saint of cooks; in one of the statues he is holding a squash. The church dates from 1727, but building by the 'Irmandade dos Pretos Cativos' (black slave brotherhood) began as early as 1708.

Opposite Praça Padre Lourival is the 18th- to 19th-century **Antiga Cadeia**, which now contains a sacred art museum devoted to St Anne (the grandmother of Christ), **Museu de Sant' Ana** ① *T032-3355 2798, www.museudesantana.org.br, Mon-Wed 1000-1900, US$1.25*. The entrance is very smart and modern, with a small café selling Cambraia coffees. You take a lift up to the museum, which is several rooms with only effigies of Santa Ana, mother of the Virgin Mary. Each image is numbered and explained on computer screens and there is a computer screen explaining everything, as well as wall plaques in Portuguese and English. The only part of the prison you see is the dungeon. It is beautifully done. Rua Direita meets the Largo das Forras at the Prefeitura Municipal, a two-storey building with an extra room under the roof. It now houses the tourist, post and phone offices.

The **Igreja São João Evangelista** ① *Largo do Sol, being restored at the time of updating this book*, is in a lovely open space. It is a simple church, built by the Irmandade dos Homens Pardos (mulattos). Next door is the **Museu Padre Toledo** ① *T032-3355 1549, Tue-Fri 1000-1700, Sat 1000-1630, Sun 0900-1500, no ticket sales 30 mins before closing time, US$2.65*, the house of one of the leaders of the Inconfidência Mineira. It exhibits some handsome colonial furniture and a painted roof depicting the Five Senses.

If you have any energy left, there are other churches and chapels in the town, including the **Igreja de Bom Jesus da Pobreza**, on the Largo das Forras. Across the river, the 18th-century **Nossa Senhora das Mercês** ① *Largo das Mercês, Sun 0900-1700*, has an interesting painted ceiling and a notable statue of the Virgin. On the grassy Morro de São Francisco is the small chapel of São Francisco de Paula (mid-18th century).

Trips from Tiradentes

Steam trains ① *Ticket office T032-3355 2789, Wed-Thu 0900-1100, 1200-1745, Fri-Sat 0900-1300, 1400-1700, Sun 0900-1400 or at Museu Ferroviário in São João del Rei (above). Runs on Fri, Sat, 1000 and 1500 from São João del Rei, returning from Tiradentes at 1300 and 1700, Sun and holidays 1000 and 1300 from São João del Rei, 1100 and 1400 from Tiradentes, US$15 return.* The steam trains, which run on the 76-cm gauge track between São João del Rei and Tiradentes (13 km), have been in continuous operation since 1881, a testament to the durability of the rolling stock and locomotives made by the Baldwin Company of Philadelphia. The maximum speed is 20 kph. To get to the railway station from the centre of the village you have to cross the river and head out of town on the Rua dos Inconfidêntes. Follow this road until it becomes the Rua Antônio Teixeira Carvalho, which carries on to the bridge over the Rio das Mortes. On the opposite bank is a small park and the station. For the railway museum at the railway station in São João del Rei, see page 181.

Walks A recommended walk from Tiradentes is to the protected forest on the **Serra de São José**. Guides are obligatory (see What to do, below). The easiest access is from behind the Chafariz, where a black door in the wall is opened at 0730 (Wednesday to Sunday). In just five minutes you are in the forest following the watercourse, where monkeys and birds can be seen. Alternatively, you can walk up into the *serra* from behind the Mercês Church; ask for directions. It is recommended that you take a guide if you wish to walk along the top of the *serra*.

There is a good one- or two-hour walk from Tiradentes to the **Balneário de Águas Santas**, which involves crossing the *serra*. At the *balneário* is a swimming pool, a lake and a *churrascaria*, **Senzala**. A map can be obtained from the Solar da Ponte, or ask locally for directions (taxi US$20). On the way you pass Parque Frei Mariano Vellozo, which contains the **Cachoeira do Mangue** falls. It is busy at weekends and can be reached by car on the old road to São João.

Listings Tiradentes *map p174*

Tourist information

Tourist office
R Resende Costa 71. Located in the prefeitura.

Where to stay

There are over 200 *pousadas* in and around town. Many are located on the main road, on the Estrada Real to São João del Rei and in the new condominiums on the edge of town. Most charge one rate for Mon-Thu and a higher rate for Fri-Sun. During festivals (especially Carnival and Semana Santa when there are Easter parades) and high season, only packages for several nights are sold. Afternoon tea is often included in the price, as well as breakfast.

$$$$ Pequena Tiradentes
Av Gov Israel Pinheiro 670, T032-3355 1262, www.pequenatiradentes.com.br.
A remarkable hotel on the road out of town, like a small town with streets between buildings which house luxurious suites, all named after famous Brazilian women. There are gardens, 2 pools, spa and fitness centre and a huge, contemporary lobby. You can buy anything you like; it even has a vast shop selling furniture and household decorations. Its restaurant, **Mandolin**, has a good reputation.

$$$$ Pousada Araújo Bazilio
R das Jacarandas 106, Condomínio Cuiabá, T032-3355 2304, www.pousadaaraujobazilio. com.br.
About 20 mins' walk from the centre, the rooms at this place are colonial style but with modern decor. It's a comfortable *pousada*, offering good service and a pool.

$$$$ Solar da Ponte
Praça das Mercês, T032-3355 1255, www.solardaponte.com.br.
The atmosphere of a country house, run by John and Anna Maria Parsons, with only 12 rooms, fresh flowers, bar, sauna, lovely gardens, swimming pool and light meals for residents only. Part of the **Roteiros de Charme** group, see page 17. Prices include breakfast and afternoon tea. Highly recommended.

$$$$-$$$ Pouso de Bartolomeu
R Herculano dos S 377, Alto da Torre, T032-3355 2142, www.pousodebartolomeo.com.br.
Outside the centre on a hillside is this place, offering pleasant rooms with 4-poster beds and good views. Set in gardens, there's also a swimming pool, but no restaurant.

$$$ Maria Fumaça Pousada
R Antonio Teixeira Carvalho 34, T032-3355 1227, www.mariafumacapousada.com.br.
By the bridge that crosses to the railway station, rooms with a/c and fan, swimming pool and gardens.

$$$ Pousada da Sirlei
R Antonio Teixeira Carvalho 113, T032-3355 1440, www.pousadadasirlei.com.
Pleasant *pousada* in a pale green building offering big tiled rooms with a/c, some with balconies, and a pool.

$$$ Pousada do Largo
Largo das Forras 48, T032-3355 1166, www.pousadadolargo.com.br.
Bright if small rooms, attractive public areas decorated with artsy Minas furniture and paintings, a tiny pool and a great location in the heart of the old town.

$$$ Pousada Mãe D'Água
Largo das Forras 50, T032-3355 1206, www.pousadamaedagua.com.br.
Large, pleasant hotel with an indoor pool, sauna and hydromassage at the back. Rates include breakfast but not tax.

$$$ Pousada Três Portas
R Direita 280A, T032-3355 1444, www.pousadatresportas.com.br.
Charming, central *pousada* in a restored townhouse, with a sauna, thermal pool, hydromassage and heating. All food served is home-produced. Recommended.

$$$-$$ Pouso das Gerais
R dos Inconfidentes 109, T032-3355 1234, www.pousodasgerais.com.br.
Central, quiet hotel offering fresh a/c rooms with marble basins, and a pool.

$$ Pousada Coração Inconfidente
R dos Inconfidentes 120, T032-3355 2464, www.pousadacoracaoinconfidente.com.br.
Simple rooms with fan along an outside passage lead to a pool. Possibly the cheapest place near the centre during the week (at weekends and festivals it's no different from others in this category).

$$ Pousada do Laurito
R Direita 187, T032-3355 1101, www.pousada dolaurito.com.br (under construction).
Central, under new ownership and being upgraded, suites with bath, many suitable for families, with fan, parking.

$$ Santa Edwiges
R Joaquim Ramalho 435, Bairro Cuiabá, T032-3355 1415, www.santaedwigespousada.com.
Some distance from the centre, not far from the Posto de Gasolina, this welcoming place has nice clean tiled rooms, and a good breakfast with home-made ingredients.

Restaurants

There are many restaurants and *lanchonetes* (snack bars).

$$$ Estalagem do Sabor
R Min Gabriel Passos 280, T032-33551144.
Excellent and generous traditional Mineira meat dishes.

$$$ Quinto de Ouro
R Min Gabriel Passos 139.
Mineira and international dishes. Recommended.

$$$ Theatro da Villa
R Padre Toledo 157, T032-3355 1275.
A gourmet restaurant with Italian, French and Brazilian fusion cooking and an excellent wine list. Good views out over the little garden and performances in summer in the restaurant's garden theatre.

Festivals

There are festivals throughout the year, at which times prices rise and the town can be full.

Jan Mostra de Cinema, www.mostra tiradentes.com.br, festival of Brazilian cinema.
Feb Carnaval is lively and popular here and going through a bit of a renaissance.
Mar Festival de Fotografia, www.fotoempauta.com.br.
Mar/Apr Lively **Easter** celebrations in Tiradentes with religious parades.
Late Apr Homage to Tiradentes, the leader of the Inconfidência.
Early May Theatre festival.
26-29 May Corpus Christi, processions with floral carpets.

Mid-Jun **Vinho e Jazz (Wine and Jazz)** festival.
Jul Lots of events during the school holidays.
Aug Jazz festival; 2nd half of the month, **Festival de Gastronomia**, www.farturagastronomia.com.br, one of Tiradentes' most popular events.

Shopping

Tiradentes shops are expensive. The main items are household decorations, furniture and some handicrafts and local produce. A lot of the furniture is made from wood reclaimed from old houses. **Bichinho**, a little town 6 km beyond Tiradentes (road paved then cobbled), specializes in this type of furniture and household items and is more expensive.

What to do

Agencies offer local excursions and can provide guides for walking on local trails and in the Serra de São José (also ask at tourist office; see under Tourist information, above). These include:
Uai Trip, *R Henrique Diniz 119, T032-3355 1161, www.uaitrip.com.br*, and **Viva Minas**, *R Custódio Gomes 13, T032-3355 1811, Facebook: AgenciaVivaMinas.*

Horse-drawn buggies do trips around town cost US$18.75 for 40-60 mins.

For horse-riding treks, contact the **Solar da Ponte**; see Where to stay, above.

Transport

Bus Last bus back to **São João del Rei** is 1940. A taxi to **Tiradentes** *rodoviária* costs US$4, while a taxi to **São João del Rei** *rodoviária* starts at US$10.75.

Train For steam trains to and from **São João del Rei**, see under Steam trains, page 176.

São João del Rei

a good base for visiting Tiradentes, a memorable steam train ride away

São João del Rei (population 79,000) lies at the foot of the Serra do Lenheiro, astride what once must have been a winding little stream. This has now sadly been transformed into a concrete gutter with grass verges. Eighteenth-century bridges cross the stream leading to streets lined with colonial buildings and plazas with crumbling churches, the most interesting and best preserved of which is the church of São Francisco.

The town feels far less of a tourist museum piece than nearby Tiradentes. There is a lively music scene, with two renowned orchestras and an annual arts festival in July, and the bars are filled with locals rather than tourists waiting for their coach.

Many streets seem to have more than one name, which can be a little confusing, but as the town centre is not large, it is hard to get lost. One such street crosses the Ponte da Cadeia from Rua Passos; it has three names: Rua da Intendência, Manoel Anselmo and Artur Bernardes. The **Secretaria de Turismo** ① *in the house of Bárbara Heliodora, T032-3372 7338, 0900-1700*, provides a free map.

Sights

The Córrego do Lenheiro, a stream with steep grassy banks, runs through the centre of town. Across it are two fine, stone bridges, **A Ponte da**

> **Tip...**
> Climb Alto da Boa Vista, where there is a Senhor dos Montes (Statue of Christ), for a good view of the town and surrounding countryside.

Cadeia (1798) and **A Ponte do Rosário** (1800), as well as several other modern bridges. Both sides of the river have colonial monuments, which are interspersed with modern buildings. On the north side are many streets with pleasant houses, but in various states of repair. Rua Santo Antônio has many single-storey eclectic houses from the imperial period, which have been restored and painted. Rua Santo Elias has several buildings all in the same style. Behind the church of Nossa Senhora do Pilar (see below), the Largo da Câmara leads up to Mercês church, which has quite a good view. Throughout the city you will see locked portals with colonial porticos. These are *passinhos*, shrines that are opened in Holy Week. They can be seen on Largo da Cruz and Largo do Rosário.

São Francisco de Assis ① *Praça Frei Orlando, Tue-Sun 0830-1700, US$1.50*, built 1774, is one of the most beautiful churches in Brazil. Although often attributed to Aleijadinho, it was designed and decorated by two almost completely undocumented artists, Francisco de Lima Cerqueira and Aniceto de Souza Lopes (who also sculpted the Pelourinho in the Largo da Câmara). The magnificent but modest whitewash and stone façade sits between two cylindrical bell towers and is decorated with an ornately carved door frame and a superb medal of St Francis receiving illumination. The *praça* in front is shaped like a lyre and, in the late afternoon, the royal palms cast shadows that interconnect to form the

São João del Rei

BACKGROUND

São João del Rei

São João del Rei is famous as the home of Tiradentes and of Tancredo Neves. The former was born in the Fazenda de Pombal, about 15 km downstream from Tiradentes on the Rio das Mortes. After his execution, the *fazenda* was confiscated. It is now an experimental station owned by Instituto Chico Mendes de Conservação da Biodiversidade (ICMBio). Tancredo Neves, to whom there is a memorial in the town, was the man who would have become the first civilian president of Brazil after the military dictatorships of the mid-20th century, had he not mysteriously died before taking office.

lyre's strings. The six altars inside have been restored, revealing fine carving in sucupira wood. Their artistry is wonderful and the three pairs of altars mirror each other, each pair in a different style (note the use of pillars and the different paintings that accompany each altar). The overall shape of the nave is elliptical, the gold altar has spiralling columns and an adoring St Francis kneels atop.

The cathedral, **Basílica de Nossa Senhora do Pilar** ① *R Getúlio Vargas (formerly R Direita), daily 1000-1600*, was built in 1721, but has a 19th-century façade which replaced the 18th-century original. It has rich altars and a brightly painted ceiling (Madonna and Child in the middle, saints and bishops lining the sides). Note the androgynous gold heads and torsos within the eight columns set into the walls either side of the main altar. There is a profusion of cherubs and plants in the carving. This abundance and angelic innocence contrasts with the suffering of the Passion and the betrayal of the Last Supper (two pictures of which are before the altar), all common themes in Brazilian baroque. In the sacristy are portraits of the Evangelists.

The **Memorial Tancredo Neves** ① *R Padre José Maria Xavier 7, Wed-Fri 1300-1800, weekends and holidays 0900-1700, US$1*, is a homage to the man and his life. A short video on São João del Rei is shown. It also holds exhibitions and has a bookshop.

The **Museu Ferroviário (Railway Museum)** ① *Av Hermílio Alves 366, T032-3371 8485, Wed-Sat 0900-1300, 1400-1700, Sun 0900-1300, ticket office Wed-Thu 0900-1100, 1200-1745, Fri-Sat 0900-1300, 1400-1700, US$2.50 (included in the train ticket to Tiradentes, see page 176)*, is well worth exploring. The museum traces the history of railways in general and in Brazil in brief. There is an informative display of the role of Irineu Evangelista de Souza, Barão de Mauá, who was a pioneer of both industry and the railways following his visit to England in 1840. The locomotive that ran on the first railway from Rio de Janeiro to the foot of the Serra do Mar was called 'A Baronesa' after his wife. The railway to São João, the Estrada de Ferro Oeste de Minas, was not a success, but it was instrumental in the development of the region. In the museum is an 1880 *Baldwin 4-4-0* locomotive from Philadelphia (No 5055) and a 1912-1913 VIP carriage, both still used on the steam journey to Tiradentes. Outside, at the end of the platforms are carriages and a small Orenstein and Koppel (Berlin) engine. You can walk along the tracks to the round house, where there are several working engines in superb condition, an engine shed and a steam-operated machine shop, still working. It is here that the engines get up steam before going to couple with the coaches for the run to Tiradentes. On days when the trains are running, you can get a good, close-up view of operations even if not taking the trip. Highly recommended. For the steam train to Tiradentes, see page 176.

Entertainment

Music

São João del Rei has 2 famous orchestras which play baroque music. In colonial days, the music master not only had to provide the music for Mass, but also had to compose new pieces for every festival. All the music has been kept and the Ribeiro Bastos and Lira Sanjoanense orchestras preserve the tradition. Both have their headquarters, rehearsing rooms and archives on R Santo Antônio (Nos 54 and 45 respectively). The **Orquestra Ribeiro Bastos** plays at Mass every Sun in São Francisco de Assis at 0915 and Fri 1900 at the Matriz do Pilar, as well as at many religious ceremonies throughout the year (eg Holy Week). The **Orquestra Lira Sanjoanense**, which is said to be the oldest in the Americas (founded in 1776), plays at Mass in Nossa Senhora do Pilar at 1900 every Thu and on Sun in Nossa Senhora do Rosário at 0830 and Nossa Senhora das Mercês at 1000, as well as on other occasions. It is best to check at their offices for full details. There are similar orchestras in Prados and Tiradentes, but the latter is not as well supported as those in São João.

Shopping

Known for furniture is **Santa Cruz de Minas**, contiguous with São João del Rei on the Estrada Real, but a separate municipality (one of the smallest in Brazil). The best value for shopping is **Resende Costa**, 14 km off the BR-040 and about 35 km from São João del Rei, where they make bedspreads, rugs, place settings, etc and the whole town is one long shopping street for nothing else.

Transport

For details of transport to and from Tiradentes, see page 179.

Bus The *rodoviária*, 2 km west of the centre, has an ATM, telephone office, toilets, luggage store, *lanchonetes* and a tourist office. *Rodoviária* platform tax US$1.20. To **São Paulo**, 8 hrs, 4 a day, US$25. **Belo Horizonte**, 7 daily, 4 hrs, US$17. To Juiz de Fora, 12 a day, US$12. To **Tiradentes**, 19 a day from 0550-1900, 9 on Sun and holidays from 0700, US$0.90. Viação Real goes to Tiradentes along the cobbled Estrada Real, 0530-2210 (from 0610 0n Sun).

Diamantina (population 48,000, altitude 1120 m) sits nestled in rugged hills 300 km north of Belo Horizonte. The town's churches are less spectacular than those in Ouro Preto or São João del Rei, but the city has a wonderful architectural unity and is better preserved and less touristy.

The Cerrado forests that swathe the countryside around the town are home to some of the rarest birds and mammals on the continent. The recently opened São Gonçalo do Rio Preto state park, 45 km from Diamantina, is the best base from which to explore them. Regular flights from Belo Horizonte to Diamantina have made visiting far easier than it used to be; it is now possible to continue overland from the town to Bahia.

> **Tip...**
> Try and visit during the regular Vesperata festivals when groups of musicians serenade passersby from balconies, especially around Praça Guerra. See Festivals, page 187.

Sights

Diamantina is easily manageable on foot; the city centre is compact and there are plenty of little street-side cafés and bars. The best place to start exploring is the **Praça Guerra** (Praça do Sé) which is dominated by the towering 1930s cathedral.

Diamantina's most interesting church, **Nossa Senhora do Carmo** ① *R do Carmo, Tue-Sat 1400-1800, Sun 0800-1200*, is a short walk west along Rua Carmo Quitanda. It is most remarkable for its beautiful interior paintings, carried out by José Soares de Araujo, a former bodyguard from Braga in Portugal. Many of the city's churches are painted by him, but this is by far his finest work. The Carmelites are said to have been founded before the time of Christ by the prophet Elijah, who is depicted on the magnificent ceiling, ascending to heaven in a chariot of fire, and brandishing a sword on one of the side altars. Another ceiling painting shows the patron saint and founder of the Third Order of Mount Carmel, the 12th-century English saint, St Simon Stock, receiving a scapular from the Virgin. The placing of the church tower at the back of the building was ostensibly to please Chica Silva, the black slave of Padre Rolim. In an era when black Brazilians were valued less than chickens she achieved liberty, married the wealthy diamond merchant João Fernandes de Oliveira and became the most influential woman in the city, living in luxury with him and their 14 children in a house overlooking the Praça Lobo de Mesquita. The house is now a museum, the **Casa de Chica da Silva** ① *Praça Lobo Mesquita 266, T038-3531 2491, Tue-Sat 1200-1730, Sun 0830-1200, free.*

Just southwest of Nossa Senhora do Carmo is the church of **Nossa Senhora do Rosário dos Pretos** ① *Largo Dom Joaquim, Tue-Sat 1400-1800, Sun 0800-1200*, designated for the black underclass who were not permitted to attend Mass at Nossa Senhora do Carmo. Its simple interior has a magical meditative silence. Outside is an original 18th-century public fountain, the **Chafariz do Rosário,** where water pours from the mouths of distinctly African faces.

São Francisco de Assis ① *R São Francisco, just off Praça JK, open only for Mass*, was built between 1766 and the turn of the 19th century. It is notable for its paintings. Other colonial churches are the small, blue and white **Capela Imperial do Amparo** ① *R do Amparo, open 0900-1120, US$0.50,* dating from 1758-1776; **Nossa Senhora das Mercês,** dating from 1778-1784; and the early 19th-century **Nossa Senhora da Luz,** the latter two both open for church services only. The **Catedral Metropolitana de Santo Antônio**, on Praça Guerra (or da Catedral), was built in the 1930s in neocolonial style to replace the original cathedral.

Diamantina has a number of other interesting small museums worth exploring. The **Museu do Diamante** ⓘ *R Direita 14, http://museudiamante.blogspot.co.uk, Tue-Sat 1000-1700, Sun 0900-1300, US$1*, in the house of Padre Rolim, has an important collection of the materials used in the diamond industry, together with some beautiful 18th- and 19th-century oratories and icons and the iron collars that were once fitted to the slaves that worked the mines.

The **Biblioteca Antônio Torres** ⓘ *R Quitanda 48, Mon-Fri 1400-1700*, is a smart 18th-century townhouse, which is also known as the Casa Muxarabie after the enclosed Moorish balcony on one of the windows.

Behind the 18th-century building that now houses the **Prefeitura Municipal** (originally the diamond administration building), at the far end of the Praça Barão de Guacuí at Praça Conselheiro Matta 11, is the municipal **Mercado dos Tropeiros (Muleteers)** ⓘ *Praça Barão*

Diamantina

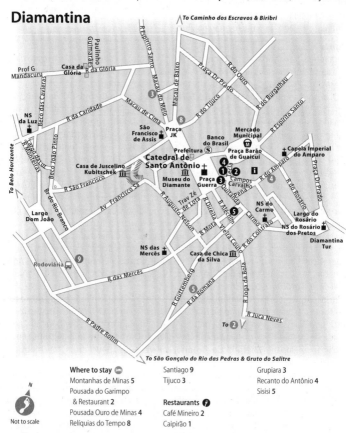

Where to stay 😴
Montanhas de Minas 5
Pousada do Garimpo
  & Restaurant 2
Pousada Ouro de Minas 4
Relíquias do Tempo 8

Santiago 9
Tijuco 3

Restaurants 🍴
Café Mineiro 2
Caipirão 1

Grupiara 3
Recanto do Antônio 4
Sisisi 5

N
Not to scale

BACKGROUND
Diamantina

Like Minas's other colonial towns, Diamantina owes its existence and colonial finery to mining wealth, in this case diamonds, which were first discovered here in 1728. The settlement became known as Arraial do Tijuco and grew rapidly into a city. As the city's wealth increased, so did the feelings of resentment at the Portuguese tyranny. The majority black and mixed-race population was treated as subhuman. They were considered of such low birth that they were banned from walking in front of façades of the white churches as it would be an affront to God. They remained largely in poverty, leading many of the citizens to sympathize with the Inconfidêntes, a group of people conspiring to free Brazil of Portuguese colonial power. One local priest, José da Silva de Oliveira Rolim (Padre Rolim), joined the movement.

de Guaicuí. It was built in 1835 as a residence and trading house before being expanded and has wooden arches.

The **Casa da Glória** ⓘ *R da Glória 297*, is the city's most photographed building. Two houses on either side of the street are connected by a covered corridor-bridge. This was once part of a convent school and the girls would laugh and flirt through the small windows. It is some distance from the centre and contains the *Instituto Eschwege de Geologia*.

President Juscelino Kubitschek, the founder of Brasília, was from Diamantina and his house is now a **museum** ⓘ *R São Francisco 241, Tue-Sat 0800-1700, Sun 0800-1300, US$1.35.*

Around Diamantina

There is a good walk along the **Caminho dos Escravos**, the old road built by slaves between the mining area on Rio Jequitinhonha and Diamantina. A guide is essential and not expensive; ask at the Casa de Cultura. Beware of snakes and thunderstorms.

About 9 km from town is the **Gruta de Salitre** ⓘ *T038-3531 2197, grutadosalitre@ biotropicos.org.br*, a big cave with a strange rock formation. There are no buses, but it is a good walk and you can find some interesting minerals along the way. Ask the tourist office for directions, or take a taxi. Closer to the town is the **Cachoeira da Toca**, a 15-m waterfall, which is good for swimming.

Along the riverbank it is 12 km on a dirt road to **Biribiri**, a pretty village with a well-preserved church and an abandoned textile factory. It also has a few bars and is popular and noisy at weekends. About halfway there are swimming pools in the river; opposite them, on a cliff face, are red animal paintings of unknown age and origin. There is some interesting plant life along the river and beautiful mountain views.

The sleepy little town of **São Gonçalo do Rio Preto**, which sits next to a beautiful mountain river, is famous for its traditional festivals. It lies some 60 km from Diamantina and 15 km from the Parque Estadual de São Gonçalo do Rio Preto – an area of stunning, pristine Cerrado filled with flowering trees and particularly rich in birdlife. There are *pousadas* in São Gonçalo and *cabañas* in the park (reachable by taxi). Guides are also available.

São Gonçalo do Rio Preto, **Serro** and many other small towns are part of the **Circuito Turístico dos Diamantes** ⓘ *Praça Barão de Guacuí 28A, Diamantina, T038-3531 8994, http://circuitodosdiamantes.com.br*, which aims to promote sustainable tourism in this region. Trips to many of the locations can be organized through **ASGITUR** (see page 187).

Tourist information

Tourist office
Casa de Cultura, Praça Antônio Eulálio 53,
T038-3531 1636, www.diamantina.mg.gov.br.
Friendly and helpful and provides pamphlets
and a reliable map, and information about
church opening times, buses and local
guides. See also www.diamantina-travel.
com.br (in English) and www.diamantina.
com.br (in Portuguese), which list hotels
and tour operators.

Where to stay

Rooms are usually half price for those
travelling alone. Unless otherwise stated,
all are within 10 mins' walk of the centre.

$$$ Pousada do Garimpo
Av da Saudade 265, T038-3532 1040,
www.pousadadogarimpo.com.br.
Plain well-kept rooms in a smart hotel on
the outskirts of town, a taxi ride from the
centre. There's a pool, sauna and a restaurant
serving some of the city's best Minas cooking
from celebrated chef, Vandeka.

$$$ Relíquias do Tempo
R Macau de Baixo 104, T038-3531 1627,
www.pousadareliquiasdotempo.com.br.
Cosy wood-floored rooms with en suites
furnished with antiques in a pretty 19th-
century house just off Praça JK. Public areas
are decorated like a colonial family home.
Breakfasts are generous. There is a heated
indoor lap pool and jacuzzi, and they have
a handicrafts shop, **Relíquias do Vale**
(R Macau do Meio 401, T038-3531 1353).

$$$ Tijuco
R Macau do Melo 211, T038-3531 1022,
www.hoteltijuco.com.br.
A wonderful Niemeyer design that looks like
a building from Thunderbird island. The large
rooms have been refurbished whilst staying

true to the original 1960s kitsch. The best
rooms are at the front with balconies and
glorious views.

$$$-$$ Montanhas de Minas
R da Romana 264, T038-3531 3240,
www.grupomontanhasdeminas.com.br.
Spacious rooms with stone floors
and en suites, some with balconies.
Decent breakfasts.

$$ Hotel Santiago
Largo Dom João 133, T038-3531 3407,
www.santiagohotel.com.br.
Plain, small but spruce rooms with
en suites. Reasonable breakfast.
Located near the *rodoviária*.

$$ Pousada Ouro de Minas
R do Amparo 90A, T038-3531 3240,
www.grupomontanhasdeminas.com.br.
Simple well-kept rooms with stone floor
rooms with tiny bathrooms in a converted
colonial house.

Camping
Wild camping is possible near the waterfall
just outside town.

Restaurants

$$$ Grupiara
R Campos Carvalho 12, T038-3531 3887.
Decent regional cooking, a convivial
atmosphere and good-value per-kilo
options at lunch.

$$ Caipirão
R Campos Carvalho 15, T038-3531 1526.
Minas cooking with a lunchtime buffet
cooked over a traditional wood-fired clay
oven and evening à la carte.

$$ Recanto do Antônio
Beco da Tecla 39, T038-3531 1147.
Minas food and decent steak served in a
chic rustic dining room in a colonial house.

$ Café Mineiro
R Beco da Tecla, at the top end. Mon-Fri
0730-2000, Sat 0800-2000, Sun 1000-1400.
A good, limited menu of freshly made
tortas and *pastéis, pão do queijo*, sweets,
coffee and drinks.

$ Sisisi
Beco da Mota 89, T038-3531 3071.
Pasta, Minas cooking and an excellent-
value *prato feito* at lunchtime.

Festivals

During the famous **Vesperatas**, a tradition
dating from the 17th century, musicians and
singers serenade from balconies along the
colonial streets and drum troupes and bands
parade along them. They usually take place
2-3 times a month on a Sat Apr-Oct; for exact
dates, contact the tourist office.

Feb Carnaval is very good here.
May-Jun Corpus Christi.
13 Jun Santo Antônio.
Jul 50 days after Pentecost, **O Divino
Espírito Santo**, is a major 5-day feast.
12 Sep O Dia das Serestas, the 'Day of the
Serenades', for which the town is famous;
this is the birthday of President Juscelino
Kubitschek, who was born here.
Oct First half of the month, **Festa do Rosário.**

What to do

There are a few tour operators in the city,
none are firmly established. The tourist office
(see Tourist information, above) can help
organize trips to São Goncalo do Rio Perto
and the surrounding area.

ASGITUR, *contact through the Secretaria de
Turismo, at pousadas, or on T038-3531 3197,
or T9-881 2119 (Aguinaldo Clemente).* This
guides' association offers city tours and a
Passeio Ecológico to the Cruzeiro da Serra for
views of the city, the Caminho dos Escravos,
Cachoeira da Sentinela, Cachoeira dos
Cristais, Biribiri (for lunch) for US$39. You can
add the Gruta do Salitre for an extra US$13.

Transport

Air There are 3 weekly flights to **Belo
Horizonte** (Pampulha Airport) with
Trip, www.voetrip.com.br.

Bus The *rodoviária* (T038-3531 9176) is
3 km east of the centre. There are 6 buses
a day to **Belo Horizonte** (US$21, 5 hrs), via
Curvelo (for connections to **Brasília**, 10 hrs),
with **Pássaro Verde**. There are daily buses to
Montes Claros, with daily connections here
for **Brasília** and **Parque Nacional Grande
Sertão Veredas**. For the **Serra do Cipó** take
the bus to Serro (2 daily) and change for Santa
Ana do Riacho and the Serra do Cipó. There is
1 bus per day to **São Gonçalo do Rio Preto**.
  If en route to Bahia, there are 2 daily buses
to **Araçuaí** (4 hrs) from here *combis* and
buses run to **Itaobim** (US$6, 2 hrs) from
where there are connections to **Vitória da
Conquista** (US$8, 4 hrs) and on to **Porto
Seguro** and other destinations in Bahia. (If
you get stuck in Araçuaí there is a **Pousada
Tropical** opposite the *rodoviária*, T038-3731
1765, with bath, clean, cheap and friendly.)
The BR-116 passes interesting rock formations
before crossing the border with Bahia.

Taxi Taxis are expensive.

Practicalities

Getting there

Air

International flights into Rio de Janeiro arrive **Tom Jobim International Airport** (also known as Galeão) on the Ilha do Governador, 16 km from the city centre (see page 99).

Prices are cheapest in October, November and after Carnaval and at their highest in the European summer and the Brazilian high seasons (generally 15 December to 15 January, the Thursday before Carnaval to the Saturday after Carnaval, and 15 June to 15 August). Departure tax is usually included in the cost of the ticket.

The best deals on flights within Brazil are available through **Azul** ⓘ *www.voeazul.com.br*; **GOL** ⓘ *www.voegol.com.br*; **TAM** ⓘ *www.tam.com.br*; and **Avianca** ⓘ *www.avianca.com.br*.

TRAVEL TIP
Packing for Brazil

Bag Unobtrusive sturdy bag (either rucksack or bag with wheels) and an inelegant day pack/bag – to attract minimal attention on the streets.

Clothing Brazilians dress casually. It's best to do likewise and blend in. Avoid flashy brands. Thin cotton or a modern wicking artificial fabric are best. Take lightweight trousers, shorts, a long-sleeved shirt, skirts, cotton or wicking socks, underwear, shawl or light waterproof jacket for evenings and a sun hat.

Footwear Light Gore-Tex walking shoes (or boots if you intend to trek) are best. Buy from a serious, designated outdoor company like Brasher or Berghaus rather than a flimsy fashion brand. Wear them in before you come. Nothing gives a tourist away more than new shoes.

Sponge bag 2% tincture of iodine; Mercurochrome or similar; athlete's foot powder; tea tree oil; antibiotic ointment; toothbrush; rehydration tablets; anti-diarrheals such as Imodium; sun protection (high factor) – this is expensive in Brazil.

Electronics UK, US or European socket adaptor; camera with case to attract minimal attention; torch (flashlight).

Miscellaneous items Ear plugs for surfing, traffic noise and cockerels at dawn; pen knife; strong string (3 m); hooks with a screw-in thread (for mosquito net); gaffer tape; sunglasses (with UV filter); money belt; a sealable waterproof bag large enough for camera and clothes.

For rural and beach destinations take a mosquito net impregnated with insect repellent (the bell-shaped models are best) and a water bottle.

What not to pack – to buy there
T-shirts (local brands make you less conspicuous and they are sold everywhere); insect repellent (Johnson's Off! aerosol is best); beachwear (unless you have neuroses about your body – no one cares if their bum looks big in anything in Brazil); flip-flops (Havaianas); painkillers; shampoo and soap; toothpaste; beach sarong (*kanga*); vitamins; hammock and rope.

Air passes

TAM and GOL offer a 21-day **Brazil Airpass**, which is valid on any TAM destination within Brazil. The price varies according to the number of flights taken and the international airline used to arrive in Brazil. They can only be bought outside Brazil. Rates vary depending on the season. Children pay a discounted rate; those under three pay 10% of the adult rate. Some of the carriers operate a blackout period between 15 December and 15 January.

Baggage allowance

Airlines will only allow a certain weight of luggage without a surcharge; for Brazil this is usually two items of 32 kg but may be as low as 20 kg for domestic flights; with two items of hand luggage weighing up to 10 kg in total. UK airport staff can refuse to load bags weighing more than 30 kg. Baggage allowances are higher in business and first class. In all cases it is best to enquire beforehand.

Sea

Travelling as a passenger on a cargo ship to South America is not a cheap way to go, but if you have the time and want a bit of luxury, it makes a great alternative to flying. The passage is often only available for round trips.

Shipping agents

Cargo Ship Voyages Ltd ⓘ *Hemley, Woodbridge, Suffolk IP12 4QF, T01473-736265, www.cargoshipvoyages.co.uk*. Other companies include **Freighter Expeditions** ⓘ *www.freighterexpeditions.com.au*, and **Stradn** ⓘ *www.strandtravelltd.co.uk*.

Cruise ships

Cruise ships regularly visit Brazil. The website www.cruisetransatlantic.com has full details of transatlantic crossings. There are often cheaper deals off season.

Getting around

First time visitors seldom realise how big Brazil is and fail to plan accordingly. The country is the world's fifth largest, making it bigger than the USA without Alaska, or the size of Australia with France and the UK tagged on. As intercity rail is non-existent (but for one irregular and inconsequential route), travelling overland within a state can involve long bus or car journeys: even the smaller states are as big, or bigger, than many European countries. Rio, for example, is a little larger than Denmark.

Air

Due to the huge distances between places, flying is the most practical option to get around. All state capitals and larger cities are linked with each other with services several times a day, and all national airlines offer excellent service. Deregulation of the airlines has greatly reduced prices on some routes and low-cost airlines offer fares that can often be as cheap as travelling by bus (when booked online). Buy your internal flights before leaving home. Paying with an international credit card is not always possible online within Brazil (as sites often ask for a Brazilian social security number), but it is usually possible to buy an online ticket through a hotel, agency or willing friend without a surcharge. Many smaller airlines go in and out of business sporadically. **Avianca** ⓘ *www.avianca.com.br*, **Azul** ⓘ *www.voeazul.com.br*, **GOL** ⓘ *www.voegol.com.br*, **TAM** ⓘ *www.tam.com.br*, and **TRIP** ⓘ *www.voetrip.com.br*, operate the most extensive routes.

Bus

Other than flying, the most reliable way of travelling is by bus. Routes are extensive, prices reasonable and buses modern and comfortable. There are three standards of intercity and interstate bus: *Comum*, or *Convencional*, are quite slow, not very comfortable and fill up quickly; *Executivo* are more expensive, comfortable (many have reclining seats), and don't stop en route to pick up passengers so are safer; *leito* (literally 'bed') run at night between the main centres, offering reclining seats with leg rests, toilets, and sometimes refreshments, at double the normal fare. For journeys over 100 km, most buses have chemical toilets (bring toilet paper). Air conditioning can make buses cold at night, so take a jumper; on some services blankets are supplied.

Buses stop fairly frequently (every two to four hours) at *postos* for snacks. Bus stations for interstate services and other long-distance routes are called *rodoviárias*. They are frequently outside the city centres and offer snack bars, lavatories, left luggage, local bus services and information centres. Buy bus tickets at *rodoviárias* (most now take credit cards), not from travel agents who add on surcharges. Reliable bus information is hard to come by, other than from companies themselves. Buses usually arrive and depart in very good time. Many town buses have turnstiles, which can be inconvenient if you are carrying a large pack. Urban buses normally serve local airports.

Car hire

Car hire is competitive with mainland Europe and a little pricier than the USA. But roads are not always well-signposted and maps are hard to come by. Use a sat nav only outside the cities. Within a city the sat nav will offer the shortest routes, which can involve potentially dangerous crossings through peripheral communities. Costs can be reduced by reserving a car over the internet through one of the larger international companies such as **Europcar** ⓘ *www.europcar.co.uk*, or **Avis** ⓘ *www.avis.co.uk*. The minimum age for renting a car is 21 and it's essential to have a credit card. Companies operate under the terms *aluguel de automóveis* or *auto-locadores*. Check exactly what the company's insurance policy covers. In many cases it will not cover major accidents or 'natural' damage (eg flooding). Ask if extra cover is available. Sometimes using a credit card automatically includes insurance. Beware of being billed for scratches that were on the vehicle before you hired it.

Taxi

At the outset, make sure the meter is cleared and shows 'tariff 1', except (usually) from 2300-0600, Sunday, and in December when '2' is permitted. Check that the meter is working; if not, fix the price in advance. The **radio taxi** service costs about 50% more but cheating is less likely. Taxis outside larger hotels usually cost more. If you are seriously cheated, note the number of the taxi and insist on a signed bill; threatening to take it to the police can work. **Mototaxis** are much more economical, but many are unlicensed and there have been a number of robberies of passengers. Taxis vary widely in quality and price but are easy to come by and safe when taken from a *posto de taxis* (taxi rank).

Brazilian etiquette

In his 1941 travel book, *I Like Brazil*, Jack Harding said of Brazilians that "anyone who does not get along with (them) had better examine himself; the fault is his." And perhaps the best writer on Brazil in English, Joseph Page, observed in his 1995 book *The Brazilians* that "cordiality is a defining characteristic of their behaviour. They radiate an irresistible pleasantness, abundant hospitality, and unfailing politeness, especially to foreigners." It is hard to offend Brazilians or to find Brazilians offensive, but to make sure you avoid misunderstandings, here are a few, perhaps surprising, tips.

Public nudity, even toplessness on beaches, is an arrestable offence.

Brazilians will talk to anyone, anywhere. "Sorry, do I know you?" is the least Brazilian sentiment imaginable and no one ever rustles a newspaper on the metro.

Walks in nature are never conducted in silence. This has led many Brazilians to be unaware that their country is the richest in terrestrial wildlife on the planet.

Drug use, even of marijuana, is deeply frowned upon. Attitudes are far more conservative than in Europe. The same is true of public drunkenness.

When driving it is normal, especially in Rio, to accelerate right up the bumper of the car in the lane in front of you on the highway, hoot repeatedly and flash your headlights. It is considered about as rude as ringing the doorbell in Brazil.

The phrase 'So para Ingles Ver' ('just for the English to see') is a common expression that means 'to appear to do something by the rule book whilst doing the opposite'.

This is the land of red tape. You need a social security number to buy a SIM card and fingerprint ID just to go to the dentist.

Never presume a policeman will take a bribe. And never presume he won't. Let the policeman do the presuming.

Never insult an official. You could find yourself in serious trouble.

Brazilians are very private about their negative emotions. Never moan for more than a few seconds, even with justification – you will be branded an *uruca* (harbinger of doom), and won't be invited to the party.

Never confuse a Brazilian footballer with an Argentine one.

Brazilians believe that anyone can dance samba. They can't.

Never dismiss a street seller with anything less than cordiality; an impolite dismissal will be seen as arrogant and aggressive. Always extend a polite "não obrigado".

Brazilian time. Peter Fleming, the author of one of the best travel books about Brazil, once said that "a man in a hurry will be miserable in Brazil." Remember this when you arrive 10 minutes late to meet a friend in a bar and spend the next hour wondering if they've already gone after growing tired of waiting for you. They haven't. They've not yet left home. Unless you specify 'a hora britanica' then you will wait. And wait. And everyone will be mortified if you complain.

Essentials A-Z

Accident and emergency

Ambulance T192. **Police** T190/197. If robbed or attacked, contact the tourist police (in Rio T021-3399 7170). If you need to claim on insurance, make sure you get a police report.

Children

Travel with children is easy in Brazil. Brazilians love children and they are generally welcome everywhere. Facilities are often better than those back home.

Some hotels charge a cheaper family rate. Some will not charge for children under 5 and most can provide an extra camp bed for a double room. A few of the more romantic boutique beach resorts do not accept children. If you are planning to stay in such a hotel it is best to enquire ahead.

Most restaurants provide children's seats and menus as well as crayons and paper to keep them happy. Children are never expected to be seen but not heard.

Children under 3 generally travel for 10% on internal flights and at 70% until 12 years old. Prices on buses depend on whether the child will occupy a seat or a lap. Laps are free and if there are spare seats after the bus has departed the child can sit there for free.

On tours children under 6 usually go free or it may be possible to get a discount.

Disabled travellers

As in most Latin American countries, facilities are generally very poor. Problems are worst for wheelchair users, who will find that ramps are rare and that toilets and bathrooms with facilities are few and far between, except for some of the more modern hotels and the larger airports. Public transport is not well geared up for wheelchairs and pavements are often in a poor state of repair or crowded with street vendors requiring passers-by to brave the traffic. The metro has lifts and disabled chair lifts at some stations (but not all are operational). Disabled Brazilians obviously have to cope with these problems and mainly rely on the help of others to get on and off public transport and generally move around. Drivers should bring a disabled sticker as most shopping centres and public car parks have disabled spaces.

Disability Travel, www.disabilitytravel.com, is an excellent US site written by travellers in wheelchairs who have been researching disabled travel full-time since 1985. There are many tips and useful contacts and articles and the company also organizes group tours.

Global Access – Disabled Travel Network Site, www.globalaccessnews.com. Provides travel information for 'disabled adventurers' and includes a number of reviews and tips.

Society for Accessible Travel and Hospitality, www.sath.org. Has some specific information on Brazil.

Brazilian organizations include: **Sociedade Amigos do Deficiente Físico**, T021-2241 0063, based in Rio and with associate memberships throughout Brazil; and **Centro da Vida Independente**, Rio, www.cvi-rio.org.br. There are a number of specialist and general operators offering holidays specifically aimed at those with disabilities. These include: **Responsible Travel**, www.responsibletravel.com; **CanbeDone**, www.canbedone.co.uk; and **Access Travel**, www.access-travel.co.uk.

Nothing Ventured, edited by Alison Walsh (Harper Collins), has personal accounts of worldwide journeys by disabled travellers, plus advice and listings.

Electricity

Generally 110 V 60 cycles AC, but occasionally 220 V 60 cycles AC is used. European and US 2-pin plugs and sockets.

Embassies and consulates

For a list of Brazilian embassies abroad, see http://embassygoabroad.com.

Gay and lesbian travellers

Brazil is a good country for LGBT travellers as attitudes are fairly liberal, especially in the big cities. Opinions in rural areas are far more conservative and it is wise to adapt to this. There is a well-developed scene in Rio. Local information can be obtained from the **Rio Gay Guide**, www.riogayguide.com.

The Rio de Janeiro Pride march (usually Jun) takes place on Copacabana and is the centrepiece of an annual event that includes numerous activities. Other festivals include the nationwide **Mix Brasil festival of Sexual diversity**, www.mixbrasil.uol.com.br.

Health

See your GP or travel clinic at least 6 weeks before departure for general advice on travel risks and vaccinations. Make sure you have sufficient medical travel insurance, get a dental check, know your own blood group and, if you suffer a long-term condition such as diabetes or epilepsy, obtain a **Medic Alert** bracelet (www.medicalalert.co.uk). Cases of **Zika virus** have been reported in Brazil and it is recommended that you check with the Foreign Office (www.gov.uk) before travelling particularly if you're pregnant or planning to become pregnant, and seek advice from a health professional.

Vaccinations and anti-malarials

Confirm that your primary courses and boosters are up to date. It is advisable to vaccinate against polio, tetanus, typhoid, hepatitis A and, for more remote areas, rabies. Yellow fever vaccination is obligatory for most areas. Cholera, diptheria and hepatitis B vaccinations are sometimes advised. Only a very few parts of Brazil have significant malaria risk. Seek specialist advice before you leave.

Health risks

The major risks posed in the region are those caused by insect disease carriers such as mosquitoes and sandflies. The key parasitic and viral diseases are malaria, which is not widespread, South American trypanosomiasis (Chagas disease) and dengue fever. **Dengue fever** (which is present throughout Brazil) is particularly hard to protect against as the mosquitoes can bite throughout the day as well as night (unlike those that carry malaria); try to wear clothes that cover arms and legs and also use effective mosquito repellent. Mosquito nets dipped in permethrin provide a good physical and chemical barrier at night. **Chagas disease** is spread by faeces of the triatomine, or assassin bugs, whereas sandflies spread a disease of the skin called **leishmaniasis**.

While standards of hygiene in Brazilian restaurants are generally very high, intestinal upsets are common, if only because many first time visitors are not used to the food. Always to wash your hands before eating and to be careful with drinking water and ice; if you have any doubts about the water then boil it or filter and treat it. In a restaurant buy bottled water or ask where the water has come from. Food can also pose a problem, be wary of salads if you don't know if it has been washed or not.

There is some risk of **tuberculosis** (TB) and although the BCG vaccine is available, it is still not guaranteed protection. It is best to avoid unpasteurized dairy products and try not to let people cough and splutter all over you.

Hospitals in Rio de Janeiro

Hospital Miguel Couto, Mário Ribeiro 117, Gávea, T021-3111 3800, free casualty ward.
Hospital Municipal Rocha Maia, R Gen Severiano 91, Botafogo, T021-2295 2295/2121, near Rio Sul shopping centre, a good public hospital for minor injuries and ailments; free, but may be queues.
Policlínica, Av Nilo Peçanha 38, T021-2517 4200, www.pgrj.org.br, for diagnosis and investigation.

Saúde dos Portos, Praça Mcal Âncora, T021-2240 8628/8678, Mon-Fri 1000-1100, 1500-1800, for vaccinations; vaccination book and ID required.

Websites
www.cdc.gov Centres for Disease Control and Prevention (USA).
www.fitfortravel. nhs.uk Fit for Travel (UK), A-Z of vaccine and travel health advice for each country.
www.fco.gov.uk Foreign and Commonwealth Office (FCO), UK.
www.itg.be Prince Leopold Institute for Tropical Medicine.
http://travelhealthpro.org.uk Useful website for the National Travel Health Network and Centre (NaTHNaC), a UK government organization.
www.who.int World Health Organization.

Books
Dawood, R, editor, *Travellers' health*, Oxford University Press, 2012.
Warrell, David, and Sarah Anderson, editors, *Oxford Handbook of Expedition and Wilderness Medicine*, Oxford Medical Handbooks 2008.
Wilson-Howarth, Jane. *The Essential Guide to Travel Health*, Cadogan 2009.

Insurance

Always take out travel insurance before you set off and read the small print carefully. Check that the policy covers the activities you intend or may end up doing. Also check exactly what your medical cover includes (eg ambulance, helicopter rescue or emergency flights back home). Also check the payment protocol. You may have to cough up first before the insurance company reimburses you. To be safe, it is always best to dig out all the receipts for expensive personal effects like jewellery or cameras. Take photos of these items and note down all serial numbers.

Internet

Internet usage is widespread. Most hotels offer in-room Wi-Fi (usually free but sometimes at exorbitant rates).

Language *See also page 207.*

Brazilians speak Portuguese, and very few speak anything else. Spanish may help you to be understood a little, but spoken Portuguese will remain undecipherable even to fluent Spanish speakers. To get the best out of Brazil, learn some Portuguese before arriving. Brazilians are the best thing about the country and without Portuguese you will not be able to interact beyond stereotypes and second guesses. Language classes are available in the larger cities and schools are listed in the What to do sections in this book.

Cactus (www.cactuslanguage.com), **Languages abroad** (www.languages abroad.co.uk) and **Travellers Worldwide** (www.travellersworld wide.com) are among the companies that can organize language courses in Brazil. **McGraw Hill** and **Dorling Kindersley** (*Hugo Portuguese in Three Months*) offer the best teach-yourself books. **Sonia Portuguese** (www.sonia-portuguese. com) is a useful online resource and there are myriad free and paid-for Portuguese apps of varying quality.

Money

Currency
£1=R$5.85; €1=R$4.26; US$1=R$3.9 (Jan 2016).
The unit of currency is the **real**, R$ (plural **reais**). Any amount of foreign currency and 'a reasonable sum' in reais can be taken in, but sums over US$10,000 must be declared. Residents may only take out the equivalent of US$4000. Notes in circulation are: 100, 50, 10, 5 and 1 real; coins: 1 real, 50, 25, 10, 5 and 1 centavo. **Note** The exchange rate fluctuates – check regularly.

Costs of travelling

Brazil is cheaper than most countries in South America though prices vary greatly. Rural areas can be 50% cheaper than heavily visited tourist areas in the big city. As a very rough guide, prices are about half those of Western Europe and a third cheaper than rural USA.

Hostel beds are usually around US$8. Budget hotels with few frills have rooms for as little as US$15, and you should have no difficulty finding a double room costing US$30 wherever you are. Rooms are often pretty much the same price whether 1 or 2 people are staying and aside from hostels prices invariably include a large breakfast.

Eating is generally inexpensive, especially in *padarias* (bakeries) or *comida por kilo* (pay by weight) restaurants, which offer a wide range of food (salads, meat, pasta, vegetarian). Expect to pay around US$4 to eat your fill in a good-value restaurant. Although bus travel is cheap by US or European standards, because of the long distances, costs can soon mount up. Internal flights prices have come down dramatically in the last couple of years and some routes work out cheaper than taking a bus, especially if booking online.

ATMs

ATMs, or cash machines, are easy to come by. As well as being the most convenient way of withdrawing money, they frequently offer the best available rates of exchange. They are usually closed after 2130. There are 2 international ATM acceptance systems, **Plus** and **Cirrus**. Many issuers of debit and credit cards are linked to one, or both (eg Visa is Plus, MasterCard is Cirrus). **Bradesco** and **HSBC** are the 2 main banks offering this service. **Red Banco 24 Horas** kiosks advertise that they take a long list of credit cards in their ATMs, including MasterCard and Amex, but international cards cannot always be used; the same is true of **Banco do Brasil**.

Advise your bank before leaving, as cards are usually stopped in Brazil without prior warning. Find out before you leave what international functionality your card has. Check if your bank or credit card company imposes handling charges. Internet banking is useful for monitoring your account or transferring funds. Do not rely on one card, in case of loss. If you do lose a card, immediately contact the 24-hr helpline of the issuer in your home country (keep this number in a safe place).

Exchange

Banks in major cities will change cash and, for those who still use them, traveller's cheques (TCs). If you keep the official exchange slips, you may convert back into foreign currency up to 50% of the amount you exchanged. The parallel market, found in travel agencies, exchange houses and among hotel staff, often offers marginally better rates than the banks but commissions can be very high. Many banks may only change US$300 minimum in cash, US$500 in TCs. Rates for TCs are usually far lower than for cash, they are harder to change and a very heavy commission may be charged.

Credit cards

Credit cards are widely used. **Visa** and **MasterCard** are the most widely used, with **Diners Club** and **Amex** a close second. Cash advances on credit cards will only be paid in reais at the tourist rate, incurring at least a 1.5% commission. Banks in remote places may refuse to give a cash advance: try asking for the *gerente* (manager).

Currency cards

If you don't want to carry lots of cash, prepaid currency cards allow you to preload money from your bank account, fixed at the day's exchange rate. They look like a credit or debit card and are issued by specialist money changing companies, such as Travelex and Caxton FX, as well as the Post Office. You can top up and check your balance by phone, online and sometimes by text.

Money transfers

Money sent to Brazil is normally paid out in Brazilian currency, so do not have more sent out than you need for your stay. Funds can ostensibly be received within 48 banking hours, but it can take at least a month to arrive, allowing banks to capitalize on your transfer. The documentation required to receive it varies according to the whim of the bank staff, making the whole procedure often far more trouble than it is worth.

Opening hours

Generally Mon-Fri 0900-1800; closed for lunch sometime between 1130 and 1400.
Banks Mon-Fri 1000-1600 or 1630; closed at weekends.
Government offices Mon-Fri 1100-1800.
Shops Also open on Sat until 1230 or 1300.

Post

To send a standard letter or postcard to the USA costs US$0.65, to Europe US$0.90, to Australia or South Africa US0.65. Air mail should take about 7 days to or from Britain or the USA. Franked and registered (insured) letters are normally secure, but check that the amount franked is what you have paid, or the item will not arrive. Aerogrammes are most reliable. To avoid queues and obtain higher denomination stamps go to the stamp desk at the main post office.

The post office sells cardboard boxes for sending packages internally and abroad. Rates and rules for sending literally vary from post office to post office even within the same town and the quickest service is **SEDEX**. The most widespread courier service is **Federal Express**, www.fedex.com/br. They are often cheaper than parcel post.

Postes Restantes usually only hold letters for 30 days. Identification is required and it's a good idea to write your name on a piece of paper to help the attendant find your letters. Charges are minimal but often involve queuing at another counter to buy stamps, which are attached to your letter and franked before it is given to you.

Safety *See also page 33.*

Although Brazil's big cities suffer high rates of violent crime, this is mostly confined to the favelas where poverty and drugs are the main cause. Visitors should not enter favelas except when accompanied by trustworthy local residents, workers for NGOs, tour groups or other people who know the local residents well and are accepted by the community. Otherwise they may be targets of muggings by armed gangs who show short shrift to those who resist them. Mugging can take place anywhere. Travel light after dark with few valuables (avoid wearing jewellery and use a cheap, plastic, digital watch). Ask hotel staff where is and isn't safe; crime is patchy in Brazilian cities.

If the worst does happen and you are threatened, don't panic, and hand over your valuables. Do not resist, and report the crime to the local tourist police later. It is extremely rare for a tourist to be hurt during a robbery in Brazil. Being aware of the dangers, acting confidently and using your common sense will reduce many of the risks.

Photocopy your passport, air ticket and other documents, make a record of traveller's cheque and credit card numbers. Keep them separately from the originals and leave another set of records at home. Keep all documents secure; hide your main cash supply in different places or under your clothes. Extra pockets sewn inside shirts and trousers, money belts (best worn below the waist), neck or leg pouches and elasticated support bandages for keeping money above the elbow or below the knee have been repeatedly recommended.

All border areas should be regarded with some caution because of smuggling activities. Violence over land ownership in parts of the interior have resulted in a 'Wild West' atmosphere in some towns, which should therefore be passed through quickly.

Red-light districts should also be given a wide berth as there are reports of drinks being drugged with a substance popularly known as 'good night Cinderella'. This leaves the victim easily amenable to having their possessions stolen, or worse.

Avoiding cons

Never trust anyone telling sob stories or offering 'safe rooms', and when looking for a hotel, always choose the room yourself. Be wary of 'plain-clothes policemen'; insist on seeing identification and on going to the police station by main roads. Do not hand over your identification (or money) until you are at the station. On no account take them directly back to your hotel. Be even more suspicious if they seek confirmation of their status from a passer-by.

Hotel security

Hotel safe deposits are generally, but not always, secure. If you cannot get a receipt for valuables in a hotel safe, you can seal the contents in a plastic bag and sign across the seal. Always keep an inventory of what you have deposited. If you don't trust the hotel, lock everything in your pack and secure it in your room when you go out. If you lose valuables, report to the police and note details of the report for insurance purposes. Be sure to be present whenever your credit card is used.

Police

There are several types of police: **Polícia Federal**, civilian dressed, who handle all federal law duties, including immigration. A subdivision is the **Polícia Federal Rodoviária**, uniformed, who are the traffic police on federal highways. **Polícia Militar** are the uniformed, street police force, under the control of the state governor, handling all state laws. They are not the same as the Armed Forces' internal police. **Polícia Civil**, also state controlled, handle local laws and investigations. They are usually in civilian dress, unless in the traffic division. In cities,

the *prefeitura* controls the **Guarda Municipal**, who handle security. **Tourist police** operate in places with a strong tourist presence. In case of difficulty, visitors should seek out tourist police in the first instance.

Public transport

When you have all your luggage with you at a bus or railway station, be especially careful and carry any shoulder bags in front of you. To be extra safe, take a taxi between the airport/bus station/railway station and hotel, keep your bags with you and pay only when you and your luggage are outside; avoid night buses and arriving at your destination at night.

Sexual assault

If you are the victim of a sexual assault, you are advised firstly to contact a doctor (this can be your home doctor). You will need tests to determine whether you have contracted any STDs; you may also need advice on emergency contraception. You should contact your embassy, where consular staff will be very willing to help.

Women travellers

Most of these tips apply to any single traveller. When you set out, err on the side of caution until your instincts have adjusted to the customs of a new culture. Be prepared for the exceptional curiosity extended to visitors, especially women, and try not to overreact. If, as a single woman, you can befriend a local woman, you will learn much more about the country you are visiting. There is a definite 'gringo trail' you can follow, which can be helpful when looking for safe accommodation, especially if arriving after dark (best avoided). Remember that for a single woman a taxi at night can be as dangerous as walking alone. It is easier for men to take the friendliness of locals at face value; women may be subject to unwanted attention. Do not disclose to strangers where you are staying. By wearing a wedding ring and saying that your 'husband' is close at hand, you may dissuade an aspiring suitor. If politeness fails, do not feel bad about showing offence and departing. A good rule is always to act with confidence, as though you know where you are going, even if you do not. Someone who looks lost is more likely to attract unwanted attention.

Student travellers

If you are in full-time education you will be entitled to an **ISIC** (International Student Identity Card), which is valid in more than 77 countries. The ISIC card gives you special prices on transport and access to a variety of other concessions and services. For the location of your nearest ISIC office see www.isic.org. ISIC cards can be obtained in Brazil from **STB** agencies throughout the country; also try www.carteiradoestudante. com.br, which is in Portuguese but easy to follow (click 'pontos de Venda' for details of agencies). Remember to take photographs when having a card issued.

In practice, the ISIC card is rarely recognized or accepted for discounts outside of the south and southeast of Brazil, but is nonetheless useful for obtaining half-price entry to the cinema. Youth hostels will often accept it in lieu of a **HI** card or at least give a discount, and some university accommodation (and subsidized canteens) will allow very cheap short-term stays to holders.

Tax

Airport departure tax The amount of tax depends on the class and size of the airport, but the cost is usually incorporated into the ticket.
VAT Rates vary from 7-25% at state and federal level; the average is 17-20%. The tax is generally included in the international or domestic ticket price.

Telephone *Country code: +55.*

Ringing: equal tones with long pauses. Engaged: equal tones, equal pauses.

Making a phone call in Brazil can be confusing. It is necessary to dial a 2-digit telephone company code prior to the area code for all calls. Phone numbers are now printed in this way: 0XX21 (0 for a national call, XX for the code of the phone company chosen (eg 31 for Telemar) followed by, 21 for Rio de Janeiro, for example, and the 8 or 9-digit number of the subscriber. The same is true for international calls where 00 is followed by the operator code and then the country code and number.

Telephone operators and their codes are: **Embratel**, 21 (nationwide); **Telefônica**, 15 (state of São Paulo); **Telemar**, 31 (Alagoas, Amazonas, Amapá, Bahia, Ceará, Espírito Santo, Maranhão, most of Minas Gerais, Pará, Paraíba, Pernambuco, Piauí, Rio de Janeiro, Rio Grande do Norte, Roraima, Sergipe); **Tele Centro-Sul**, 14 (Acre, Goiás, Mato Grosso, Mato Grosso do Sul, Paraná, Rondônia, Santa Catarina, Tocantins and the cities of Brasília and Pelotas); **CTBC-Telecom**, 12 (some parts of Minas Gerais, Goiás, Mato Grosso do Sul and São Paulo state); **Intelig**, 23.

National calls

Telephone booths or *orelhões* (literally 'big ears' as they are usually ear-shaped, fibreglass shells) are easy to come by in towns and cities. Local phone calls and telegrams are cheap.

Cartões telefônicos (phone cards) are available from newsstands, post offices and some chemists. They cost US$3 for 30 units and up to US$5 for 90 units. Local calls from a private phone are often free. *Cartões telefônicos internacionais* (international phone cards) are increasingly available in tourist areas and are often sold at hostels.

Mobile phones and apps

Cellular phones are widespread and coverage excellent even in remote areas, but prices are extraordinarily high and users still pay to receive calls outside the metropolitan area where their phone is registered. SIM cards are hard to buy as users require a CPF (a Brazilian social security number) to buy one, but phones can be hired. When using a cellular telephone you do not drop the zero from the area code as you have to when dialling from a fixed line.

Some networks, eg **O2**, provide an app so you can use the time on your contract in your home country if you access the app via Wi-Fi. Internet calls (eg via **Skype**, **Whatsapp** and **Viber**) are also possible if you have access to Wi-Fi.

There are many Brazilian travel guide apps available only a fraction of which are thoroughly researched. Fewer still are updated regularly. You are far better off using **Google Maps** and asking in the hotel or from local people.

Time

Brazil has 4 time zones: Brazilian standard time is GMT-3; the Amazon time zone (Pará west of the Rio Xingu, Amazonas, Roraima, Rondônia, Mato Grosso and Mato Grosso do Sul) is GMT-4, the State of Acre is GMT-5; and the Fernando de Noronha archipelago is GMT-2. Clocks move forward 1 hr in summer for approximately 5 months (usually between Oct and Feb or Mar), but times of change vary. This does not apply to Acre.

Tipping

Tipping is not usual, but always appreciated as staff are often paid a pittance. In restaurants, add 10% of the bill if no service charge is included; cloakroom attendants deserve a small tip; porters have fixed charges but often receive tips as well; unofficial car parkers on city streets should be tipped R$2.

Tourist information

The **Ministério do Turismo**, www.braziltour. com, is in charge of tourism in Brazil Local tourist information bureaux are not usually helpful for information on cheap hotels – they generally just dish out pamphlets. Expensive hotels provide tourist magazines for their guests. Telephone directories (not Rio) contain good street maps.

Other good sources of information are: **LATA**, www.lata.org. The Latin American Travel Association, with useful country information and listings of all UK operators specializing in Latin America. Also has up-to-date information on public safety, health, weather, travel costs, economics and politics highlighted for each nation. Wide selection of Latin American maps available, as well as individual travel planning assistance. **South American Explorers**, T607-277 0488, www.saexplorers.org. A non-profit educational organization functioning primarily as an information network for South America. Useful for travellers to Brazil and the rest of the continent.

Tour operators

UK
Brazil specialists

Bespoke Brazil, T01603-340680, www.bespokebrazil.com. Tailor-made trips throughout the country, even to the lesser-known areas.
Brazil Revealed, T01932-424252, www.brazilrevealed.co.uk. A specialist, boutique and bespoke operator with excellent in-country contacts.
Culture Explorers, www.culturexplorers. com. First-class sustainable travel in the Amazon and southeast, including a wonderful gastronomic tour.
Journey Latin America, T020-8600 1881, www.journeylatinamerica.co.uk. An enormous range of Brazil trips, including bespoke options.

Sunvil Latin America, T020-8758 4774, www.sunvil.co.uk. Quality packages and tailor-made trips throughout the country.
Veloso Tours, T020-8762 0616, www.veloso. com. Imaginative tours throughout Brazil; bespoke options on request.

Olympics
Cosport, T020-7478 0673, www.cosport. co.uk. The official Olympic ticket sales agency offers hotel and tickets packages, all of which are Rio-based. Prices depend on the event. See also page 44.

Villas
Hidden Pousadas Brazil, www.hidden pousadasbrazil.com. A choice of tasteful small hotels and homestays hand-picked from all over the country and ranging from chic but simple to luxe and languorous.
SJ Villas, T020-7351 6384, www.sjvillas. co.uk. Luxurious beach houses around Rio de Janeiro and the Bahian beaches.

Wildlife and birding specialists
Naturetrek, T01962-733051, www.nature trek.co.uk. Wildlife tours throughout Brazil with bespoke options and specialist birding tours of the Atlantic coastal rainforests.
Ornitholidays, T01794-519445, www.ornit holidays.co.uk. Annual or biannual birding trips throughout Brazil; usually to the Pantanal, Atlantic coast rainforest and Iguaçu.
Reef and Rainforest Tours Ltd, T01803-866965, www.reefandrainforest.co.uk. Specialists in tailor-made and group wildlife tours.

North America
Brazil For Less, T1-877-565 8119 (US toll free) or T+44-203-006 2507 (UK), www. brazilforless.com. US-based travel firm with a focus solely on South America, with local offices and operations, and a price guarantee. Good-value tours, run by travellers for travellers. Will meet or beat any internet rates from outside Brazil.

Culture Explorers, www.culturexplorers. com (see UK operators, above).
Ladatco Tours, T1800-327 6162, www. ladatco.com. Standard tours to Rio.
Mila Tours, T847-248 2111, T800-387 7378 (USA and Canada), www.milatours.com. Itineraries to Rio.

Wildlife and birding specialists
Field Guides, T1-800-7284953, www. fieldguides.com. Interesting birdwatching tours to all parts of Brazil.
Focus Tours, T(505)216 7780, www. focustours. com. Environmentally responsible travel throughout Brazil.

Brazil
Dehouche, T021-2512 3895, www.dehouche. com. Upmarket, carefully tailored trips throughout Brazil, including Rio and Búzios.
Matueté, T011-3071 4515, www.matuete. com. Bespoke luxury options around Brazil with a range of private house rentals. Places include Rio, Angra dos Reis, Paraty and Búzios.
Tatur Turismo, T071-3114 7900, www. tatur.com.br. Very helpful and professional bespoke Bahia-based agency who can organize tours throughout Brazil, especially in Bahia, using smaller hotels.
whl.travel, T031-3889 8596, www.whl.travel. Online network of tour operators for booking accommodation and tours throughout Brazil.

Wildlife and birding specialists
Andy and Nadime Whittaker's Birding Brazil Tours, www.birdingbraziltours.com. Another good company, based in Manaus. The couple worked with the BBC Natural History Unit on David Attenborough's *The Life of Birds* and are ground agents for a number of the major birding tour companies from the US and Europe.
Birding Brazil Tours, www.birdingbrazil tours.com. First-class bespoke options throughout the country.
Edson Endrigo, www.avesfoto.com.br. Bespoke options only.

National parks

National parks are run by the Brazilian institute of environmental protection, **Ibama**, T061-3316 1212, www.ibama.gov.br (in Portuguese only). For information, contact **Linha Verde**, T0800-618080, linhaverde.sede@ibama.gov.br. National parks are open to visitors, usually with a permit from Ibama. See also the **Ministério do Meio Ambiente** website, www.mma. gov.br (in Portuguese only).

Useful websites

www.brazil.org.uk Provides a broad range of info on Brazilian history and culture from the UK Brazilian embassy.
www.brazilmax.com Excellent information on culture and lifestyle, the best available in English.
www.visitbrazil.com The official tourism website of Brazil, and the best.
www.gringos.com.br An excellent source of information on all things Brazilian for visitors and expats.
www.ipanema.com A quirky, informative site on all things Rio de Janeiro.
www.maria-brazil.org A wonderfully personal introduction to Brazil, specifically Rio, featuring Maria's cookbook and little black book, features and reviews.
www.socioambiental.org Invaluable for up-to-the-minute, accurate information on environmental and indigenous issues. In Portuguese only.
www.survival-international.org The world's leading campaign organization for indigenous peoples with excellent information on various Brazilian indigenous groups.
www.worldtwitch.com Birding information and comprehensive listings of rainforest lodges.

Visas and immigration

Visas are not required for stays of up to 90 days by tourists from Andorra, Argentina, Austria, Bahamas, Barbados, Belgium, Bolivia, Chile, Colombia, Costa Rica, Denmark, Ecuador, Finland, France, Germany, Greece, Iceland, Ireland, Italy, Liechtenstein, Luxembourg, Malaysia, Monaco, Morocco, Namibia, the Netherlands, Norway, Paraguay, Peru, Philippines, Portugal, San Marino, South Africa, Spain, Suriname, Sweden, Switzerland, Thailand, Trinidad and Tobago, United Kingdom, Uruguay, the Vatican and Venezuela. For them, only the following documents are required at the port of disembarkation: a passport valid for at least 6 months (or *cédula de identidad* for nationals of Argentina, Chile, Paraguay and Uruguay); and a return or onward ticket, or adequate proof that you can purchase your return fare, subject to no remuneration being received in Brazil and no legally binding or contractual documents being signed. Venezuelan passport holders can stay for 60 days on filling in a form at the border.

Citizens of the USA, Canada, Australia, New Zealand and other countries not mentioned above, and anyone wanting to stay longer than 180 days, *must* get a visa before arrival, which may, if you ask, be granted for multiple entry. US citizens must be fingerprinted on entry to Brazil. Visa fees vary from country to country, so apply to the Brazilian consulate in your home country. The consular fee in the USA is US$50. Students planning to study in Brazil or employees of foreign companies can apply for a 1- or 2-year visa. 2 copies of the application form, 2 photos, a letter from the sponsoring company or educational institution in Brazil, a police form showing no criminal convictions and a fee of around US$70 is required.

Extensions

Foreign tourists may stay a maximum of 180 days in any 1 year. 90-day renewals are easily obtainable, but only at least 15 days before the expiry of your 90-day permit, from the Polícia Federal. The procedure varies, but generally you have to: fill out 3 copies of the tax form at the Polícia Federal, take them to a branch of **Banco do Brasil,** pay US$15 and bring 2 copies back. You will then be given the extension form to fill in and be asked for your passport to stamp in the extension. According to regulations (which should be on display) you need to show a return ticket, cash, cheques or a credit card, a personal reference and proof of an address of a person living in the same city as the office (in practice you simply write this in the space on the form). Some offices will only give you an extension within 10 days of the expiry of your permit.

Some points of entry, such as the Colombian border, refuse entry for longer than 30 days, renewals are then for the same period, insist if you want 90 days. For longer stays you must leave the country and return (not the same day) to get a new 90-day permit. If your visa has expired, getting a new visa can be costly (US$35 for a consultation, US$30 for the visa itself) and may take anything up to 45 days, depending on where you apply. If you overstay your visa, or extension, you will be fined US$7 per day, with no upper limit. After paying the fine to Polícia Federal, you will be issued with an exit visa and must leave within 8 days.

Officially, if you leave Brazil within the 90-day permission to stay and then re-enter the country, you should only be allowed to stay until the 90-day permit expires. If, however, you are given another 90-day permit, this may lead to charges of overstaying if you apply for an extension.

Identification

You must always carry identification when in Brazil. Take a photocopy of the personal details in your passport, plus your Brazilian immigration stamp, and leave your passport in the hotel safe deposit. This photocopy, when authorized in a *cartório*, US$1, is a legitimate copy of your documents. Be prepared, however, to present the originals when travelling in sensitive border areas. Always keep an independent record of your passport details. Also register with your consulate to expedite document replacement if yours gets lost or stolen.

Warning

Do not lose the entry/exit permit they give you when you enter Brazil. Leaving the country without it, you may have to pay up to US$100 per person. It is suggested that you photocopy this form and have it authenticated at a *cartório*, US$1, in case of loss or theft.

Volunteering

Task Brasil Trust, T020-7735 5545, www. taskbrasil.org.uk. A small UK-based charity set up to help abandoned street children in Brazil. It runs various projects to improve the lives of children and pregnant teenage girls, especially those living on the streets of Rio de Janeiro. You can get involved as a volunteer in Brazil, to help the children with sports, reading and writing, music, art and computer skills. Volunteer at the UK or US offices, or make a donation.

Weights and measures

Metric.

Footnotes

Basic Portuguese for travellers

Learning Portuguese is a useful part of the preparation for a trip to Brazil and no volume of dictionaries, phrase books or word lists will provide the same enjoyment as being able to communicate directly with the people of the country you are visiting. It is a good idea to make an effort to grasp the basics before you go. As you travel you will pick up more of the language and the more you know, the more you will benefit from your stay.

General pronunciation

Within Brazil itself, there are variations in pronunciation, intonation, phraseology and slang. This makes for great richness and for the possibility of great enjoyment in the language. A couple of points which the newcomer to the language will spot immediately are the use of the tilde (~) over 'a' and 'o'. This makes the vowel nasal, as does a word ending in 'm' or 'ns', or a vowel followed by 'm' + consonant, or by 'n' + consonant. Another important point of spelling is that for words ending in 'i' and 'u' the emphasis is on the last syllable, though (unlike Spanish) no accent is used. This is especially relevant in place names like Buriti, Guarapari, Caxambu, Iguaçu. Note also the use of 'ç', which changes the pronunciation of c from hard [k] to soft [s].

Personal pronouns

In conversation, most people refer to 'you' as *você*, although in the south and in Pará *tu* is more common. To be more polite, use *O Senhor/A Senhora*. For 'us', *gente* (people, folks) is very common when it includes you too.

Portuguese words and phrases

Greetings and courtesies

hello	*oi*
good morning	*bom dia*
good afternoon	*boa tarde*
good evening/night	*boa noite*
goodbye	*adeus/tchau*
see you later	*até logo*
please	*por favor/faz favor*
thank you	*obrigado* (if a man is speaking)/ *obrigada* (if a woman is speaking)
thank you very much	*muito obrigado/muito obrigada*
how are you?	*como vai você tudo bem?/tudo bom?*
I am fine	*vou bem/tudo bem*
pleased to meet you	*um prazer*
no	*não*
yes	*sim*
excuse me	*com licença*
I don't understand	*não entendo*
please speak slowly	*fale devagar por favor*
what is your name?	*qual é seu nome?*
my name is…	*o meu nome é…*
go away!	*vai embora!*

Basic questions

where is?	*onde está/onde fica?*
why?	*por que?*
how much does it cost?	*quanto custa?*
what for?	*para que?*
how much is it?	*quanto é?*
how do I get to…?	*para chegar a…?*
when?	*quando?*
I want to go to…	*quero ir para…*
when does the bus leave?/arrive?	*a que hor sai/chega o ônibus?*
is this the way to the church?	*aquí é o caminho para a igreja?*

Basics

bathroom/toilet	*banheiro*
police (policeman)	*a polícia (o polícia)*
hotel	*o (a pensão, a hospedaria)*
restaurant	*o restaurante (o lanchonete)*
post office	*o correio*
telephone office (central)	*telefônica*
supermarket	*o supermercado*
market	*o mercado*
bank	*o banco*
bureau de change	*a casa de câmbio*
exchange rate	*a taxa de câmbio*
notes/coins	*notas/moedas*
traveller's cheques	*os travelers/os cheques de viagem*
cash	*dinheiro*
breakfast	*o caféde manh*
lunch	*o almoço*
dinner/supper	*o jantar*
Meal	*a refeição*
drink	*a bebida*
mineral water	*a água mineral*
soft fizzy drink	*o refrigerante*
beer	*a cerveja*
without sugar	*sem açúcar*
without meat	*sem carne*

Getting around

on the left/right	*à esquerda/à direita*
straight on	*direto*
to walk	*caminhar*
bus station	*a rodoviária*
bus	*o ônibus*
bus stop	*a parada*
train	*a trem*
airport	*o aeroport*
aeroplane/airplane	*o avião*
flight	*o vôa*

first/second class	*primeira/segunda clase*
train station	*a ferroviária*
combined bus and train station	*a rodoferroviária*
ticket	*o passagem/o bilhete*
ticket office	*a bilheteria*

Accommodation

room	*quarto*
noisy	*barulhento*
single/double room	*(quarto de) solteiro/(quarto para) casal*
room with two beds	*quarto com duas camas*
with private bathroom	*quarto com banheiro*
hot/cold water	*água quente/fria*
to make up/clean	*limpar*
sheet(s)	*o lençol (os lençóis)*
blankets	*as mantas*
pillow	*o travesseiro*
clean/dirty towels	*as toalhas limpas/sujas*
toilet paper	*o papel higiêico*

Health

chemist	*a farmacia*
doctor	*o coutor/a doutora*
(for) pain	*(para) dor*
stomach	*o esômago (a barriga)*
head	*a cabeça*
fever/sweat	*a febre/o suor higiênicas*
diarrhoea	*a diarréia*
blood	*o sangue*
condoms	*as camisinhas/os preservativos*
contraceptive (pill)	*anticoncepcional (a pílula)*
period	*a menstruação/a regra*
sanitary towels/tampons	*toalhas absorventes/absorventes internos*
contact lenses	*lentes de contacto*
aspirin	*a aspirina*

Time

at one o'clock (am/pm)	*a uma hota (da manhã/da tarde)*
at half past two/two thirty	*as dois e meia*
at a quarter to three	*quinze para as três*
it's one o'clock	*é uma*
it's seven o'clock	*são sete horas*
it's twenty past six/six twenty	*são seis e vinte*
it's five to nine	*são cinco para as nove*
in ten minutes	*em dez minutos*
five hours	*cinco horas*
does it take long?	*sura muito?*

Days

Monday	*segunda feiro*
Tuesday	*terça feira*
Wednesday	*quarta feira*
Thursday	*quinta feira*
Friday	*sexta feira*
Saturday	*sábado*
Sunday	*domingo*

Months

January	*janeiro*
February	*fevereiro*
March	*março*
April	*abril*
May	*maio*
June	*junho*
July	*julho*
August	*agosto*
September	*setembro*
October	*outubro*
November	*novembro*
December	*dezembro*

Numbers

one	*um/uma*
two	*dois/duas*
three	*três*
four	*quatro*
five	*cinco*
six	*seis* ('*meia*' half, is frequently used for number 6 ie half-dozen)
seven	*sete*
eight	*oito*
nine	*nove*
ten	*dez*
eleven	*onze*
twelve	*doze*
thirteen	*treze*
fourteen	*catorze*
fifteen	*quinze*
sixteen	*dezesseis*
seventeen	*dezessete*
eighteen	*dezoito*
nineteen	dezenove
twenty	*vinte*
twenty-one	*vente e um*
thirty	*trinta*
forty	*cuarenta*
fifty	*cinqüe*

sixty	*sessenta*
seventy	*setenta*
eighty	*oitenta*
ninety	*noventa*
hundred	*cem, cento*
thousand	*mil*

Useful slang

that's great/cool	*que legal*
bloke/guy/geezer	*cara* (literally 'face'), *mano*
cheesy/tacky	*brega*
in fashion/cool	*descolado*

Glossary

azulejo	tile	*forró*	music and dance style from northeast Brazil
baía	bay		
bairro	area or suburb	*frevo*	frenetic musical style from Recife
bandas	marching bands that compete during Carnaval		
		gaúcho	cowboy, especially from Rio Grande do Sul
bandeirantes	early Brazilian conquistadors who went on missions to open up the interior		
		garimpeiro	miner or prospector
		igreja	church
barraca	beach hut or stall	*ilha*	island
berimbau	stringed instrument that accompanies *capoeira*	*jangada*	small fishing boats, peculiar to the northeast
		jardim	garden
biblioteca	library	*lanchonete*	café/deli
bilhete	ticket	*largo*	small square
botequim	small bar, open-air	*leito*	executive bus
caboclo	rural workers of mixed descent	*litoral*	coast/coastal area
cachaça	cane liquor	*mata*	jungle
cachoeira	waterfall	*mercado*	market
caipirinha	Brazilian cocktail, made from cachaça, lime, sugar and ice	*Mineiro*	person from Minas Gerais
		mirante	viewpoint
câmbio	bureau de change	*mosteiro*	monastery
candomblé	African-Brazilian religion	*Paulista*	person from São Paulo
capela	chapel	*ponte*	bridge
capoeira	African-Brazilian martial art	*praça*	square/plaza
Carioca	person from Rio de Janeiro	*praia*	beach
carnaval	carnival	*prancha*	surfboard
cerrado	scrubland	*prefeitura*	town hall
cerveja	beer	*rio*	river
churrascaria	barbecue restaurant, often all-you-can-eat	*rodoviária*	bus station
		rua	street
empadas	mini pasties	*sambaquis*	archaeological shell mounds
estrada	road	*sertão*	arid interior of the northeast
favela	slum/shanty town	*Sertanejo*	person who lives in the *sertão*
fazenda	country estate or ranch	*vaqueiro*	cowboy in the north
feijoada	black-bean stew		
ferroviária	train station		

Acronyms and official names

FUNAI	Fundação Nacional do Índio (National Foundation for Indigenous People)
IBAMA	Instituto Brasileiro do Meio Ambiente E Dos Recursos Naturais Renováveis (Brazilian Institute of Environment and Renewable Natural Resources)
MPB	Música Popular Brasileira
RAMSAR	Wetlands Convention

Index

Entries in bold refer to maps

FOOTPRINT

Features

Credits

Footprint credits
Editor: Jo Williams
Production and layout: Emma Bryers
Maps: Kevin Feeney
Colour section: Angus Dawson

Publisher: Felicity Laughton
Patrick Dawson
Marketing: Kirsty Holmes
Sales: Diane McEntee
Advertising and content partnerships:
Debbie Wylde

Photography credits
Front cover: Luiz Rocha/Shutterstock.com
Back cover top: Alex Robinson Photography
Back cover bottom: Alex Robinson Photography
Inside front cover: Alex Robinson Photography

Colour section
Page 1: Alex Robinson Photography
Page 2: Alex Robinson Photography
Page 4: Alex Robinson Photography
Page 5: Alex Robinson Photography
Page 7: Alex Robinson Photography
Page 8: Alex Robinson Photography

Duotones
Page 30: Curioso/Shutterstock.com
Page 144: Curioso/Shutterstock.com

Printed in Spain by GraphyCems

Publishing information
Footprint Rio de Janeiro
3rd edition
© Footprint Handbooks Ltd
February 2016

ISBN: 978 1 910120 64 4
CIP DATA: A catalogue record for this book
is available from the British Library

® Footprint Handbooks and the
Footprint mark are a registered
trademark of Footprint Handbooks Ltd

Published by Footprint
6 Riverside Court
Lower Bristol Road
Bath BA2 3DZ, UK
T +44 (0)1225 469141
F +44 (0)1225 469461
footprinttravelguides.com

Distributed in the USA by
National Book Network, Inc.

Every effort has been made to ensure that
the facts in this guidebook are accurate.
However, travellers should still obtain advice
from consulates, airlines, etc about travel
and visa requirements before travelling.
The authors and publishers cannot
accept responsibility for any loss, injury
or inconvenience however caused.